Clocks and Watches in Colour

Clocks and Watches in Colour

Andrew Nicholls and Richard Good

Photography by Bob Loosemore

New Orchard Editions

Originally published as two volumes by Blandford Press Ltd.

Clocks in Colour Copyright © Blandford Press 1975
Watches in Colour Copyright © Richard Good 1978

ISBN 1-85079-019-1

This combined edition published 1985 by
New Orchard Editions Ltd
Robert Rogers House
New Orchard
Poole
Dorset
BH15 1LU

Printed in Great Britain by
Garden City Press, Letchworth, Herts.

Contents

I

Early History

The wheel, the steam engine and the aeroplane have each transformed life in their turn, but perhaps the clock affects our daily lives more than any other invention. The measurement and subdivision of time have very ancient roots in the science of astronomy. By observing the apparent movements of the sun and moon, men arrived at a system in which the year is divided into days and months. In the Middle Ages European life was based upon agriculture and controlled by the seasons. Ancient manuscripts show that events could only be recorded as occurring at, for example, dawn or mid-day, since no precise time could be given.

The monasteries, which were the centres of learning, had their days divided into the seven canonical hours of Matins, Lauds, Prime, Terce, Sext, None and Vespers. At these times a bell was tolled to call the monks to prayer. The only way of knowing the time was by unreliable time-candles, waterclocks and sandglasses, all of which would be checked against the sun dial. Since the monasteries urgently needed an improved timekeeper, it seems probable that the mechanical clock was invented by monks, and indeed may have been developed independently in several different countries.

Certainly by 1300, the new invention was known in most European countries, and many clocks were constructed in public places so that the whole community could regulate its day. At first these clocks had no dials and simply struck the hours on a large bell, the period of day and night now being divided into twenty-four equal hours. The provision of a dial to mark the time was a small step forward and

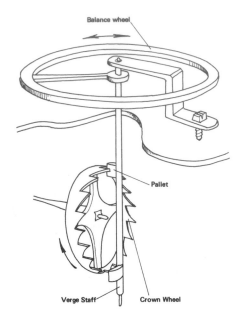

Balance wheel

Pallet

Verge Staff

Crown Wheel

1. VERGE ESCAPEMENT
CONTROLLED BY BALANCE
WHEEL

only required a simple arrangement of wheels to drive the hand or hands from the main mechanism. But, even as late as the eighteenth century, turret clocks were made with no dial and so many village church clocks still only struck the hours.

The clock was by no means the first instrument to function by means of cogs or toothed wheels. For example, the machinery of windmills and watermills is very similar, but instead of using the power of wind or water, the clock uses the constant force of a weight to turn its wheels.

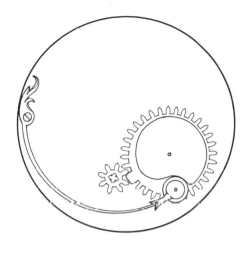

The Verge Escapement

Any mechanical clock requires some device to regulate the speed at which the wheels rotate. This is known as an escapement, since it allows one tooth of a wheel to escape at each swing of the regulator, which is usually a balance of some form or a pendulum. The first form of escapement was the verge, and it was universally employed until about 1670. In the early weight-driven clocks the part of the escapement which actually controlled the clock's speed was the foliot (plate 1). This consisted simply of a horizontal bar, with adjustable weights on the ends, mounted on the verge staff. The further from the centre of oscillation they were placed, the slower the foliot would swing. Another early form of regulator was the balance wheel (fig. 1). Unlike the foliot it had no form of adjustment, so that the only way to make fine changes in the rate of the clock was to add or subtract small weights from the driving weight.

The Spring-Driven Clock

Even the smallest weight-driven clocks were not portable and could not conveniently be moved from one room to another. The coiled spring-driven clock solved this problem and gave rise to the table clock. Recent research indicates that the coiled spring was being used in the early fifteenth century on the continent of Europe. The production of the spring itself was most difficult. There would be many failures before a reliable spring was made.

An immediate drawback of the coiled spring is that it exerts a greater force when fully coiled than when it is nearly run down. To equalise the force the early German makers sometimes used a device known as stackfreed (fig. 2). A strong spring, carrying at its end a small roller, presses against a shaped cam mounted on a toothed

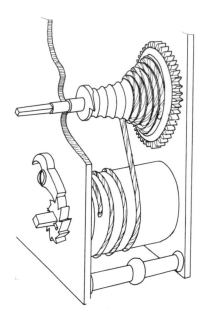

3. FUSÉE CONNECTED TO SPRING BARREL BY A GUT LINE

wheel not fully cut. A pinion on the mainspring arbor strikes the stop on the wheel after only a few turns, thus preventing overwinding and ensuring that only the turns of the spring which are nearly equal in force are used. As the mainspring unwinds so the shaped cam revolves and the friction caused by the little roller decreases. The stackfreed, however, was inefficient and little used.

The fusée was a much simpler and more effective device in use by the mid-fifteenth century. In medieval Latin *fusata* meant a spindle full of thread which the fusée resembled (fig. 3). The principle of the fusée is that of the lever. When the spring is fully coiled and the gut is all wound onto the cone-shaped fusée, the pull from the spring acts upon the smallest diameter. As the spring unwinds, the extra leverage of the increased diameter of the fusée equalises the force transmitted to the train of wheels.

The Pendulum

Although great advances had been made, until the mid-seventeenth century few clocks could keep time to within a quarter of an hour a day. The use of a pendulum to regulate a clock changed this. Both Leonardo da Vinci and Galileo are known to have realised the possibility of controlling clockwork with a pendulum, and it is believed that Galileo partially constructed a pendulum clock but died before it was completed. The Campani brothers of Rome also experimented with pendulum clocks in the 1650s, but it was the Dutch scientist, Christian Huygens, who put the principle into practical use in 1657. Very soon the pendulum clock was widely adopted in Europe (fig. 4).

The advantage of the pendulum was that it was isochronous – that is, its swing was always equal and depended only on its length. Neither its own weight, nor the angle of arc through which it swung, altered the time that each swing took. Within six months of the introduction of the pendulum, clocks could be made to keep time to within a minute or two a day. This made it practical to fit a minute- as well as an hour-hand, although this was not a universal practice.

During the next fifteen years, under the patronage of Charles II, English makers invented a new escapement, the anchor, for use with

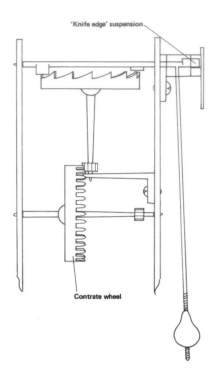

'Knife edge' suspension

Contrate wheel

4. VERGE ESCAPEMENT AND
BOB PENDULUM

a long pendulum (fig. 5). Although it is thought to have been Dr Robert Hooke who realised the added advantage of the long pendulum, both he and the clockmakers, William Clement and Joseph Knibb, have a claim to the invention of the anchor escapement.

By the early eighteenth century it was realised that the recoil of the anchor escapement produced too much friction, thus interfering with the pendulum's swing and reducing the clock's accuracy. Around 1715 George Graham, Thomas Tompion's successor, invented a dead beat escapement (fig. 6). The drawing shows how the pallet has two faces instead of the single curved one of the anchor. When

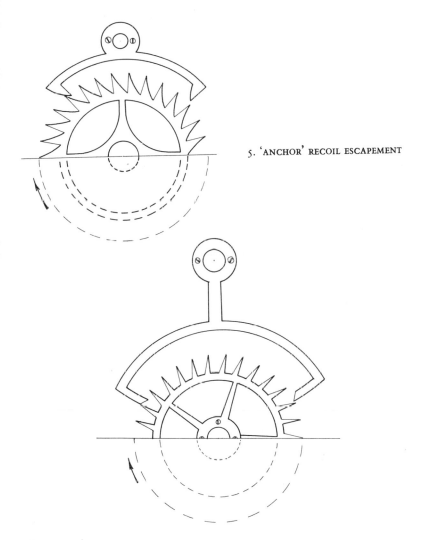

5. 'ANCHOR' RECOIL ESCAPEMENT

6. GRAHAM'S DEAD BEAT ESCAPEMENT INVENTED IN THE EARLY EIGHTEENTH CENTURY

a tooth is released it falls onto a locking face which does not cause the wheel to recoil, since the face is part of an arc centred at the pallet arbor. As the pendulum returns, the tooth gives the pendulum an impulse as it moves down the impulse face.

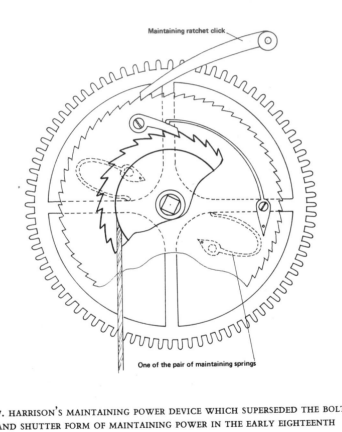

Maintaining ratchet click

One of the pair of maintaining springs

7. HARRISON'S MAINTAINING POWER DEVICE WHICH SUPERSEDED THE BOLT AND SHUTTER FORM OF MAINTAINING POWER IN THE EARLY EIGHTEENTH CENTURY

Maintaining Power

When a clock is being wound and the motive power is removed, it is possible for the clock to stop or the escape wheel may even trip backwards. As well as losing time it is also possible for the escapement to be damaged if a heavy pendulum causes the pallets to fall upon an idling escape wheel, which in a precision clock is likely to have delicate teeth. To overcome this, Harrison invented a form of maintaining power in the early eighteenth century (fig. 7). Its action is very simple in theory but not so easy to illustrate. The system works automatically. Two small but powerful springs are screwed to a large ratchet wheel, they act upon the spokes of this wheel and are therefore constantly under pressure. As the clock is being wound the pressure is released, the springs slowly uncoil by pushing the great wheel round and so they keep the clock going. This system may be used on weight-driven clocks and on fusée spring-driven clocks.

Compensated Pendulums

Metal expands and contracts with changes in atmospheric temperature, and of the two metals most commonly used in clock construction brass has a greater coefficient of expansion than steel. With an accurate regulator the very small changes in the length of a seconds pendulum would affect the rate of the clock if it were not fitted with a compensated pendulum.

George Graham invented the first temperature-compensated pendulum for use with his dead beat escapement. This is the mercury pendulum (fig. 8) which consists of a steel rod and the bob takes the form of a glass jar nearly filled with mercury. As the temperature rises the steel rod lengthens, but at the same time the mercury expands upwards in the jar so keeping the centre of oscillation constant. This method works extremely well when properly constructed, and was generally used for nineteenth-century English regulators.

The efforts made to produce an especially accurate timepiece in the early eighteenth century were partly to meet the requirements of astronomers who wished to time their observations to a split second. A reliable timekeeper was also needed for use on board ships to calculate their longitude when at sea. Both John and James Harrison

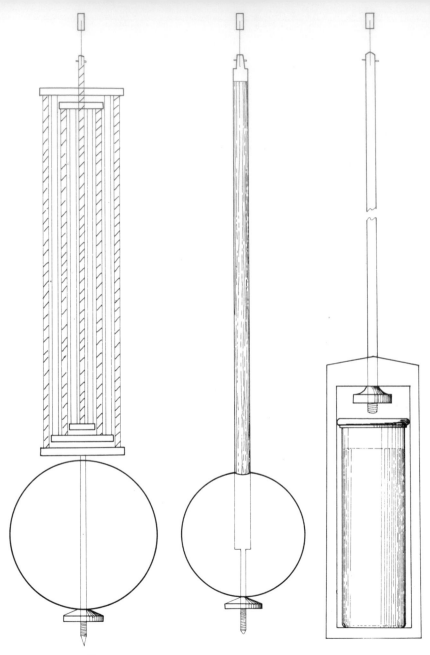

8. TEMPERATURE COMPENSATING PENDULUMS
HARRISON'S BI-METALLIC OR 'GRIDIRON' PENDULUM
WOOD ROD PENDULUM
GRAHAM'S MERCURIAL PENDULUM

spent much of their working lives perfecting such an instrument. To James Harrison is ascribed the invention of the popular gridiron-pendulum, used almost without exception on French regulators. As the drawing of this pendulum (fig. 8) shows, the steel rods are always longer than the brass ones. But, because the expansion of steel is less than that of brass, the greater expansion of the brass rods makes up for their shorter lengths and so keeps the length of the pendulum constant.

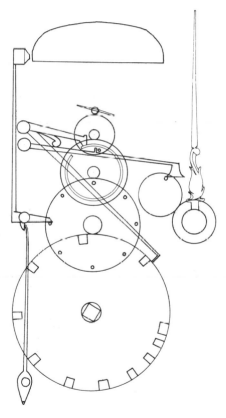

9. COUNTWHEEL STRIKING MECHANISM

Although this book is concerned only with domestic clocks, we will find that they sometimes incorporate escapements and pendulums devised for use on regulators made for astronomical or other specialised purposes. A third type of compensating pendulum is more commonly used on domestic clocks than the mercury and gridiron ones: this is the wooden rod pendulum, which is cheap, effective and has a lead or cast-iron bob. The wood must always be well-seasoned, with perfectly straight grain.

Striking Mechanisms
The countwheel or locking plate type of striking mechanism (fig. 9) was used on the very earliest clocks and continued in use well into the nineteenth century. To the striking train is geared a disk with notches cut in its perimeter. The notches are cut at an increasing distance from

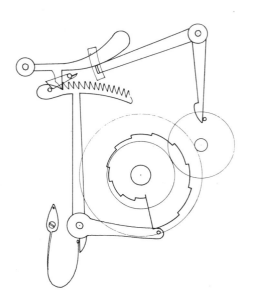

10. RACK STRIKING MECHANISM
INVENTED BY EDWARD
BARLOW IN 1676

one another for the hours one to twelve. Once the striking train is released by the going train, the clock continues to strike until the lever falls back into the next notch in the countwheel. With this system it is possible for the number of hours struck to become out of sequence with that indicated by the hand on the dial. This can usually only be remedied by releasing the striking mechanism manually and letting it sound each hour until it is back in phase with the hands. With a countwheel strike, it is thus impossible to have a pull-repeat mechanism to sound the last hour.

In 1676 the Reverend Edward Barlow invented a system known as the rack and snail (fig. 10), which makes it impossible for the hour struck to become out of sequence with the hands. The hour hand carries with it, behind the dial plate, a stepped snail-shaped disk, each step corresponding to an hour. At the hour the depth of the step determines how far the rack will fall and consequently how many teeth of the rack are to be gathered in again by the striking train. Each tooth gathered represents one stroke of the bell.

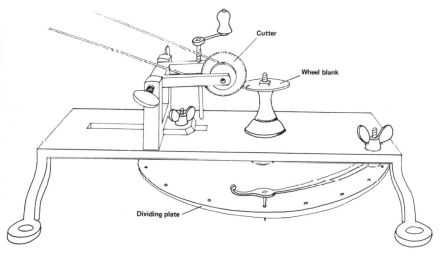

11. WHEEL CUTTING MACHINE OF THE EIGHTEENTH CENTURY

2

Germany, Austria, Switzerland

Gothic Chamber Clocks

After the public or turret clock had become established, scaled-down versions began to be made for domestic use. The earliest domestic chamber clocks had only an hour-hand as they were not sufficiently accurate for a minute-hand to be worthwhile. Sometimes the dial was made with small knobs or 'touch pieces' at each hour so that the time could be felt by hand at night. Some chamber clocks stood on solid brackets fixed to the wall, but many were too heavy and stood on a pedestal on the floor. The earliest surviving chamber clocks date back to *c.* 1400.

Plate 1 – This sixteenth-century chamber clock still closely resembles a turret clock in construction. It stands about 60 cm (2 ft) high and is made entirely of iron. The foliot is clearly visible with its adjustable weights. Like all medieval chamber clocks, the four posts of the frame are made to resemble the buttresses of a church topped by pinnacle-like finials. The framework and the cruciform-shaped plates between which the wheels are pivoted are all fixed together by means of wedges. The hours are struck on the large bell. The alarm mechanism can be clearly seen mounted in one corner of the movement. The alarm hammer is mounted on the end of a verge staff and actuated by a crown wheel. Within the centre of the dial is a toothed wheel to which the hour-hand is fixed. To set the alarm, a peg is pushed into one of the twelve holes in this wheel. As the wheel rotates the peg lifts a lever which releases the alarm.

Perhaps the best-known clocks of the period were produced in Switzerland by the Liechti family. Until the seventeenth century most of their work was signed and dated, a practice which makes the study of antique clocks very much easier. The first clockmaking member of this family was born in 1480 and the business continued through twelve generations until 1857. Their early Gothic clocks are normally very decorative with elaborately painted dials. Every part of these old clocks was made by hand including the wheels, each tooth of which was scribed and cut or filed by hand. The wheels usually consist of two separate parts. The circular rim into which the teeth are cut is riveted or jointed onto the spokes which in turn are riveted or pinned to the arbor. It was not until the second half of the seventeenth century that wheel cutting machines, which divided and cut the teeth of the wheel in one operation, were widely used.

The Guilds of Southern Germany

In southern Germany the towns of Nuremberg and Augsburg were the unrivalled centres of clockmaking. In the early records of Nuremberg, fifteenth- and sixteenth-century clockmakers were referred to as locksmiths, because they were apprenticed to this trade and were members of the locksmiths' guild. In 1565, however, three craftsmen who made watches requested the city fathers to allow them to create a masterpiece which would confirm watchmaking as a separate craft. Their wishes were granted on condition the pieces were completed within one year. The first test piece was to be a clock or watch small enough to hang from a cord around a man's neck, it was to strike the hours and contain an alarm mechanism. Such watches were not small by our standards, being up to three inches in diameter. They were, in fact, miniature table clock movements.

The second piece was to be a tabernacle or belfry clock (plate 2). This was to show the twenty-four hours of the day and night, the quarter hours and the moon's phases. At the rear of the clock was to be an annual calendar dial, a planetary dial and another showing the changing lengths of the day and night. These requirements laid great stress on complexity, with no mention of accuracy. The

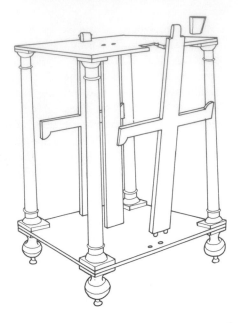

12. FOUR POSTER FRAME SHOWING METHOD OF REMOVING 'CRUCIFORM'
PLATES

requirements were later altered and required the tabernacle clock to
show the minutes, strike the hours and contain an astrolabe as well
as an alarm mechanism.

This demand for elaborate dialwork and the strict guild laws led
to the decline of the German industry and, by the eighteenth century,
France and England had taken the lead.

The Renaissance
As the sixteenth century progressed more and more artists, designers
and craftsmen absorbed the ideas of the Italian Renaissance. As a
result, Gothic chamber clocks were made alongside weight- and
spring-driven clocks of a distinctly classical style.

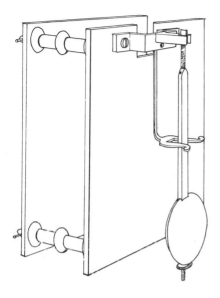

13. PLATED CONSTRUCTION OF
CLOCK MOVEMENT

Augsburg, a town in Bavaria, was perhaps the chief centre of clockmaking in Europe during the Renaissance. The quality of workmanship was consistently high, while the cases show great individuality and variety of design. Clocks were rarely signed although they often bear the town's stamps A.G. or a pineapple. At this period makers usually used their initials when signing a piece of work.

Spring-driven clocks can be easily classified by the construction of the movement. First there is the 4-post method of construction. Here the frame of the movement is a fixed unit and the vertical plates in which the wheels are pivoted and fitted into the frame by means of wedges. Secondly there is the plated method of construction. Here the plates in which the wheels are pivoted form part of the framework and are separated by decoratively turned pillars. One end of the pillar is riveted into one plate and the other plate is secured to the opposite end of the pillar by tapper pins. The advantage of the plated movement is that it can be very compact, since both sets of wheels can be laid out between the same two plates. At first they were placed horizontally with the dial on top of the clock.

A type of clock often associated with southern Germany, particularly Augsburg, is the so-called belfry or tabernacle clock. As the name implies, it takes the form of a tower. There are also examples from Austria, Italy and Holland which date from the mid-sixteenth century to the early eighteenth century.

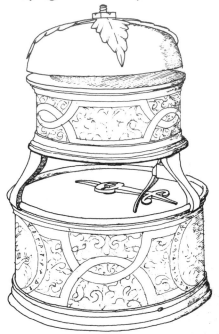

14. A SIXTEENTH–CENTURY
TABLE CLOCK WITH A
DETACHABLE ALARM
MECHANISM. THE HAND
TRIPS A LEVER TO SET OFF
THE ALARM BELL

Plate 2 – An Augsburg table clock of the early seventeenth century, of the belfry or tabernacle type. The gilt brass case is modelled on classical architecture. The main dial shows mean solar time and lunar time. The phases of the moon can be seen in a circular aperture in the disk carrying the moon pointers. The centre of the dial is an astrolabe and shows the position of the sun, moon and a number of other stars in the heavens. The lower left-hand dial shows the Dominical Letter for the year and the number of the year in the solar cycle. On the left side of the clock is a small dial to indicate which quarter was last sounded, while on the right side is another dial to show which hour was last struck. The large dial on the rear of the clock originally gave the minutes and the hours on the 2 × 12 system, and also Italian hours. Small dials also on the rear of the clock show the day of the week and the position of the sun in the zodiac.

The movement was originally controlled by a balance wheel. After the invention of the pendulum in 1657 many clocks, including this one, were converted to pendulum control. The pendulum clock was a prized object and so the pendulum was often made to swing in front of the dial where all could see it.

Many clocks made before the eighteenth century show the time on two or three dials. In Europe there were three methods of counting the hours. By the late sixteenth century the double twelve-hour count had become almost universal, except in Rome where a six-hour dial was used and in Germany where the twenty-four-hour dial was used.

Plate 3a – A German drum-shaped table clock made *c.* 1580. The dial has an outer ring of roman numerals from 1–12 and an inner ring of arabic numerals 13–24. It is also fitted with touch knobs for feeling the time in the dark. Such clocks were sometimes supplied or fitted with a detachable alarm mechanism (fig. 14). The movement of a drum clock may be controlled by a balance wheel or by what is called a 'dumb-bell' balance, which is a minute foliot looking like a dumb-bell.

The Baroque

During the seventeenth century the classical lines of the Renaissance gave way to the elaborate and vigorous designs of the Baroque which developed most vigorously, and even excessively, in Germany. The inventiveness of the German designers is particularly illustrated in the clock cases. Some have a globe supported on a pillar or by a group of youths, with the hour numerals on the globe rotating past a fixed pointer. Similar clocks represent Christ on the cross, or the Virgin and Child surmounted by a crown on which are the hour numerals.

Plate 4 – A novelty clock in the form of a globe mounted on the trunk of a palm tree. This early seventeenth-century clock is basically a drum-shaped table clock on an elaborately moulded base. The hour-hand arbor is mounted off-centre and continues up the trunk of the tree, on the end of which is the globe bearing the hour numerals. As the hour strikes, the man's head moves and the dog at his feet moves as if running.

Plate 5 – An early seventeenth-century clock case of novel design from southern Germany. Many such animal clocks have the animal standing or seated upon an ebony case with little windows on each side. At each hour the griffon's wings flap and its beak opens and closes. The brass tube running into its chest drives the mechanism animating the bird. By its feet are dials to show which hour and quarter-hour were last struck.

Other clocks even used their own weight to turn the wheels. The rack clock is an example of this. A drum-shaped clock is mounted over a toothed vertical pillar. To wind it, the clock is lifted to the top of the rack and its descent is regulated by the escapement.

The most excessive design of the Baroque was the 'Prunk Uhr' or cabinet clock. This was occasionally so elaborate that it became a sizeable piece of furniture incorporating numerous little cupboards and secret compartments; usually, however, it stood upon a stand or table. Most were made of wood or metal, but some are masterpieces of the silversmith's art: set with precious and semi-precious stones, embossed, engraved or enamelled. They are often decorated with groups of twisted columns supporting a massive superstructure of balustrades, pediments and figures which symbolise the arts or Roman gods. The movements are seldom as complicated as those of tabernacle clocks. Sometimes the dial or dials are so insignificant that it takes a few moments to recognise that what one is looking at is indeed a clock.

The Thirty Years' War, which began in 1618 between Catholics and Protestants, so disrupted life in Germany that between 1618 and 1645 the number of clockmakers in Augsburg dwindled from forty-three to seven. During this same period the French centres of Blois, Lyon and Paris, and the Swiss and English centres of Geneva and London, were growing rapidly.

Small table clocks, very often hexagonal in shape, were still made in the early eighteenth century, two hundred years after their first appearance. These later clocks are in less decorative cases, with badly proportioned mouldings. They usually have little windows in their sides and have a minute as well as an hour-hand.

Plate 3b – An hexagonal table clock about 12 cm (5 in) in width. Notice the champlevé chapter ring. This is where the depth of the chapter ring is reduced between the numerals, the lower portions usually being matted. The champlevé dial must not be confused with the skeleton chapter ring where areas of the ring between the numerals are cut out completely. One of the spring barrels can be seen through the bevelled glass window and is covered with engraving, while the hour bell can just be seen, mounted below the movement. Similar clocks were also made in Austria and many have fictitious London makers' names engraved upon the dial.

The Eighteenth Century
The eighteenth century was a time of a great expansion in the clock-making industry in Austria, especially in Vienna, and in Switzerland, which concentrated mainly on watch production. Augsburg was not the great centre it had once been, but its influence was still widely felt. A form of clock which had been made in Augsburg as far back as the early seventeenth century was the Teller Uhr or plate clock, so called because of the shape and nature of its dial. These were made in southern Germany and Austria until the late eighteenth century.

The Teller Uhr, which hangs from a hook on the wall, had a spring-driven movement controlled by a watch escapement or later by a cow's tail pendulum, a short pendulum which swings in front of the dial. The dial can vary from about 15 cm (6 in) to 45 cm (18 in) in diameter. Many are surrounded by an embossed and sometimes silvered brass plate, while the seventeenth-century examples may have no surround at all. The Zappler is a very similar clock, but it is made to stand on a table or cabinet top and was made well into the nineteenth century. The later Viennese makers often made small examples, some of them no more than a few centimetres high. Like carriage clocks, both the Zappler and the Teller Uhr have become specialised areas of collecting.

English clocks were very highly regarded throughout Europe in the early eighteenth century and the work of leading makers was not only copied but their proportions and design had a noticeable influence on the work of many Austrian and German makers.

Plate 6 – This clock shows how English bracket clock design was interpreted by Austrian makers of the late eighteenth century. The fruitwood case has a brass carrying handle, four finials and brass feet. All other gilt ornamentation on the case is of carved wood. The brass dial is signed 'Ge. Preisacher, Clostemenburg'. The arch contains a large calendar dial with the signs of the zodiac. The two subsidiary dials are for strike/silent and chime/silent. The backplate is engraved with a central cartouche of scrolls and foliage. The case is quite shallow compared to those of contemporary English bracket clocks.

Plate 7 – A good example of the kind of bracket clock produced in Austria and southern Germany during the latter half of the eighteenth century. The maker, Adalbertus Hockenadl, was one of a family of Viennese clockmakers who also sold, and possibly even made, clocks in Venice. This example is signed 'Venetia'. As is usual with Austrian bracket clocks it has only a 40-hour movement. The going train has a chain fusée, while the chiming part has a gut fusée. The striking train, however, has a going barrel; such a mixture is common in Austrian work. The going barrel is fitted with stop-work so that it cannot be overwound. The movement has heavy rectangular plates and is closer to English work of the period than to French. As well as chiming the quarter-hours on eight bells it has an alarm mechanism. The dials in the arch are for chime/silent and pendulum regulation.

The pendulum hangs upon a silk suspension. The chapter ring is secured by four tiny screws, a feature never found on English and seldom on French work. Austrian clocks often have the dial centre engraved to match the engraving in the arch. The painted wooden case with its sprays of flowers and blue interior is particularly beautiful. Ebonised, walnut veneered and marquetry cases were also popular.

Another major influence was the rococo, which is best illustrated by the Swiss Neuchâtel bracket clocks, named after the horological centre of that country. These eighteenth-century clocks were copies of the waisted French bracket clock in plate 29. Later a more individual style, with restrained gilt mounts, evolved. The case of wood was often lacquered and decorated with flowers or *chinoiserie*.

P. Jaquet-Droz of Neuchâtel made superb bracket clocks in the French style and in some of them he is known to have included complicated chiming and musical movements. Both Pierre and his son Henri became celebrated clock, watch and automaton makers. Many complicated watches were exported to China in the late eighteenth century, as well as wonderful automata such as that of a human figure who can write with pen and ink upon paper. Henri also worked in collaboration with Henri Maillardet from 1775, who was a member of another distinguished clock- and automata-making family, much of whose work also went to China. Henri Maillardet devised a single whistle with a moving piston to alter the note for mechanical singing birds, and with it was able to reproduce bird song almost perfectly.

In the last quarter of the century high quality machine-made watches began to be made in Switzerland. F. Japy was the first to manufacture watch *ébauches* by machines. In 1818 Japy opened a factory for the production of clock *ébauches* in Baderel.

The Swiss combined inventiveness, mechanical ingenuity and superb craftsmanship. Some of the leading makers in France and England such as Berthoud, Breguet, Recordon and Emery were, in fact, Swiss. By 1800 the Swiss industry had overtaken England and France in the production of watches of quality, which were also cheaper and more compact. During the nineteenth century Switzerland secured a virtual monopoly of the Chinese market. Many watches had elaborate repeating mechanisms which made figures on the dial strike little bells. Others contained minute musical box movements which played a tune at the hour or at will.

Plate 8 – A Swiss bracket clock or Neuchâteloise of the early nineteenth century. This style of clock evolved in the Neuchâtel district of Switzerland. The case sits upon a matching wall bracket. The cast brass bezel around the dial and that surrounding the pendulum aperture are in one piece. The long plain pointer on the enamelled dial is the alarm setting hand. The rear of the case can be removed to gain access to the movement. The movement of this clock has *grande sonnerie* striking, that is it sounds each quarter on two gongs and the last hour on a bell. All the lifting levers and racks for the chiming are mounted on the back plate.

There were no craftsmen of the influence of Sheraton or Adam in Germany and so clock case design was influenced by both English and French styles in the eighteenth century and many local styles also developed. Both longcase and bracket clocks were popular in Germany. Like the French and Dutch the *bombé* base was much used on longcase clocks. Veneers were often inlaid in panels of parquetrie, and the trunks were often shaped, swelling in rococo curves at the level of the pendulum bob. By the 1750s most German states had adopted the French rococo style. The fashionable court of the Elector of Bavaria at Munich, for instance, employed craftsmen trained in Paris. The famous Roentgen workshops at Neuwied produced some of the most beautiful furniture.

Abraham Roentgen, 1711–93, worked in Holland and England in his early years, and his son, David, later had considerable influence on German furniture. His designs were light and graceful and not over-elaborate. Many of his longcase clock cases display very fine pictorial marquetry on the trunk and base. The designs for this inlay (a specialty of his) were often taken from the paintings of Januarious Zick.

Clockcases by Roentgen usually contain movements by Kinzing. In one clock made by this partnership in 1805 Kinzing used Benjamin Franklin's unique dial layout. This uses one hand which makes one

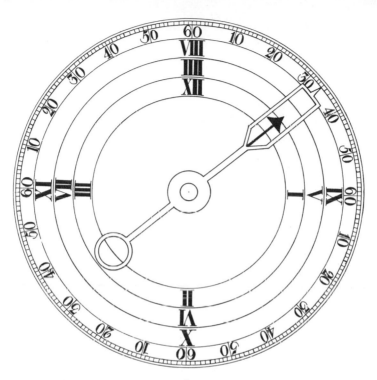

15. THE DIAL OF BENJAMIN FRANKLIN'S ONE-HANDED CLOCK AS MADE BY SEVERAL MAKERS IN GERMANY AND ENGLAND

revolution of the dial every four hours, and shows the minutes. It also has a 'window' along its length in which is another pointer indicating the hours. This second pointer adjusts itself to the appropriate ring after each 4-hour period.

The idea of the picture clock is a very old one, since it is known that as early as 1700 a certain Friedrick Christian Hirt made clocks fitted into church towers within landscape paintings. In the early nineteenth century the Swiss cashed in on this idea which the French were making popular. Characteristically the Swiss were seldom content to make do with an ordinary striking movement and often fitted a comb musical box which played a tune every hour.

Nineteenth-century Vienna

Viennese clocks echoed both the French rococo and the neoclassical styles. Gilt cartel clocks were a popular type, but instead of being of cast bronze they were made of carved and gilt wood, like those in England. Carved and gilt wood mantel clocks were also made towards the end of the eighteenth century in the neoclassical designs fashionable in Paris. The gilt is often of several shades and burnished in parts. The dials are usually enamelled and the 30-hour movements often chime and repeat the quarter-hours at will. It is not unusual to find examples with sweep-centre calendar hands.

The nineteenth century saw a considerable growth in the Viennese industry, partly due to the increased export trade to eastern Europe and Italy. Large numbers of mantel clocks made at this time were variations of the four-pillar or portico style of case seen in plate 36. Mahogany and ebonised cases were particularly popular, with columns of alabaster, glass or gilt wood framing mirror glasses or even delicate paintings by artists such as Wiegand, who painted architectural subjects. The dials may be of engine-turned brass, or enamelled. Sometimes, on especially fine pieces, the centre of the dial may feature an automaton scene set off as the clock strikes. Another particularly charming feature is the musical box fitted in the base of some clocks which is set off by the clock at the hour. The disadvantage of so many Viennese clocks is that they are only of 30-hour duration. Only special 'one off' pieces were of 8-day duration.

Plate 9 – An Empire or Biedermeier period mantel clock of about 1825 standing 45·7 cm (18 in) high. The case, which is designed as an obelisk on a plinth, is of mahogany with ebony mouldings and brass mounts. The enamelled dial has Breguet style hands and a centre calendar pointer. It is signed 'Niederlags Compagnie in Wien' and has a quarter-striking movement. The pendulum regulation square can be seen over the figure twelve.

The clock for which Vienna is renowned is, of course, the Vienna regulator, a name used indiscriminately today to describe any wall regulator with glass front and sides even if it is a mass-produced article from the U.S.A. or Germany. The movements are of fine quality and were secured to the back of the case by cast brass brackets. The pendulum was also suspended from a bracket on the back board and not from the back plate of the movement. Many of these clocks are not true regulators since they also strike the hour or even chime the quarters. Even so they are all fitted with temperature-compensating pendulums, a dead beat escapement and maintaining power.

Plate 10 – This is a striking Vienna regulator movement of the second half of the nineteenth century and is typical of Austrian work. It is instructive to compare this with movements of a similar period made in France (plate 37), England (plate 57), and America (plate 73). English movements of the period are extremely weighty while American movements are very flimsy. Austrian work is closest to that of France.

Plate 11a – A longcase regulator in a burr walnut case with inlaid lines of contrasting white wood. The inside of the case is also finely veneered. The sides of the case have windows as well as the hood and trunk. The severe architectural style of the case is typical of the first quarter of the nineteenth century. The clock has a massive pendulum bob and wooden rod which, like pendulums on all Vienna regulators, swings through an exceedingly small arc. The glass dial is not uncommon on Vienna regulators. The counter-balanced minute- and hour-hands are in the form of arrows. In a sense this clock is not a true regulator since it strikes the hours and also chimes the quarters. The clock stands slightly over 1·8 m (6 ft) high. In the background is a reproduction of a late 18th-century Neuchâtel bracket clock in a red lacquer case with matching wall bracket and brass mounts.

Plate 11b – A wall regulator dating from the latter half of the nineteenth century. Early nineteenth-century wall regulators were designed like the longcase clock in plate 11a with a hood trunk and glazed base in which the pendulum bob swung. The ebonised case of this clock is conceived as a single unit enlivened by finials and a central cresting. The dial is of two pieces with a recessed centre.

3

Black Forest

The Black Forest area of Germany includes the provinces of Baden and Württemberg bordered to the south and west by the Rhine. The northern border of Switzerland is included within the area which is referred to as the Black Forest school of clockmaking.

The hard winters which the area experiences encouraged local people to find new indoor occupations, and by the second half of the seventeenth century a cottage clockmaking industry was established. The area had always been known for its glass manufacture, and some clocks may even be found with glass bells. In an area such as the Black Forest there was a great tradition of woodworking and carving and it was to this material that the clockmakers naturally turned. The local timber is mainly coniferous, and it is probable that much of the hardwood used for the intricate work of making the plates and wheels was imported. The dials and side doors were the only parts made of the local soft woods. The plates, arbors and (on early examples) the wheels were made of beech.

The tools which the craftsmen used were as unusual as the construction of the wooden movements. The region has some fine museums (such as those at Furtwangen and Triberg) where one can see both the clocks and also reconstructions of typical nineteenth-century clockmakers' workshops, complete with lathes and wheelcutting machines constructed mostly of wood to individual designs. The massiveness of these treadle-operated machines with their heavy stone flywheels produced a very sure and steady action.

As in any clockmaking community, no one man made a complete clock. Much of the work would be done in farmers' cottages, collected and assembled in larger workshops. Each man would specialise in the production of a particular part, so there would be dial makers, dial painters, frame makers, chain makers and so on.

Like the clocks produced in the Morbier district of France, designs varied little over many generations. The foliot, for example, was probably used until as late as the 1740s. Few early clocks have survived and it is rare to come across an eighteenth-century example. It is very difficult to date these clocks with any accuracy, since styles changed so slowly. Towards the close of the eighteenth century brass began to be produced locally, and this was used for making the wheels.

Plate 12a – This movement is of the mid-nineteenth century. The brass wheels are mounted on wooden arbors often painted to imitate steel. The pivots are of wire set in brass bushes sunk into the wooden plates. The pinions are of the lantern form, with wire leaves. The striking is the countwheel type.

Plate 12b – It is interesting to see how the clocks were fitted with different dials to suit the taste of the country to which they were to be exported. The shield dial on this clock was the traditional design which was popular in the Low Countries and with the French, who liked them gaily painted with flowers in the spandrels. This one is only 20·3 cm (8 in) high. The movement is an alarm timepiece although the central alarm disk is not original.

Hexagonal dials were favoured in Scandinavia, while those exported to England were mostly in the style of the English fusée dial clock. Some of the more elaborate cases were made in England to house these Black Forest movements.

The Black Forest clocks have often been mistakenly called Dutch clocks, a corruption of the word Deutsch. These clocks were sold by travelling salesmen. Each salesman would hire a room and have a number of clocks delivered there. He would then set out each day carrying his wares on a *tragstuhl*, a form of carrying frame. These travelling salesmen became the subject of a clock, made of painted cast iron, where one of their number is seen carrying two clocks, one of which contains a miniature verge spring-driven movement. Good reproductions of these clocks are now being made.

Another notable miniature was the weight-driven Jockel clock. The pendulum swings outside the case, which is kept a centimetre or two away from the wall by wooden spikes. The dials are normally of fired enamel surmounted or surrounded by a repoussé brass shield.

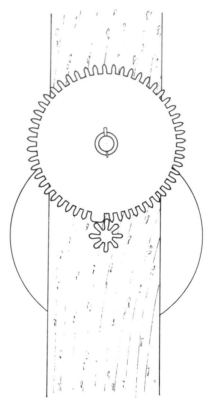

16. STOP WORK ON BLACK
FOREST SPRING-DRIVEN
CLOCKS

Late nineteenth century Jockel clocks were also made with dainty porcelain cases.

Quarter-chiming clocks were made with elaborately shaped arch dials and an aperture in which figures can be seen striking the bells.

Another elaborate clock was the cuckoo clock, invented in about 1730 by Anton Ketterer of Schonwald, but it did not gain universal popularity until the nineteenth century. The bird sound is produced by small bellows blowing air through the wooden pipes, like an organ. Ketterer never knew that the cuckoo clock was eventually to become the most famous product of the Black Forest. The cuckoo clocks of about 1800–20 were simply wooden shield dials with a little door in the arch where the bird appears.

Plate 12c – By the mid-nineteenth century more elaborate examples appeared with the movement completely enclosed within a soundly made case. The clock illustrated has a chalet style case with brass inlaid lines. The painted dial surround is of tin, the dial itself is enamelled on copper.

To have the striking train positioned behind the going train of weight-driven clocks resulted in a very deep frame, which subsequently tended to twist the movement out of shape (see plate 12a). To overcome this some clocks were made with the trains mounted side-by-side.

Competition from America

The export trade flourished until Jerome and other American factories began to export cheap clocks in sophisticated-looking cases to Europe. From about 1845 competition became increasingly tough, and eventually the Black Forest was forced to turn to mass production techniques.

The success of American and French spring-driven clocks may have tempted Black Forest makers to introduce spring-driven wall clocks.

Plate 12d – This is a wooden plated 8-day spring-driven wall clock. It is fitted with stop work to avoid overwinding (see diagram). Some of these clocks, especially mantle clocks, were even fitted with fusées. The case is veneered in walnut with brass inlaid lines and is a close copy of English wall clocks. One way to distinguish a Black Forest-made case from an English one is that the Black Forest case will have a removable back to allow access to the movement. The zinc dial painted cream, is signed 'Beha Lickert & Co. of Norwich' who was the retailer of the clock.

Mass Production

To match American competition, factory production was started in the 1850s in Schwenningen by Johannes Burk, followed soon after by Erhard Junghans at Schramberg. Junghan's brother had actually worked in an American clock factory and was able to bring valuable information to the family business. Their clocks were exact replicas of American products except that instead of rolled brass for the plates and stamped out wheels, the Germans used castings which were heavier and show the marks of hand finishing.

The idea of making American clocks in Germany was taken to extraordinary lengths. Printed labels showing the factories or coats of arms were pasted inside the cases, and printed and coloured designs were applied to the glass panels below the dials. Even the numerous companies which grew up took on American-sounding names, such as the Teutonia Clock Manufactory, The Hamburg American Clock Co., and the Union Clock Co. Often it is very difficult to differentiate between the products of the two countries.

Plate 13a – Three German clocks of typical American shelf clock form. The left-hand one is by the Union Clock Co. of Furtwangen and is the closest to its American prototypes. The case is painted with false rosewood graining and is decorated with gilt mouldings. The zinc dial is not painted but is faced with printed paper; note the shaped centre and the alarm disk. The right-hand clock is displayed with the dial removed to show the mass-produced movement and the label of the Union Clock Co. This clock was probably made in the early 1900s. The movement in the centre clock is of finer quality. It has solid cast brass plates stamped 'W. & H. Sch.' for Winterhalder and Hoffmeier of Schramberg, and also has stop work. It was retailed in England by Camerer Kuss and Co. who had premises in New Oxford St., Bloomsbury, and Shepherd's Bush, London. Their label advertises 'a large assortment of curiosity and cuckoo clocks always on sale'. This clock in its sombre ebonised case probably dates from the 1880s.

Many popular styles of American clocks were copied by German factories. They also produced cheap copies of the very popular Vienna regulator, many fitted with spring-driven movements and sham gridiron pendulums. The popularity of these wall clocks helped to kill the Dutch clockmaking industry which, like the English, was too slow and reluctant to change its production methods. Junghan's also made longcase clocks after 1900. The models with chiming movements playing on gongs sold well in England. They had glass doors through which could be seen the brass pendulum bob and weights. The movements of most German clocks made in the years leading up to World War I were of good quality despite being mass-produced; indeed some of them approached the quality of French clocks, with heavy plates and well-cut wheels.

Plate 13b – A cuckoo clock of the second half of the nineteenth century. It has a brass movement and heavily carved case in the form of oak, ivy or vine leaves inhabited by birds and animals. The white-painted hands may not be original. Many carved cuckoo clocks were originally fitted with matching carved wood pendulum bobs.

Plate 13c – This is a typical cuckoo clock movement of cast brass from the second half of the nineteenth century. It is quite easy to see the file marks where the rough castings were finished. The pipes which produce the bird sound are to the left and right of the movement, the little bellows above each are actuated by wires from the striking train.

Plate 14 – Even in the 1900s, when mass production was the rule rather than the exception, wooden plated movements were still being made. The most usual form was known as the postman's alarm, here seen with the dial painted on the reverse of a sheet of glass enabling it to be kept clean without damaging the numerals. This particular example was first purchased by a gentleman who worked for the Great Western Railway in Exeter, England, in 1914.

A very successful clock of novel design was the 400-day clock with a torsion pendulum invented by Anton Harder. The pendulum consists of a very fine brass strip from which hangs the slowly-turning balance. These clocks are housed under a glass dome and have sold in huge numbers and in dozens of slightly different designs from the 1880s to the present day. The same torsion principle was employed again in the Atmos clock (plate 42).

4 *Holland*

Like most European countries, Holland had an established clock-making trade by the Middle Ages. Examples do exist of Gothic weight-driven chamber clocks with the familiar features of 4-poster movements with buttress-shaped posts and tall, tapering pinnacle-like finials.

By the mid-seventeenth century Dutch chamber clocks were placed on purpose-built wooden brackets not unlike the Stoel clocks of a later period. The posts of the movement were of a truly classical architectural design – Tuscan columns standing upon square pedestals. Strangely, these beautiful columns were enclosed within the undecorated side doors and do not form a part of the external design. In this respect there is a link with the so-called lantern clocks of Japan.

The Invention of the Pendulum

The Hague was to earn a reputation for itself during the latter part of the seventeenth century since it was near where Christian Huygens, the scientist, worked. By the age of twenty-six, in 1655, he had already discovered a new satellite of Saturn with a telescope which he had constructed himself, and it was to assist his astronomical observations that he turned his mind to making an improved timepiece. He was also concerned with producing a clock which would function well enough aboard ship to be used for finding longitude and so improve navigation.

Although Huygens was not the first to use a pendulum to control clockwork he was certainly responsible for its successful application in Holland, France and England. He constructed his first model in 1656 and within the following months Solomon Coster, a clockmaker who worked for Huygens, took out a patent on the new invention, which gave him sole rights to make and sell pendulum clocks in the Netherlands for twenty-one years. Huygens probably took a share of the profits. The granting of this patent may explain why the Dutch industry did not expand as fast as would be expected at this time. Huygens also tried to secure a patent for his invention in France but his requests were repeatedly refused. The French, especially Parisians, ordered many pendulum clocks from makers in the Hague, but by 1662 Huygens himself admitted that the French were making superior clocks to those of the Dutch, especially regarding finish. By this date it is possible that French taste was demanding a more ornate article than the Dutch were making.

Plates 15 and 16 – This clock is very similar to the first pendulum clocks made in the Hague, from where its name, Haagse clock, originates. It is signed 'Van Ceulen' and dates from about 1675. The going and striking trains are both driven from one spring. The pendulum is suspended between curved 'cycloidal cheeks'. When these cheeks are of the correct curvature the pendulum describes a cycloidal arc and not the arc of a circle. In this cycloidal arc the time of each swing of the pendulum is equal, regardless of the size of the arc of the swing. Very few clockmakers fully understood this principle and many makers fitted curved cheeks although they were of the wrong shape. Notice the beautifully decorated wings to the back cock and the pierced frets to the striking lifting and locking piece arbors. The dial is hinged to the case to allow easy access to the movement. The chapter ring, supported by a figure of Father Time, is cut out or skeletonised and each minute is engraved around its edge. Notice that the bell is not fitted to the movement but is mounted on top of the case, behind the open arched pediment. The rings on the back of the case are to secure the clock to the wall, but it could equally well be used as a table clock.

Plate 17 – A magnificent silver-cased clock, with a movement by Adriaen Van den Bergh of the Hague, and a case signed J. H. C. Breghtel. The extremely elaborate case displays more German than

Dutch characteristics and must surely have been inspired by the decorative pieces of Augsburg and Nuremberg. The silver case which stands about 75 cm (2 ft 6 in) high is covered with fretted and engraved silver of an intricate floral design. The clock has dials on two sides and was evidently intended to stand in the centre of the room, or at least somewhere where all sides could be seen.

Plate 18 – At first sight this clock could easily be mistaken for an English production. It is by Roger Dunster, who was evidently so well-known that he thought it unnecessary to mention on the dial that he worked in Amsterdam. This clock is of about 1745 and is very like the fine clocks made by Benjamin Gray and Vulliamy in London at this time. Within the arch is a pendulum regulation dial, a large calendar dial and a strike/silent lever. The central alarm disk is very typically Dutch. The clock is controlled by a short pendulum and verge escapement; the false pendulum aperture above the centre of the dial shows that the clock is going and can be used to set the pendulum in motion after rewinding.

English designs at this period had a great influence on Dutch makers, especially in the field of bracket clocks where there was no traditional Dutch design.

The idea of fraudulently engraving famous makers' names onto clock dials is by no means a modern one. In 1704 the master of the London clockmakers' company complained that 'certain persons at Amsterdam were in the habit of putting the names of Tompion, Windmills, Quare, Cabrier, Lamb and other well-known London makers on their works and selling them as English'.

Weight-driven Wall Clocks
The Zaanse clock, believed to have originated in the Zaan region, is probably the earliest of the numerous styles of wall clock. The weight-driven wall clock was without question the most popular clock in Holland, the longcase and bracket clocks being made mostly in the cities. The movements of Zaanse clocks are usually quite simple, while the strap-type frame can be traced back to medieval clocks. To dismantle the framework a wedge is removed from the hinged top plate. Zaanse clocks may date back to the 1650s and have verge

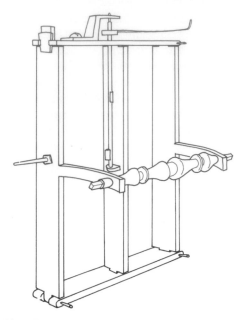

17. STRAP FORM OF CONSTRUCTION OF THE ZAANSE CLOCK SHOWING HOW MOVEMENT IS HINGED AND WEDGED TOGETHER. ALSO SHOWN IS THE VERGE STAFF AND CRUTCH

escapements. The verge staff is placed vertically, as it would be if the clock had a balance wheel, and is connected to the pendulum by a long wire. The pendulum is contained within the box-like wall bracket which is usually elaborately shaped. This wall bracket supports the wooden cased clock itself. The case sits upon turned feet and often has twisted baroque columns at the corners. Examples with arched dials and moon work appear to have been made in the seventeenth century, pre-dating the popularity of the arch dial in England by a good twenty years. The cases are invariably surmounted by very ornate cast brass crestings, the front one often incorporating an arched open pediment on which stand figures of Faith, Hope and Charity.

44

Inside the crestings are the two bells for the hours and half hours on which stand the figure of Atlas or Minerva. Zaanse clocks usually have pear-shaped brass-cased weights suspended on a rope.

Plate 19 – Two Zaanse clocks. The one on the left is signed 'Groot 1725'. The simple turned corner columns to the case support a horizontal entablature surmounted by the normal metal cresting. The dial is velvet covered, onto which are applied a wide chapter-ring and cherub's head spandrels. A similar clock is seen to the right but this has a painted dial plate.

A more common type of wall clock is the Stoel clock or little chair clock, so-called because the 4-poster movement sits upon a wooden stool supported by the wall bracket. This type of clock was made in large numbers in Freisland – the northern part of Holland. The polished wood cases of the Zaanse clocks are quite sombre compared with the Stoel clocks which display a mass of gaily coloured paint-work.

The movements of early eighteenth-century Stoel clocks are very similar to the movements of some mid-seventeenth-century wall clocks. During the eighteenth century the classical style of the corner posts gave way to more imaginative turning, similar to that of the Staart clock movement in plate 22.

Before 1750 the raised chapter ring of silvered brass was usually mounted on a painted dial plate which might depict landscape scenes, figures or flowers. Above and below the dial plate were pierced metal castings of leafy scrolls often incorporating heraldic motifs. The metal used, often lead, was always painted gold. Occasionally examples can be found with this kind of decoration sprouting from all four sides of the dial. The wall bracket itself was shaped on either side in the form of painted mermaids or vase handles. To the top of this wall board a canopy is fixed which may protect the movement from dust although its main function was decorative. While the weights of the Zaanse clock are normally hung on plaited ropes, those of the Stoel clock and Staart clock are hung on chains of a particular kind. Each link is a figure of eight with the two circles of the figure twisted at right angles to one another. In other words, one link of this chain corresponds to two links of a normal chain.

Plate 20 – A Stoel clock with a verge escapement positioned, as in a Zaanse clock, with a vertical verge staff. The 4-post movement has thin turned brass posts connecting the iron top and bottom plates. This clock does not strike the hours but has an alarm mechanism mounted on the rear of the back plate. The cast brass hour-hand has a large central boss on which are marked the hours for the small iron alarm pointer. The short pendulum is mounted from a peg on the back board.

The basic types of wall clock are fairly distinct, but there are transitional types which may have features of both Zaanse and Stoel or may appear to be a cross between Stoel and Staart clocks.

The Staart clock or tail clock is so named because of the great length of the wall board which is, like the Zaanse clock, of box-like construction to contain the pendulum. The Staart clock is a more refined and imposing clock than the Stoel clock which it eventually superseded. Its hood is like that of a longcase clock and the movement, which is similar to the Stoel clock movement, is bolted to a base board. Variations of the Staart clock were made, one with a short trunk is known as a *Kortkast*. Very small examples were made for use on the barges using Holland's inland waterways and these are known as little ships' clocks or *Schippertjes*. They have short pendulums within the hood and have verge escapements which performed better than the more usual anchor which would have been upset by the movement of the vessel. Staart clocks were made from the late eighteenth century to about 1880. The town of Joure seems to have been the main centre of their production, which was at its height in the mid-nineteenth century.

Plates 21 and 22 – A Staart clock in an oak case stained to simulate mahogany. The 30-hour movement has one brass-bound weight. The iron dial is elaborately painted, while under the chapter ring is a coastal scene with a rocking ship, a windmill with rotating sails and a fisherman whose rod is constantly rising and falling. The position of the automata scene is unusual, as it generally is in the arch. The movement (plate 22) shows that the countwheel is cut for Dutch double-striking. The hour is sounded on the larger bell, then at the half-hour it is sounded again on the smaller bell (a replacement). The automated ship and fisherman are actuated from the crutch to the pendulum, while the windmill is connected to a wooden pulley on the escape wheel arbor (the pulley on the windmill is a replacement and the pulley cord is missing).

It is almost impossible to date Staart clocks precisely, since they were made to the same design for nearly a century. This one is probably late eighteenth century or early nineteenth century.

Lastly under the heading of wall clocks must be mentioned the Amsterdamse hanging clocks. These clocks predate the Staart clock but are similar in concept; the most noticeable difference is in the movement. The movements of Amsterdamse hanging clocks are like those of good quality 30-hour longcase clocks. They are plated and have brass dials often with a seconds dial, alarm and moon phases in the arch. The hood is identical in design to good quality Amsterdam longcase clocks, usually veneered in walnut with an elaborate scroll top surmounted by a dome and figures of Atlas and trumpeting angels. The wall board contains the pendulum which is seen through a lenticle in the short door.

The Longcase Clock

While the wall clock was certainly the favourite clock of Holland, longcase clocks were made throughout the eighteenth century, first appearing in about 1680 and closely resembling English clocks of the period. The popular velvet-covered dial plate was used on many early examples. The hands of early Dutch longcase clocks are often very much finer than English examples. When the velvet overlay was used, the hands were of beautifully pierced, engraved and gilt brass, while the hands for dials with matt brass centres were of blued steel. The cases of late seventeenth-century longcase clocks were of walnut or covered in parquetry or marquetry designs.

Plate 23a – This clock marks the peak of the longcase clock and was made by Roger Dunster of Amsterdam, a leading eighteenth-century maker. The exotic-looking veneer is mulberry wood, which is inlaid with ebony stringing and has ebonised mouldings. The base has *bombé* sides. The cast brass mount to the lenticle on the trunk door figures the rape of Europa. The movement is a musical one, with a selection of twelve tunes and is similar to that seen in plate 24. Apart from the signature, the arch contains a painting of musicians in classical costume. This imposing piece is nearly 2·7 m (9 ft) high.

Plate 23b – Another fine longcase clock made in Amsterdam this time by Jan Van Brussel. The 8-day movement also shows the moon's phases in the arch. There is an alarm disk in the dial centre, and within the seconds dial is a square aperture showing the day of the month and below the dial centre is the day of the week. The finely veneered walnut case has a *bombé* base, common to much Dutch furniture of the mid-eighteenth century. The whole clock stands 2 m (7 ft) high.

Plate 24 – A musical longcase clock movement made by Franciscus Bavius of Leeuwarden, in northern Holland, in about 1760. The dial of this clock has subsidiary dials for strike/not strike and chime/not chime, and also has segment-shaped calendar apertures for the month and day of the week. The clock had two interchangeable musical barrels with twelve tunes on each. The musical longcase clock was very much more popular in Holland than in England, where even a clock which chimes the quarter-hours is a rarity. By mounting the musical barrel horizontally across the back plate, it was possible to accommodate this movement within a case of fine proportions a little larger than a normal case. There are two hammers to each bell which allows one note to be repeated in very quick succession to produce lively and interesting tunes. The hours are struck on the large bell nestling between the dial and the musical bells, and the half-hours are struck on the smaller bell mounted on the back plate.

The wall clock outlived the longcase in popularity since the Staart clock was still made in very large numbers in the 1850s. This was just the time when cheap and mass-produced American and Black Forest clocks were beginning to arrive in England and Holland in large numbers. These low-priced clocks were, however, surprisingly reliable and would keep reasonable time and were consequently most popular with working people. The middle classes also bought the more elegant and decorative mass-produced imports.

According to E. J. Tyler in *European Clocks*, Dutch retailers encouraged demand for German-made clocks by giving a rebate on old Dutch clocks brought in for part exchange. The heavy brass movements were then sold as scrap metal, the cases (even today) sold for firewood and movements thrown away by the ill-informed. In my own experience no fine old movement or shattered case is beyond restoration and is always well worth the effort and expense.

5 *France*

The Renaissance

It is the spring-driven clocks which have survived best of the clocks of the sixteenth century. Because they are small and very decorative they have always been looked upon as something precious, even if out of order. Unlike Germany, where the guild laws forbade the use of precious metals by clockmakers, the French made full use of silver and even gold in their table-clock cases. As might be expected the majority of these have been broken up for their valuable metal content, consequently the existing clocks give a very unbalanced picture of early clockmaking in France.

Plate 25 – The hexagonal clock was the most popular type during the sixteenth century. The trains are mounted one above the other in the case which is designed as a miniature tower with columns at each corner and surmounted by a pierced dome housing the bell. The movements of these clocks are equally architectural: the plates or 'floors' of the movement are supported by pillars at each corner. The movement, often standing on squat feet, is inserted into the case from below and held in position by the tightly-fitting base. The clock is also wound from below which means that the going fusée arbor on the top floor extends down to the bottom of the case. Similarly, the bell hammer has to be extended from the striking train mounted beneath up into the dome where the bell is mounted. The dial is always a part of the movement and appears through an aperture in the case.

French Renaissance clocks do not display quite the same grandeur or variety as their German counterparts until the end of the sixteenth century when new types, inspired by German designs, were adopted It is interesting to notice that the shape of the case of Renaissance clocks is determined by the construction of the movement – the two parts are inseparably related. Only later in the seventeenth century does the case become independent from the shape of the movement.

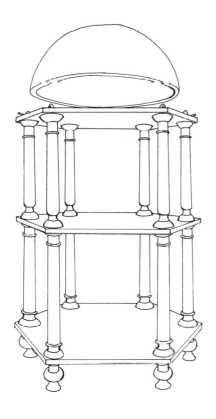

18. TWO TIER PLATED MOVEMENT OF SIXTEENTH-CENTURY TABLE CLOCKS. THE TOP PLATE IS PINNED ON WHILST THE BOTTOM PLATE IS REMOVED BY UNSCREWING THE FEET

During the period 1590 to 1610 the hexagonal shape almost disappeared, to be replaced by the recently-introduced square form. The architectural details of these square cases are less pronounced than on the former hexagonal ones. The four sides were often exquisitely engraved with foliage and flowers. Within France were numerous clockmaking centres, including Blois, Paris, Lyons, Marseilles, Abbeville and Autun. Each major centre had its own craft guilds.

The Paris Guilds

The Paris Guild of Clockmakers had its statutes changed a number of times between its formation in 1544 and 1691 when, in Louis XIV reign, its laws were rewritten. An apprentice was bound for eight years, although he could spend these years under more than one master. A master was allowed only one apprentice, although he could have numerous assistants. The laws were rather restrictive, allowing seventy-two qualified members of the Guild at any one time, and sons of established members were given special privileges.

Each craft had its own guild, cabinet-makers, gilders, founders, engravers, enamellers and so on. This resulted in perhaps half a dozen workshops working on or producing parts for one clock. Inevitably this caused friction between the various groups of craftsmen; arguments even arose from deciding who should transport a piece from one workshop to another. Variations in quality between constituent parts of a case can sometimes be detected.

Certain groups of craftsmen had the opportunity to streamline their production because they were free of the laws of the guilds and worked in districts controlled by the church or the king. These craftsmen could have as large a workshop and as many apprentices as they could manage. Within the Louvre were lodged many of the most distinguished craftsmen, including cabinet-makers and clockmakers working wholly or partly for the king.

Louis XIII and XIV

The seventeenth century saw a dramatic decline in clock production as the fashion for carrying watches on the person increased. The clocks of this period display wonderful quality, which probably reflected the precise and decorative work required in the making of watches.

By 1653 when Louis XIV came to the throne, the French clockmaking industry was dead. This explains why the early French pendulum clocks were such faithful copies of Dutch ones. For the first time clocks were housed in wooden cases whose size and shape were not strictly dictated by that of the movement. The pendulum clock was such a great improvement in accuracy that clocks once more became fashionable, and Paris now became firmly established as the centre of the French clockmaking industry.

The early pendulum clocks were known as *Pendules Religeuse* because their black ebony veneer gave them such a sombre appearance. Such a modest-looking clock could hardly satisfy for long the requirements of the aristocracy who, under the leadership of Louis XIV, were furnishing their houses in the most elaborate style based loosely on classical forms. The development of the Religeuse into a highly decorative article designed to fit in with the elaborate bronze mounted and inlaid furniture was rapid and predictable.

By the 1670s the square, box-like case had become embellished with baroque columns or pillasters at the corners, an elaborate entablature supported a shallow dome top surmounted with gilt finials. The veneer was usually tortoiseshell inlaid with pewter lines and foliage. The square dial aperture was now arch-topped and below the chaptering was often a figure of Father Time or some other allegorical figure in cast and gilt bronze. In the 1690s enamel plaques for each hour numeral were introduced. The minutes were still engraved around the edge of the dial. By the end of the century the lower portion of the dial was left open, except perhaps for a figure or name plaque and the inlaid interior of the clock could be seen.

Plate *26* – This is an elaborate *Pendule Religeuse* of the late seventeenth century. The wooden case is inlaid with tortoiseshell, brass and a white metal, most probably pewter. The shaped apron below the dial was a common feature of French pendulum clocks at this early date. The movement has a plain back plate engraved with the maker's name. The pendulum is suspended between cycloidal cheeks. Both going and striking trains have going barrels. As in the early

Dutch pendulum clock seen in plate 16, the striking, lifting and locking detent arbors have pierced steel 'gates' which are purely decorative.

The Royal manufactory at the Gobelin's on the outskirts of Paris was the birth-place of the Louis XIV style. It was set up in 1667 under the control of Le Brun, who employed not only French craftsmen, but also Flemish and Italians skilled in metal inlaying and tapestry. Here the classical baroque style matured, and no expense was spared to produce the very best of everything for the King's palace at Versailles.

During the last decade of the seventeenth century André Charles Boulle (1642–1732) was to become one of the most influential of cabinet-makers. In collaboration with Jean Berain he made magnificent pieces of inlaid furniture with marquetry of tortoiseshell and brass, pewter, silver, mother-of-pearl and numerous other materials. The designs are of linear arabesques combined with scrolling leafy foliage from which emerge grotesques and mythological creatures. The cast metal mounts on Boulle's own work tend to be secondary to the form of the piece and serve to enhance the inlay work.

During the first years of the eighteenth century the pedestal clock became very popular. The mounting of a spring-driven clock on a matching pedestal produced a very impressive piece of furniture. Drawings attributed to Oppendard exist showing weight-driven longcase clocks of about 1720, and some examples survive from as early as 1680 but they are most uncommon. At no period in French history was the weight-driven longcase clock produced in large numbers.

Plate 27 – A pedestal clock by Mynuel of Paris (1694–1750). The spring-driven movement sounds 'ting-tang' quarter-hours and is contained in a gilt bronze case with brass and dark brown tortoiseshell inlay. The bronze dial is finely chased and each hour numeral consists of a separate enamel plaque. The hands are of blued steel. The dial no longer fills the door aperture, and the inlaid and bronze mounted interior can be seen through the glass panel below the dial.

This is a clock of Boulle's period and it will be noticed that the decoration is always symmetrical. The motifs in use at this period include masks, shells, goats' heads, rearing seahorses, allegorical figures, lions' paws and the inevitable acanthus leaves. The inlay work of the late seventeenth and early eighteenth centuries is always of outstanding quality: the pieces fit perfectly and show no sign of the thickness of a saw cut. The metal inlay is always engraved.

Plate 28 – An early example of a cartel clock (from the Italian *cartela*, a bracket). The cartel clock, normally of gilt bronze, hangs on the wall and can range in size from 30 cm to 1·5 m (1 ft to 5 ft) in height. This clock was made by J. Thuret of Paris who was clockmaker to the king from 1694 to 1712, as his father had been before him. The design is perfectly symmetrical, incorporating festoons of flowers and rams' heads. The bronze case, basically of lyre form, contains a dial with enamelled plaques for the hours with the figures in blue. The hands at this period were almost a standard design and were of steel. Parts of the case are burnished, while others are left as a contrasting light matt gilt.

During the early eighteenth century a new feeling in furniture design was emerging. The weight of Louis XIV gave way to a freer and lighter style and for the first time asymmetrical designs appeared, especially in cartel clocks. The waisted shape became almost universal for bracket clocks, many of which still survive, together with their matching brackets. By about 1715–20 the enamelled dial centre was introduced. Throughout the century clock movements became more standardised. The bell was now often mounted on the back plate of the drum-shaped movement, since an increasing number of bronze cases now being made had restricted space for the movement. This period is rich in eminent craftsmen. Cressent, Caffieri, Meisonnier and Gaudreau were all men of creative genius, who made clock cases that were often superb pieces of sculpture in their own right.

Louis XV

Louis XV reigned from 1723 to 1774 and during these years styles changed dramatically. This period saw the rococo style come and go, being replaced by a much purer classical style than that of Louis XIV. The rococo is often thought of as a style in its own right, but strictly it is the last phase of the baroque style. There is no break in the development of styles from Louis XIV to the mid-eighteenth century as there is between the rococo and the neoclassicism which followed. Rococo designs combine abstract curves and scrolls with shell- and coral-like shapes, as well as flowers and leaves and, later, Chinese and Gothic motifs.

One of the most popular types of clock was the waisted bracket clock. At first it was veneered with tortoiseshell and brass inlay with gilt mounts. Later examples are sometimes veneered in brightly coloured horn, and sometimes inlaid with flowers in contrasting colours. Others were lacquered and painted with flowers while some of the most superb are of bronze.

Plate 29 – An ornate rococo waisted bracket clock with its original wall bracket. The flat, one-piece enamelled dial is signed 'F. Lownoy A Paris' while the case is signed 'F. Goyer and J M E'. The wooden case is veneered with green shell inlaid with engraved brass flowers, mostly carnations. This piece is about 91 cm (3 ft) high, including the bracket.

Plate 30 – A small ormolu bracket clock, the movement by Stollework of Paris, who was master in 1746. This piece stands less than 30 cm (1 ft) high, and a cherub plays the pipes above the enamelled dial. This kind of case was to, be copied extensively in England by some leading makers of the early nineteenth century.

When a clock with a particularly complex movement was required, it usually took the form of a tall clock. Very often it was made to look rather like a bracket clock on a pedestal, although it was in fact weight-driven. Rococo tall clocks are usually of exotic woods like kingwood, or inlaid with contrasting woods in delicate leafy designs. Invariably they are mounted with bronze. The designs of tall clocks are not always so successful or pleasing as the majority of bracket and cartel clocks, even though made by eminent cabinet-makers. From the horologist's viewpoint, however, tall clocks are among the most interesting. The movements are usually by leading makers and invariably have interesting escapements and other complicated features.

It was not uncommon for clocks to be incorporated effectively within pieces of furniture. Such great *ebonistes* as Nicholas Pineau,

Van Risen Burgh and Jacques Dubois made cabinets, desks and over-mantles in which clocks were set. The latter two craftsmen were also well-known for their lacquered furniture. As in England the craze for oriental decoration was long-lived. Panels of true Chinese and Japanese lacquer, usually of dark brown or black, were cut out of screens and fitted into cabinets and commodes. The French lacquer sometimes imitated oriental lacquer very closely, especially when a dark ground colour was used; however very brightly coloured pieces were also popular.

Oriental objects were sometimes included in animal clocks and the figures of a bull, elephant or horse supporting the clock may be of oriental porcelain. The animals of the French rococo may be of porcelain, or gilt or patinated bronze. The clock may be surmounted by a little figure of a Chinaman, a much-loved figure of rococo ornament.

The continuing search for new materials is reflected by the intro-duction of cases made wholly of porcelain. Such cases were somewhat impractical. Fitting a comparatively heavy movement into a fragile case is not easy. They can display wonderful intricacy, sometimes with branches of bronze wire supporting flowers and leaves. Invariably they stood on scrolled bronze bases.

Plate 31 – This beautiful porcelain case from the Meissen factory contains a movement by Etienne Lenoir of Paris. Below the dial emerges the winged torso of Father Time, while the clock is sur-mounted by a figure of Plenty, her basket overflowing with flowers.

The primary function of this piece as a clock is still quite evident, but some porcelain cases become a riot of flowers, figures and branches, making the clock dial look quite insignificant. Such pieces sometimes contain only a watch movement and are of little horo-logical interest.

The lyre clock is a type associated particularly with the reign of Louis XVI (1774–89). It incorporates marble, onyx or porcelain with bronze to produce what must surely be one of the most beautiful of clock forms.

Plate 32 – A fine example of a lyre clock by Lenoir of Paris, delicately combining cream marble with gilt mounts. The pendulum

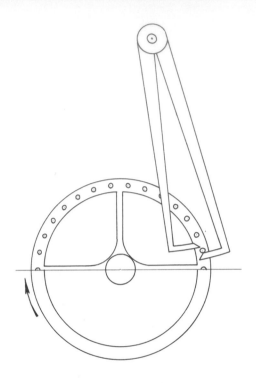

19. PIN WHEEL ESCAPEMENT. A FORM OF DEAD BEAT ESCAPEMENT INVENTED BY AMANT IN 1749 AND USED IN FRENCH REGULATORS AND TURRET CLOCKS

is formed by the ring of paste brilliants which encircles the prettily enamelled dial. The pendulum rod is in the form of the strings of a lyre, arranged as on a gridiron compensating pendulum.

Plate 33 – An important Louis XVI longcase regulator. The ebony case has gilt bronze mouldings and restrained mounts, and gives a false impression of being tapered. The enamelled dial is signed Ferdinand Berthoud. A calendar disk is visible through an aperture above the figure twelve. The steel pointer shows the equation of time, that is, how much faster or slower solar time is than mean time.

Within the trunk door is an aperture containing a barometer. The massive gridiron pendulum is supported from an equally massive bracket fixed to the back board. The clock has count wheel striking, and stands about 2·2 m (7 ft 6 in) high.

At no other time had France possessed so many great clockmakers. Berthoud, Janvier, Lepaute, Robin and the greatest of them all, Breguet, were all men of genius who raised the industry to its greatest heights. Encouraged by Louis XVI, who took a personal interest in horological matters, the very first horological school was formed in 1786. Unfortunately it was a short-lived venture, since only three years elapsed before the Revolution.

Provincial Clockmaking
Paris had long been the only great centre of clockmaking in France, but mention must be made of the type of clock traditionally made in the Morbier area of the French Jura. The Comtoise clock, as it is known, was first made during the eighteenth century and (like those of the Black Forest) was made to the same design from one generation to the next. The weight-driven movements are made of iron and brass in the 4-poster manner. The pendulum hangs at the front of the movement and operates either an anchor escapement, or a verge when the crown wheel is mounted upside down. A unique system of rack striking is used which is often arranged to sound the last hour again two minutes after the hour. The fly on the striking train consists of four vanes instead of the usual two. The movements which are of 8-day duration, and occasionally of a month's duration, have iron doors to the sides and can be used as wall clocks or fitted into a tall case.

Plate 34a – This beautiful Comtoise longcase clock is signed on the enamelled dial 'Bailly A. Prémery'. The dial has a thin pressed brass surround of baroque scrolls and festoons of fruit and foliage. The lyre-shaped case follows that of the pendulum, and the decoration on the case is not inlaid but painted. The faked walnut graining is painted in lines of contrasting colours around the edges of the case.

Plate 34b – A Comtoise clock used as a wall clock.

The Neoclassic Period

A curious situation arose in the second half of the eighteenth century: at the height of the rococo the classical style reappeared. This was a very different classicism to that of Louis XIV. It was a rebellion against the extravagances of the rococo and arose from a desire to find a new basis of simplicity and rationality. Laugier's *Essay on Architecture* of 1753 praises classical architecture as an economic expression of man's basic need for shelter. The Pantheon in Paris, designed by Souflot and begun in 1757, was the first truly neoclassical building in Paris. The neoclassical style emphasised the correct use of the orders, and the furniture of the period is linear, with decoration in low relief applied to the flat surfaces.

Clock cases in the new style were based on architecture. The clock might be set into a column of marble or porcelain or made as the pedestal for a small urn. The Sèvres factory produced porcelain vases of classical design into which clock movements were set. The chapter ring sometimes took the form of a horizontal band round the rim of the vase. The hours and minutes rotated past a fixed pointer. Figures from classical mythology also formed major parts of the case designs.

The Revolution of 1789 greatly disrupted the clockmaking and cabinet-making industries. Without the patronage of the aristocracy, few could carry on a successful business. However, the Directoire, formed in 1795, brought a stable government and in 1797 commerce was stimulated by the first of many industrial exhibitions held in Paris. The craft guilds had been dissolved in 1791 which meant that standards could be allowed to fall, while it had the advantage that makers could form businesses incorporating every branch of manufacture.

It was also a time of wonderful archaeological discoveries in Greece and Italy and this stimulated an academic interest in classical architecture and interior decoration. Many designers advocated the use of strict classical forms, a move led by such men as George Jacob, Percier and Fontaine and the artist David, who later became court painter to Napoleon.

Napoleon became Emperor in 1804 and saw himself as the head of a vast empire which would include the ancient Roman Empire. Along with the armies he took to Egypt went artists, designers and antiquarians who collected material at first hand. As a result, Empire furniture displays a mixture of classical and Egyptian forms.

Plate 35 – An Empire period mantel clock of about 1810 made in Paris. The drum-shaped striking movement has an enamelled dial with Breguet-style hands. A very rich effect is achieved by the application of the gilt reliefs on a coloured background. The use of individual motifs in low relief is typical of Empire decoration. An exciting contrast is made between the clock case and the boudoir scene which surmounts it.

Something must now be said of France's most gifted maker, Abraham Louis Breguet, who was born in 1742 near Neuchâtel, the great watchmaking centre of Switzerland. Nothing is known of his early career in Switzerland, but by 1787 he was making fine watches with lever escapements in Paris. All his work has a distinctive character and superb finish. He introduced many improvements for watches, one of the most important being a system of shock-proofing for the balance staff pivots. He made clocks and watches with perpetual calendars which allowed for the short months and for leap years. He also made a number of calendar clocks in silver cases which were designed for travelling. They are fitted with watch escapements mounted on the back-plate. These clocks were much copied. After his death in 1823 the business was carried on by his son and subsequently by his grandson.

Plate 36 – The influence of the Empire style continued well into the mid-nineteenth century. This 4-pillar clock supporting a heavy entablature was made in the 1830s, but the style originated in the 1800s. Although the form of the clock is very severe, the inlay and decorative pendulum and dial surround heralds the return of the fussy and sometimes over-elaborate designs of the later nineteenth century.

Mass Production
The introduction of steam-powered machinery led to great advances in production methods. French movements which had become

standardised in the eighteenth century were now produced in very large numbers and put into a wide range of cases. It was a period when designers sought novelty rather than elegance.

Plate 37a and b – This picture clock reflects the growing interest in the Gothic which was evident by the 1830s. Behind the canvas, and mounted within a shallow box, is a quarter-striking ting-tang movement, the dial of which appears through a hole in the canvas. The movement is identical to thousands of others made throughout the century and is stamped GANCHY. The hour is struck on the larger of the two gongs. The clock's silk suspension is regulated by the small arbor which protrudes through the top of the front plate.

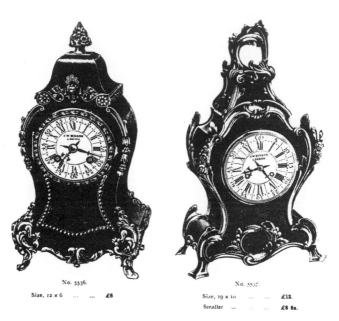

No. 5536.

Size, 12 x 6   ...   ...   **£6**

No. 5537.

Size, 19 x 10   ...   ...   **£12.**

Smaller   ...   .   **£8 8s.**

20. BUHL CLOCKS FOR DINING ROOM, DRAWING ROOM OR BOUDOIR. A PLATE FROM THE CATALOGUE OF J. W. BENSON LTD., *c.* 1890

Plate 38 – A novelty clock known as a *Mysterieuse*, dating from the second half of the nineteenth century. The drum-shaped striking movement is contained in the marble base and the bronzed spelter figure holding the pendulum stands on a base connected indirectly to the escapement. The base rotates through a minute angle to keep the pendulum in motion. The glass pendulum bob is signed 'S. D. McKellen, Paris'. Some *Mysterieuse* clocks have the movement in the pendulum bob.

In the 1880s a great many cheap reproductions of earlier styles were introduced. The accompanying photograph shows a page from the catalogue of Bensons' of Ludgate Hill, London, advertising 'Buhl' bracket clocks in wooden cases with brass mounts. Earlier examples

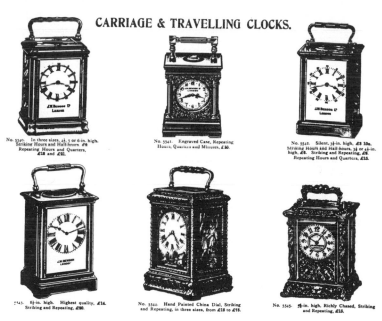

CARRIAGE & TRAVELLING CLOCKS.

No. 5540. In three sizes, 4½, 5 or 6-in. high. Striking Hours and Half-hours, £9. Repeating Hours and Quarters, £18 and £21.

No. 5541. Engraved Case, Repeating Hours, Quarters and Minutes, £30.

No. 5542. Silent, 3½-in. high, £3 10s. Striking Hours and Half-hours, 3½ or 4½-in. high, £6. Striking and Repeating, £9. Repeating Hours and Quarters, £15.

No. 5543. 8½-in. high. Highest quality, £24. Striking and Repeating, £30.

No. 5544. Hand Painted China Dial, Striking and Repeating, in three sizes, from £15 to £18.

No. 5545. 5½-in. high, Richly Chased, Striking and Repeating, £15.

21. SELECTION OF FRENCH CARRIAGE CLOCKS FROM THE CATALOGUE OF J. W. BENSON LTD., *c.* 1890

have brass and tortoiseshell inlay, but the quality bears no comparison with eighteenth-century work.

The same catalogue illustrates a wide range of carriage clocks, but although they display Bensons' name they are entirely of French manufacture.

Plate 39 – Another novelty clock, a carriage clock surmounted by an animated bird which can be made to twitter and flap its wings. The subsidiary dial is for setting the alarm. Clocks intended to be used as travelling clocks were sold with close fitting wooden cases covered with leather to protect them during the journey. They were certainly never intended for use in a carriage as the English name implies.

Makers such as Breguet had produced carriage clocks as early as 1810, but their large-scale production did not commence till the 1840s–1850s and it continued unchanged well into the present century. The movements were made in various provincial towns, such as Lyons and St Nicholas, and were sent to the numerous Paris workshops to be finished to the required standard. From these workshops they would be sent to the retailer whose name would appear on the dial. The cases would be ordered from specialist case makers, as were the platform watch-type escapements which were made by craftsmen working in towns on the Swiss border.

Plate 40a – Nowhere is the continuing influence of neoclassicism more evident than in the heavy marble mantle clocks of the late nineteenth century. This green onyx and brass example is unusually decorative for such clocks. The design of the case is surely inspired by the Parthenon.

The majority of so-called black marble cases are actually made of polished slate and are cemented together with a compound of Russian tallow, brick dust and resin. Not all marble clocks are of mediocre quality. Brocot (d. 1878) made some fine calendar clocks with moon phase dials and other complicated refinements.

Plate 40b – A small, travelling alarm clock of the early twentieth century complete with its tightly-fitting turned wooden box and instruction label (fig. 23). The clock is unusual in that it is controlled by a pendulum only 5 cm (2 in) long. The long dial pointer sets the alarm. The maker's name, T. Maurel, is engraved on the back cover

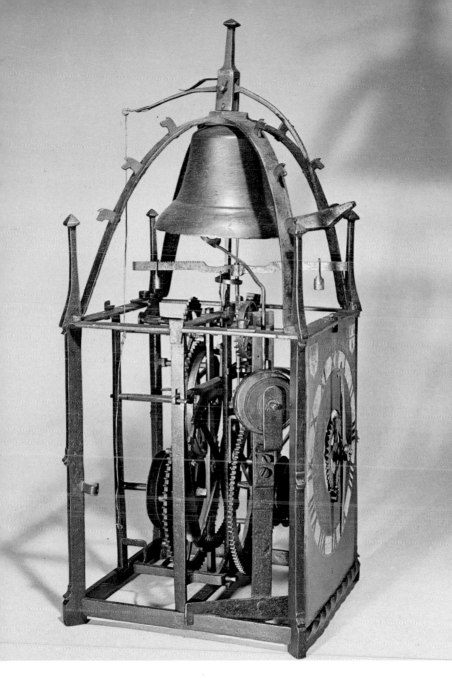

1 An iron Gothic chamber clock with verge escapement and foliot suspended by a thread.
   This clock strikes the hours and has an alarm.

2 A gilt brass cased Augsburg table clock or tabernacle clock, early 17th century. It has been converted to a pendulum control from a balance wheel. The silver dials retain traces of the original coloured enamel in the deep engraving.

3a An anonymous drum-shaped table clock of about 1580. The little
    knobs at each hour are for feeling the time in the dark.

3b A hexagonal brass table clock of about 1700 by Mayer of Augsburg.
    Similar clocks are found bearing English makers' names at this period.

4 An early 17th-century table clock incorporating animated figures. The Negro who points to the hour with his spear moves his head when the hour is struck and the dog appears to run at his feet.

5   Another clock incorporating an animated figure. The griffon holding the dial flaps its
wings and moves its beak as the hour is struck.

6   An Austrian fruitwood bracket clock signed on the chapter ring, 'Ge. Preisacher,
Clostemenburg'. In the arch is a central calendar dial and two subsidiary dials for the
strike/silent and chime/silent. In the centre of the backplate is a large engraved cartouche.

7   A beautiful pale yellow lacquered bracket clock by Adalbertus Hockenadl of the late 18th century. It stands 21 in. (53 cm) high, and its 40 hour movement chimes the quarter hours on eight bells.

8 A Neuchâteloise or Swiss bracket clock from the Neuchâtel region. This early 19th-century example has a rosewood brass inlaid case and sits upon an integral bracket on the wall. The movement has *grande sonnerie* quarter striking.

9 A Biedermeier period mantel clock of about 1825, 18 in. (46 cm) high, signed 'Niederlags Compagnie, in Wien'. It has a quarter chiming movement and the pendulum regulation square can be seen over the figure 12.

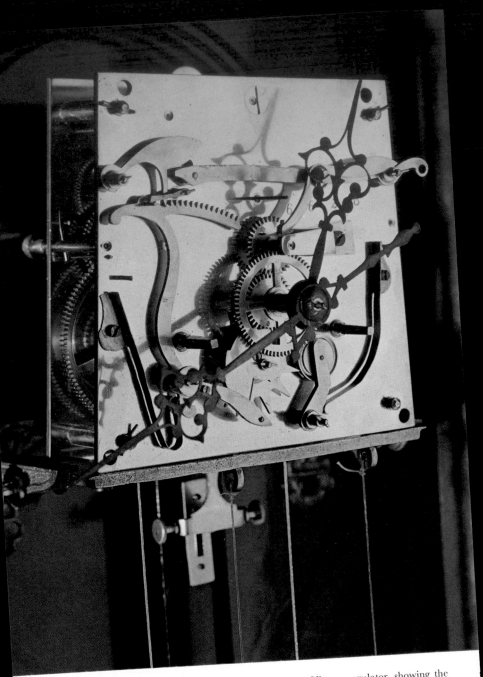

10   The finely made movement from a late 19th-century Vienna regulator, showing the excellent finish found on all Austrian clocks of the 19th century.

11a A longcase Vienna regulator chiming the quarters. The fine and severe design of the case is typical of early 19th-century Vienna regulators.

11b A later 19th-century Vienna regulator. The case is becoming more fussy with a cresting and finials.

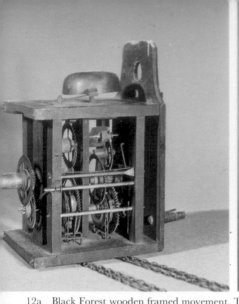

12a Black Forest wooden framed movement. The wooden arbors are often painted silver to
     imitate steel.

12b Traditional Black Forest shield dial.

12c An early cuckoo clock with enamelled dial.

12d Spring driven wall clock with wooden framed movement.

13a   Three mass produced Black Forest shelf clocks.

13b   Late nineteenth-century cuckoo clock.

13c   Movement of a simple mass produced cuckoo clock showing the bellows.

14 The so-called postman's alarm. The final development of the Black Forest clock with wooden plates. This one was retailed in 1914.

15   Early Haagse clock movement, signed 'J. Van Ceulen, Hague'. The dial is hinged to the case to allow easy access to the movement.

16   The Haagse clock to which the movement in Plate 15 belongs. The plain ebony-veneered case has delicate mouldings and is architectural in style. The skeleton chapter ring and Father Time are mounted on a velvet-covered dial plate.

A magnificent silver and gilt cased clock by Adriaen Van den Bergh of The Hague, late 17th century. A masterpiece of decorative metalwork.

18   A striking and alarm bracket clock in an ebonised case by Roger Dunster of Amsterdam, of about 1745. A Dutch example of an English style. The central alarm disk is typically Dutch, rarely found on similar English clocks.

19 Two Zaanse clocks; that on the left is signed 'Groot, 1725', has double striking and strikes once at the quarters. The clock on the right has a painted dial plate.

20 A Friesland Stoel clock of the 18th century. This alarm clock has a verge escapement but does not strike the hours. Clocks with similar movements were made as early as the mid-17th century and may have inspired the design of Japanese 'lantern' clocks.

21 A Staart clock, probably late
18th century. The nicely
painted dial has a com-
plicated automaton scene
below the chapter ring. The
windmill sails turn with the
escape wheel whilst the ship
and the fisherman's rod move
with the swing of the pendulum.

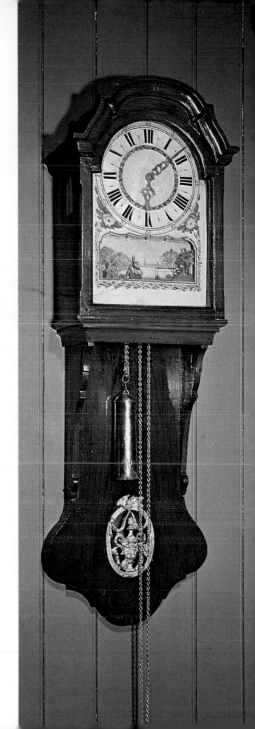

22 The 30 hour movement of Plate 21 has well turned corner posts and hammer arbor. It has an anchor escapement and strikes the hours on the large bell and again at half past on the small bell.

23a   A magnificent mulberry-veneered and ebony-moulded long case clock by Roger Dunster of Amsterdam, *c.* 1760. The musical movement plays twelve tunes on a massive pin barrel mounted across the backplate.

23b   A walnut-veneered longcase clock by Van Brussel of Amsterdam. It has a buttressed *bombe* base and fine wooden frets to the front and sides of the hood.

24 A musical longcase movement of the mid-18th century by F. Bavius of Leeuwarden. The lever to select the tunes can be seen on the barrel arbor to the left. The fly for regulating the musical train can be seen on the back plate with its adjustable vanes.

25 A 16th-century hexagonal French table clock, less than 6 in. (15 cm) high, designed like a
    tower with pillasters at each corner. The dial seems very deeply set since it is fixed to the
    movement rather than the case. Through the side windows can be seen the two tier
    movement. This clock may originally have stood on a moulded wooden plinth.

26 A late 17th-century *Religeuse* clock, a development of the Dutch Haagse clock. The silk pendulum suspension hangs between cycloidal cheeks. The bell is mounted in the dome. The case is covered in marquetry of tortoise-shell, brass and pewter. Note the shaped apron below the dial.

27 An important Boulle marquetry pedestal clock. The movement made by Mynuel of Paris, sounds ting-tang quarter hours. The case may be from C. A. Boulle's own workshop.

28 An early 18th-century bronze-cased cartel clock by J. Thuret of Paris (1694-1712). A fine example of the symmetrical baroque ornamentation of the Louis XIV period.

29 A decorative rococo clock on its matching bracket. The movement is by Lournoy of Paris. The wooden case veneered with green-tinted shell is inlaid with brass and is signed by F. Goyer and stamped 'J.M.E.'

30 A small ormolu bracket or mantel clock. The word ormolu means ground gold and may be used to describe any gold plated metal. The movement with silk suspension and numbered countwheel is by Stollewerk of Paris (*c* 1740-70).

31 A Louis XV mantel clock. The gilded bronze and Meissen porcelain case contains a Paris made movement.

32 A fine lyre clock by Lenoir of Paris. The pendulum bob is formed by the ring of paste
brilliants which encircles the dial. The restrained elegance of this clock is characteristic of
the Louis XVI period at its best.

33   A very fine Louis XVI long-
     case weight driven regulator
     of ebony. The precision
     movement is signed 'Fer-
     dinand Berthoud'. A ba-
     rometer is mounted in the
     trunk.

34a   A Comtoise clock used as a wall clock. The enamel dial has a thin *repoussé* brass surround and the movement is contained within iron dust covers.

34b   A fine Comtoise longcase clock signed 'Bailly a Prémery'. The surface of the case is painted.

35   An Empire period mantel clock on top of which is a delicate boudoir scene. The clock is contained under a glass dome.

36　A four pillar or pediment clock of the 1830's in rosewood with gilt mouldings.

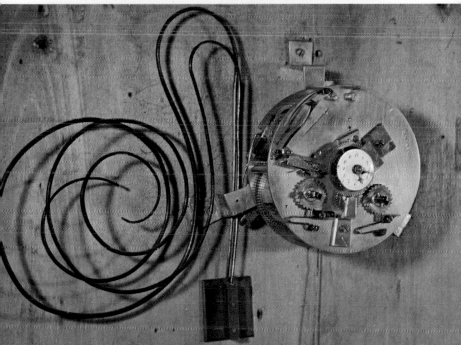

37 A 19th-century picture clock and its movement. The picture is in oils on canvas and the ting-tang quarter striking movement is contained within a shallow box behind the frame.

38 A novelty clock known as a *Mysterieuse*. The pendulum bob is signed in gilt lettering 'S. D. McKellan, Paris'.

39 A 19th-century brass carriage clock surmounted by an automated singing bird in a cage.

40a A green marble mantel clock of the late 19th century.

40b A travelling alarm clock of the early 20th century complete with its protective box.

41   The Bulle electric clock designed by Fauvre-Bulle. An early example of electrically driven
        domestic clocks.

42   An early Atmos clock. Invented by J. E. Reutter in Paris in 1913, it uses the constant changes in atmospheric temperature to keep the mainspring fully wound.

43 A mid-17-century table clock by David Bouquet of London. The square movement is shown standing on its side. The striking train going barrel is finely pierced.

44   An English lantern clock made wholly of iron except for the brass chapter ring and hand.
The front fret bears the signature 'John Holloway at Lavington 1611'. Apart from the
rather unusual hexagonal corner columns this clock is identical to later brass lantern
clocks.

45a   A brass lantern clock signed by Hercules Hastings of Burford contained in a heavy oak case with side doors to the hood.

45b   A small ebony veneered long case clock by Ahaseurus Fromanteel with verge escapement and short pendulum of about 1665.

46 A fine silver-mounted quarter-repeating bracket clock of veneered ebony made by
Thomas Herbert of London, clockmaker to the King. He worked from 1676 to 1708.

47 A well engraved back plate from a bracket clock of about 1715 made by James Blackborow. Notice the catch to the rear right of the dial which when turned secures the clock in the case. The clock repeats the quarter hours at will on six bells.

48a   A very decorative late 17th-century marquetry longcase clock by Daniel Quare. Above the dial is a *repoussé* brass frieze. The hour hand is particularly finely pierced. Notice the alternate use of ebony and walnut for the mouldings.

48b   A magnificent early 18th-century lacquered longcase clock signed 'Marwick Londini', with its original domed top and silvered finials intact.

49   An English eight-day longcase clock movement of about 1720 by Windmills, showing the rack striking work normally hidden by the dial. The English longcase clock movement remained unchanged for the next 150 years except for decorative details.

50 A bracket clock by Joseph Windmills of London made especially for the German market where the use of mirror glass on furniture was very fashionable at this period. The simple arch top to the case was not usual on English bracket clocks but avoided having to make a complicated dome in glass. This clock can be dated about 1715-1720.

51 A rare example of a bracket clock made to one of Thomas Chippendale's designs in the
mid-18th century. The beautiful case of carved mahogany contains a movement by
Archambo and Marchant of London. The original verge escapement has been converted
to anchor. The clock stands about 2 ft. (61 cm) high.

52 A London made gilt wood cartel clock with verge escapement signed 'Wintmills' of about 1775. An English example of a French type.

53   A very beautiful Chelsea porcelain flower clock containing a watch movement. The dial is about 1½ in. (3.75 cm) in diameter. An almost identical piece containing a movement by John Fladgate exists. This case would originally have been mounted upon a scrolling ormolu stand.

54   A late 18th-century gilt metal case made by Matthew Boulton of Birmingham after a design by Sir William Chambers. The movement is by Eardley Norton and the dial was enamelled by Weston of Smithfields.

55 An ebonised bracket clock made for the Turkish market in the 1790's by Recordon and Dupont. The painted dial bears Turkish numerals and in the arch are strike/silent and pendulum regulation dials. The elaborate side frets and dome are typical of clocks exported to the Near East.

56   A late 18th-century ebonised bell-top bracket clock with a Bilston enamel dial.

57 A bracket clock movement typical of early 19th-century English work. The cord is for pull repeat. The strike/silent lever can be seen in front of the bell.

58a   A fine provincial longcase clock of about 1780 by John Whitehurst of Derby.

58b   A unique Scottish longcase clock designed as a fluted Doric column. The cresting may or may not be original.

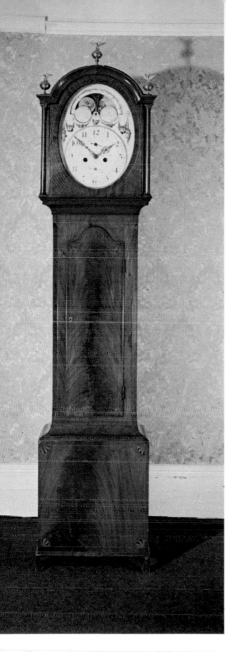

59a   An elegant Sheraton period mahogany longcase clock. The oval painted dial contains a universal tidal dial signed 'Gowland of Blyth'.

59b   A small 8 in. (20 cm) dial wall clock. The eight day striking weight-driven movement is contained within tin dust covers and is fixed to the wall by a hook and spikes.

60a A beautifully cased domestic regulator in a Gothic style mahogany and ebony case. The regulator dial has a central minute hand, a seconds dial below the figure 60 and the hour dial above the figure 30.

60b A London mahogany longcase clock signed on the full arched painted dial and on the back plate by French, Royal Exchange, London. The hands are of brass *c* 1820.

a An English dial clock. The wooden dial is signed 'Alcock and Wright' whilst the movement was actually made by Handley and Moore of London. The spade hands are of brass dating about 1800.

b A painted iron dial wall clock by Barwise with a ½-seconds pendulum encased within a figured mahogany trunk.

62   'Hope' style clock by Desbois & Wheeler of Gray's Inn Passage.

63   Chamfer top bracket clock of perfect proportions by D. & W. Morice, Cornhill.

64   Gothic style chiming clock by Viner and Co.

65   A high quality regulator. The silvered dial signed 'Tupman, London'.

66   A Victorian skeleton clock in the form of Lichfield Cathedral. Its glass dome is not shown in the photograph.

67a   Mahogany cased tall clock by Isaac Doolittle of New Haven, Conn. of the mid-18th century.

67b   Fine cherrywood-cased tall clock by Thomas Harland of Norwich. Conn. c 1790.

67c   Thirty hour tall clock by Eli Terry in a cherry wood case of about 1800 with wooden movement and dial.

68 Pillar and scroll clock. 30 hour weight-driven wood movement made by Ephraim Downes for George Mitchell of Bristol Conn. *c.* 1827.

 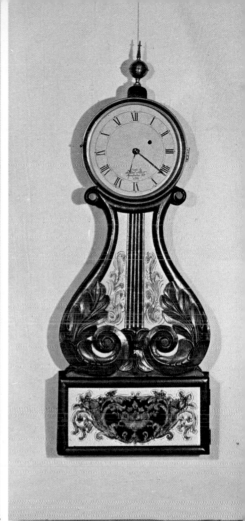

69a   Banjo clock by Simon Willard, Roxbury, Mass. of about 1820.

69b   Llyre clock by Samuel Abbot, Montpelier, Vermont, 1810. Brass eight day weight-driven
movement.

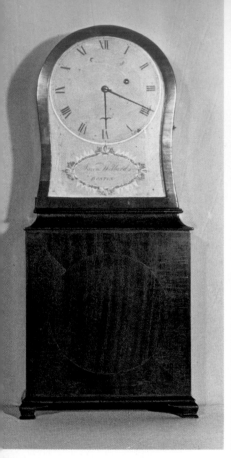

70a   Massachusetts shelf clock by Aaron Willard of Boston, Mass. It has an eight day brass weight-driven movement *c.* 1800.

70b   Wagon spring clock by Joseph Ives, Brooklyn, New York, *c.* 1825. Compare case style with that of the contemporary clock on Plate 62.

71   The works of a wagon spring clock. The system of levers amplifies the movement of the
spring.

72 a   The dial and movement of a hanging wall clock made to one of Benjamin Franklin's
& b   designs.

72c   Thirty hour O.G. shelf clock. Brass weight-driven movement of the second half of 19th
century.

72d   Eight day column shelf clock, after 1860, by Seth Thomas.

73a   Marbled wooden-cased mantel clock by the Waterbury Clock Co.

73b   Small alarm shelf clock by Seth Thomas.

73c   Steeple clock by Jerome of New Haven.

73d   *Fusée* movement by Jerome, *c.* 1853.

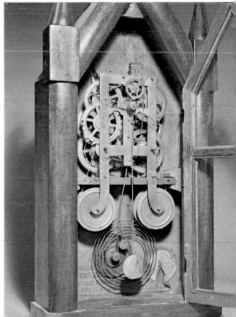

74a   Mantel clock of cast iron imitating French clocks of the period.

74b   'Anglo' wall clock made for the British market.

74c   A good quality four glass clock by the Ansonia Clock Co.

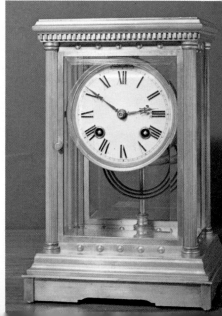

75a   A Japanese print showing in the background a lantern clock on its stand. Notice its height in relation to the seated figure.

75b   A Japanese painting on silk by Nishikawa Sukenobu (1671-1751) showing a lady winding up a lantern clock hanging from the wall.

75c   A 19th-century lantern clock on its wooden stand covered by an ornamental hood. The clock is controlled by a double foliot.

76 Two views of a Japanese
bracket or table clock, one
showing the clock in its case
and the other showing the
back plate of the clock out of
its case.

77 A small table clock about 5 in. (13 cm) wide with the front plate beautifully decorated with *cloisonné* enamel. The rotating dial shows hours and half-hours on adjustable plates. This clock is controlled by a bob pendulum and has a glazed wooden protective case not shown in the photograph.

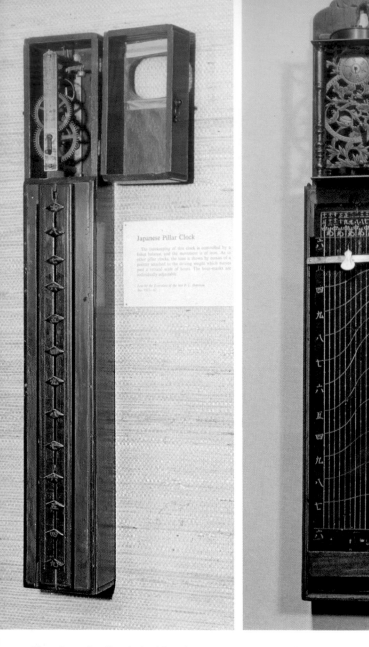

78a   An early pillar clock with an iron movement controlled by a foliot. Down the front of the case are the adjustable hour numerals.

78b   An elaborate pillar clock showing the hours on a graduated scale, the movement which has a very beautiful front plate is controlled by a balance wheel.

79   A rare inro clock 2½ in. (7 cm) high. The tiny spring driven movement with a verge and balance wheel fits snugly into the inro case. A small pointer marks the hour which rotates past a hole in the case. The movement can be wound without removing it from its case.

80 A drum-shaped Chinese table clock with verge escapement and balance wheel. The Chinese hour characters are on an outer enamelled ring whilst the twenty-four European hours are engraved upon an inner brass ring. The clock also has an alarm mechanism. The decorative sides to the case depict the Pa Chi-Hsiang or eight Buddhist symbols.

22. PIN PALLET ESCAPEMENT INVENTED BY ACHILLE BROCOT OF PARIS (1817–1878) USING AGATE PALLETS

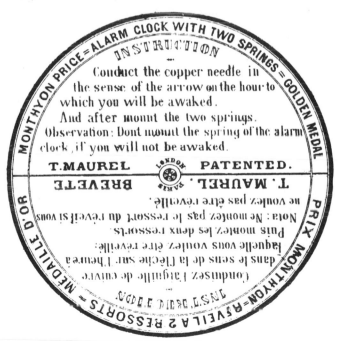

23. INSTRUCTION LABEL FROM THE TRAVELLING ALARM CLOCK SEEN IN PLATE 40b

of the case. This clock was a cheaper substitute for the heavy and more easily damaged carriage clock.

Twentieth-century Inventions

By the early nineteenth century the possibility of electrically-operated clocks was demonstrated by J. A. De Luc in France, F. Ronalds in England and by Professor Ramis in Munich. However it was another century before electric clocks were made economically for domestic use. The two most well-known were the Eureka clock and the Bulle clock. The principle of these clocks, however, had been developed by Alexander Bain in 1843.

Plate 41 – This is the Bulle clock designed by Fauvre-Bulle. On the end of the pendulum is a solenoid which encircles a consequent pole magnet. The clock is battery operated and receives an impulse to the pendulum in one direction only; the contact is made on one side only of the crutch-like lever, which engages with a silver pin on the pendulum. The actual swinging of the pendulum pushes the wheels of the clock round one tooth at a time. The delicate ratchet work can be seen within the dial centre and to its left can be seen the contact breaker. A number of different models were made, some housed in wooden mantel and wall cases, while others stood under a glass dome.

The Eureka clock works on the same principle, but instead of a pendulum it has a very heavy balance wheel running on glass roller bearings.

Plate 42 – The Atmos clock invented by J. E. Reutter of Paris in 1913. He used the constant changes in atmospheric pressure to wind the mainspring of a clock, but his idea was apparently not put into production at that time. The clock which was produced some years later makes use of temperature instead of pressure changes. A bellows within the drum-shaped cover behind the clock is filled with ethyl chloride which is highly sensitive to temperature changes. The movement is controlled by a heavy slow-moving temperature-compensated balance suspended on an invar strip. The dial of this example, probably made in the late 1930s, is signed 'ATMOS *pendule perpetuelle*, France'. The modern Atmos clock is made in Switzerland.

6

England

New Standards Introduced from the Continent

Henry VIII took a great interest in the arts and sciences, and was determined to make his palaces as sumptuous as those of his French contemporary Francis I. To achieve this he had to employ many craftsmen and artists from the Continent, who brought with them Renaissance ideas and designs. However the style was slow to mature, and shows a mixture of Gothic, Italian and Flemish features.

In 1517 the London apprentices rioted in protest against the number of foreign craftsmen in the city. A contemporary writer commented that 'the poore English artificers could skace get any livinge; and most of all the straungers were so proud that they disdained, mocked and oppressed the Englishmen'. They also 'much surpassed the Englishe in dexterity, industry and frugality'. But it was the standards introduced by these men, which the English adopted, that led to England's clockmaking supremacy by 1700. In the late sixteenth century English work, whether made by Englishmen or by French or Flemish craftsmen working in London, was very similar to work produced on the other side of the Channel. Table clocks had plated movements and can be compared with plate 25.

Plate 43a – A mid-seventeenth century square table clock by David Bouquet of London. This maker was a Frenchman free of the Blacksmith's Company in 1628, and was one of the first members of the Clockmakers Company on its incorporation in 1632. The 12-hour dial has a single hand and has 'touch pieces'. The pierced circles in the sides of the case are to let out the sound of the bell which is mounted in that corner.

Plate 43b – The movement of the Bouquet table clock. It is positioned to show the going train fusée, the hour bell and the striking train going barrel which is pierced and engraved. The balance wheel is pivoted in a pierced and engraved cock, the foot of which is similarly decorated. Below the balance lies the iron count-wheel. The stop work for the striking train is also pivoted beneath a beautifully decorated cock. The fusée set-up ratchet is on the right. The notched disks at opposite corners of the back plate are to secure the movement in its case.

Plate 44 – During the seventeenth century English clocks took on a recognisable national character as London became an important clockmaking centre. This clock owes little to continental types and is immediately recognisable as English. The use of iron in the frame-work is reminiscent of Gothic chamber clocks, while the classical Doric columns at the corners and the urn finials are typical of English lantern clocks. The name lantern clock may have arisen because of its loose resemblance to a lantern, but may also be a corruption of the old English word *latten* meaning brass in beaten sheet form.

Most lantern clocks were made to hang on the wall or to sit on a wooden bracket on the wall. After the introduction of the longcase clock some were made with free-standing cases, while in provincial areas open frameworks, usually of oak, were made to support them.

Plate 45a – A fine example of a late seventeenth-century brass lantern clock mounted in a panelled oak case. It has no central finial over the bell since this would not be seen through the hood aperture. This clock, which is signed by Hercules Hastings of Burford, was almost certainly made in the workshops of the famous Knibb family of Oxford and is fitted with a tic-tac escapement which spans only two teeth of the escape wheel. At the time the Knibbs were experimenting with the tic-tac escapement which it was thought would be more suited to a short pendulum than the recently invented anchor, although the action of the two is similar.

The Worshipful Company of Clockmakers

In 1631 Charles I granted the clockmakers of London a Charter of Incorporation for their own company. The Company, a descendant of the craft guilds, had wide powers over any clockmaker working within ten miles of the city. They made sure the work was of a high standard and their officers had the power to search workshops and order poor quality work to be destroyed.

An apprentice served seven years. He then had to spend two years as a journeyman and produce his 'masterpiece' before he could gain the 'freedom' of the Company. Not until a man became a Master Warden or Assistant of the Company could he take on more than one apprentice and then the maximum was only two at any one time.

The Golden Age of English Clockmaking

No other era of horological history has been so thoroughly researched as the first years of the pendulum clock. As soon as Huygens had produced his first pendulum clock, Ahaseurus Fromanteel, working in London, sent his son Johannes to work for Huygens. Johannes stayed in the Hague from September 1657 to May 1658, just long enough to learn about the new invention. By November the same year his father was advertising the first pendulum clocks to be made in England. Why Huygens apparently had no objection to the English learning of the pendulum at first hand is something of a mystery, especially as he tried several times to patent his invention in France as he had done in Holland. Fortunately there were no such restrictions in England and soon many makers had started making clocks with pendulums.

Under Charles II these makers introduced many improvements. The first spring-driven clocks made by Fromanteel were very closely based on Coster's work. There were no fusées, the dials were rectangular and hinged to the case to allow access to the movement attached to the rear of the dial. The cases were of ebony veneered oak, very plain in appearance and they could be used as table clocks or wall clocks. It is generally believed that it was common practice at this period to gild the brass plates and wheels, and blue the steel work of the movement. To blue the steel the pieces were laid in a tray of sand and evenly heated. As the temperature rose the steel changed from silver through yellow brown and eventually to blue, when it was quenched in oil. Not only does such treatment enhance the appearance of the movement but also protects it against rust. This practice, however, only lasted a few years – perhaps up to the 1670s.

Until that date both spring-and weight-driven clocks were fitted into ebony cases which followed very closely the architectural ideas of Palladio; all the mouldings, columns and proportions were in

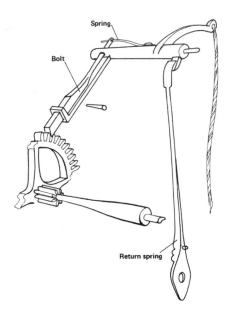

24. BOLT AND SHUTTER
MAINTAINING POWER
(SHUTTERS OMITTED)

accord with the classical principles which Sir Christopher Wren was also using on his great London churches.

Plate 45b – A longcase clock of about 1660–65 by Ahaseurus Fromanteel. It may, however, have started life as a wall clock, since it is unusual to find inverted finials below the hood moulding of a longcase, but it was certainly cased very shortly after it was made. The 8-day movement has a bob pendulum and verge escapement and, as is normal with very early longcase clocks, it also has bolt and shutter maintaining power. When a cord is pulled or a lever depressed the shutters which normally cover the winding squares are moved aside and at the same moment a sprung ratchet, the bolt, operates upon the centre wheel which keeps the going train in motion while the clock is being wound.

Around 1670 the anchor escapement was invented for use with the long pendulum which Dr Hook had demonstrated would improve timekeeping. Some makers used a 1·5 m (5 ft) $1\frac{1}{4}$ seconds beating pendulum, which was the longest a longcase clock could conveniently accommodate with the bob swinging in the base. The seconds pendulum, about a metre long, which enabled a dial showing exact seconds to be fitted, was soon universally adopted. However, the seconds pendulum could not be housed in the very narrow cases which had been made for the clocks with verge escapement and bob pendulum. At much the same time as the cases became wider to accommodate the seconds pendulum the architectural style of case went out of favour together with the use of ebony for longcase clocks.

An interesting description of a bracket clock of the 1660–70 period appeared in *The Postman* in the year 1700: 'Stolen from Mr Chute's house the upper end of Bedford Row Near Grays Inn, on Saturday 29th June last, between 10 and 11 at night a large old heavy pendulum table clock made by Fromantle [sic] and his name engraven on the back plate, a little silver cherub's head at each corner of the dyal plate, fixt in an ebony case of about a foot square made in the form of a house.' It is interesting to note that a spring-driven clock was then known as a table clock.

On 24th June 1664 Samuel Pepys wrote in his diary that in the

Queen's bed chamber was 'nothing but some pretty pious pictures and books of devotion, and her holy water at her head as she sleeps with her clock by her bedside, wherein a lamp burns that tells her the time of night at any time'. This clock may well have been made by Edward East or Fromanteel. It could even be that Johannes Fromanteel had learnt the principle of the night clock while working in the Hague.

The first night clocks of this kind were made in Italy by the Campani brothers of Rome. English clocks have engraved and painted dials, the painting, Flemish in character, usually shows figures in landscape. In the upper portion of the dial is a semi-circular aperture divided into the quarter hours and minutes of one hour and across which pass each hour numeral in turn. The cut out quarters and hour numerals are illuminated from behind by an oil lamp mounted within the clock. Both longcase and table night clocks were made, but they constituted something of a fire risk and needed nightly attention to set the lamp. They were superseded by the pull quarter repeat mechanism which sounded the time to the nearest quarter of an hour on bells at the pull of a cord.

Plate 46 – A beautiful quarter repeating clock sounding the quarters at will on three bells. Only just over 30 cm (1 ft) high, it is suitable for carrying from one room to another. It was made c 1685 by Thomas Herbert who worked between 1676 and 1708 and was clockmaker to the King. The mounts on this clock are of solid silver as are the cherub head spandrels. The shallow dome or basket top had superseded the architectural top and by 1700 had become very elaborate.

At this period tortoiseshell was being increasingly used in England as a veneer for bracket clocks. When used as a veneer the shell, usually tinted red on the reverse and combined with silver or gilt mounts, gave a very rich effect. It was obtained from the Hawksbill turtle and the largest pieces were only 30–38 cm (12–15 in) in diameter. When heated it becomes pliable and can be moulded and stamped and retains its shape on cooling. It can also be welded together, thus increasing its thickness or area.

The French used tortoiseshell and various metals in marquetry.

This kind of inlay, made popular by C. A. Boulle, was also used on some clocks, longcase and bracket, by a number of leading makers in London. These clocks were probably made for continental customers and the inlay work may well have been carried out by French craftsmen in London. Other continental customers would order an English movement and have it cased up in France or Germany to suit their decorative schemes.

All kinds of exotic materials were used for bracket clock cases. Recently a bracket clock veneered completely in mother-of-pearl was discovered. Travelling clocks and miniature bracket clocks were often made with silver or gilt brass cases.

The back plate of a bracket clock presents a large area of brass which, on the architectural cased clock, is usually relieved only by the engraved signature of the maker. By 1675 back plates often display lively engraved tulip designs of a pronounced Dutch character.

Plate 47 – The back plate of a clock c 1720 by James Blackborow, of London. Here the large flowing tulips of the seventeenth century have developed into a tighter design of scrolling foliage and arabesques with a basket of flowers in the centre.

Perhaps the finest engraved designs were executed in the early eighteenth century. Among the foliage may be found birds, animals, cherubs, serpents, grotesque heads and often a shaped cartouche bearing the maker's name. Some of the best engraving was done by Frenchmen who were well known for their excellent work. The records of the Clockmakers Company show that a number of French craftsmen were admitted as brothers of the Company and described simply as engravers. Such men would work for a number of clockmakers. The engraved back plate in plate 47, for example, is identical in design and workmanship to another on a clock by the Royal clockmaker Thomas Cartwright.

Many of the decorative features introduced during the late seventeenth century can be traced back to Holland. Joseph Knibb, for instance, made bracket clocks with velvet-covered dial plates, silver hands and chapter rings. The Dutch mania for flowers, especially tulips, is reflected not only in back plate designs but in the engraving on lantern clocks and in the floral designs on marquetry cases.

After ebony went out of favour for longcase clocks walnut was used, as were laburnum and olivewood which were often cut across the branch in what is known as oyster-cut veneers for use in parquetry. (The term parquetry covers the use of veneers in any geometric design.) The difficulty in cutting large sheets of veneers probably accounts for the large output of inlaid pieces. The finest of the early inlay work was executed by Dutch and French craftsmen working in London. The latter were Huguenot refugees, who had fled from the Continent on the Revocation of the Edict of Nantes (1685).

Plate 48a – A fine 8-day clock by Daniel Quare of London, dating c. 1690. The designs are nicely drawn and many coloured woods are used which produces a lively and realistic appearance. Green stained bone is often used for leaves.

The Eighteenth Century

By the beginning of the eighteenth century numerous types of marquetry had appeared. To save time, two, three or four sheets of veneer would be cut together, so that the waste of one panel formed the ground of the next and vice versa.

England's links with Holland were further strengthened when William of Orange became King of England through his marriage to Mary, the granddaughter of Charles I. During their reign many products of both countries were almost indistinguishable. By the late seventeenth century the Dutch had perfected a method of imitating Chinese lacquer for the decoration of furniture. The technique appears in England by about 1670 but it was not until around 1700 that it was used extensively on clock cases. Deal was used almost exclusively for seventeenth-century lacquered pieces, since the gesso ground adhered to it well. Unfortunately the use of this soft wood has led to a high mortality rate through rot and woodworm. Consequentely, lacquered cases before 1700 are rare. Many blacked pine cases found today were probably originally lacquered. During the eighteenth century oak was increasingly used in the carcasses of lacquered cases.

Plate 48b – A particularly fine example of a rare pale blue lacquered longcase clock c. 1725, by Marwick of London. The elegance and splendour of fine town and country houses is well reflected in this imposing clock which stands over 2·4 m (8 ft) tall. Few clocks of this period have survived with their original elaborate tops and double plinth to the base. Mirror glass was sometimes inset into the trunk door of lacquered longcase clocks at this time. In the past, dealers and collectors alike have believed that many of these lacquered cases were decorated in the East Indies. However, there is no proof of this and it is known that 'japanners' were working in London in the late seventeenth century. In 1694 a contemporary writer notes that 'the Japan is brought to that perfection that it not only outdoes all that is made in India, but also vies for its lacquer with the Japan lacquer itself, and there is hope of imitating its best draught and figures'. Certainly, by the early eighteenth century, there were a great number of japanners to meet the ever-increasing demand. One establishment would build the carcase which would then be sent for decoration to a specialist, such as Richard Jones, at the sign of the 'Japanned Cabinet' near King Edward's Stairs, Wapping, or James Bradford, japanner, at the sign of the 'Angel', Fleet St.

English lacquer tended to be even more colourful than eastern lacquer, because while eastern lacquer was usually dark brown or black, in England the ground colours included black, yellow, dark and pale blue, various reds, olive, dark green, lapis lazuli, imitation tortoiseshell and marble. The quality of a piece depends not only on the fineness of the drawing but also on the smoothness and polish of the ground colour. During the eighteenth century the polishing process was often dispensed with and replaced by varnish which was painted on before the raised and gilt decoration was applied. Consequently many of the later cases are dull in colour because the varnish has turned brown. By 1750 a wide variety of decorative types had been introduced. The *chinoiserie* was not always in relief. Sometimes it was combined with a coloured etching or a painting on canvas to form a centre panel on the trunk door. The whole of the front of a case is sometimes decorated with a polychromatic design of flowers or fruit or with a romantic subject derived from the French rococo artists, Lancret and Watteau.

Plate 49 – A longcase clock movement with its arched dial removed to show the rack striking mechanism, which became universal for 8-day clocks from about 1730. This 8-day movement by Thomas Windmills of London dates from about 1720. A notable point is the sturdy bracket in which the rack itself is pivoted. The tail of the rack is sprung to avoid it being damaged if the clock should be turned past 12 o'clock without striking. The aptly named snail is clearly visible.

Plate 50 – Another clock from the Windmills workshop in Tower Street, London. It was made by Joseph Windmills, the father of Thomas and was intended for the German market where mirror veneered pieces were popular.

During the eighteenth century France was the unrivalled leader of fashion in furniture, interior design and costume. French themes influenced every area of design. That very English cabinet-maker, Thomas Chippendale, and his contemporaries Ince and Mayhew and Vile and Cobb were all much influenced by the French rococo. Unlike many designers who produced pattern books, Chippendale included a number of designs for longcase clocks and bracket clocks. Some of these designs were made and contain movements by some of the leading makers of the day.

Plate 51 – A bracket clock by Archambo and Marchant, London, *c.* 1750. This partnership made both longcase and bracket clocks in cases of carved mahogany taken straight from Chippendale's *Directar*. Although many clocks, especially longcase clocks of provincial manufacture, are loosely described as Chippendale, there are very few which adhere closely to his designs. Chippendale also advocated the tapered trunk for longcase clocks to imitate the French pedestal clock, but examples are exceedingly rare.

Plate 52 – The cartel clock, a true French type, was copied closely in England. This one, *c.* 1760, is a well carved gilt wood model of English make. The workmanship of the case is very close to that of contemporary picture and mirror frames.

Plate 53 – This piece from the Chelsea factory is not a true clock since it contains a watch movement. The Chelsea factory followed French taste very closely, which is not surprising considering that two successive managers, Gouyn and Sprimont, were French.

An influential figure in the second half of the century was Sir William Chambers, who became the greatest official architect of his time. He studied in France under J. F. Blondel in 1749 and then in Italy until 1755. The following year he became the Prince of Wales' tutor and by 1760 he was the King's Architect with Robert Adam. His work always kept rigidly to the strict neoclassicism of his French contemporaries with whom he had worked in Paris. However, he also studied eastern architecture of which he gained first-hand knowledge when, as a young-man, he served with the Swedish East India Co. A survival of his work in this field is the Great Pagoda in the Royal Botanical Gardens at Kew.

Plate 54 – Chambers also designed furniture and clockcases, of which this is a typical example. The first clock of this design was made for the King and is part of a *garniture du chemine* now in Windsor Castle. Chambers' original drawings for this clock show it supported by a pair of winged sphinx. The case was made by Matthew Boulton who, in 1762, built an extensive factory at Soho, near Birmingham, which produced all manner of silver, ormolu and Derbyshire 'Blue John' articles. For his designs he took ideas from the work of men such as Chambers, Flaxman and James Stuart. Both Whitehurst of Derby and the royal clockmaker, Thomas Wright, made movements for Boulton's cases. The pedestal supporting the central urn of this clock is of Derbyshire felspar.

Equally elaborate ormolu clocks were made especially for the Chinese market. The name of James Cox immediately springs to mind in this respect. His ormolu and ormolu-mounted bracket clocks are of superb quality. The designs, however, are often far from classical, and are sometimes extraordinarily imaginative and not always aesthetically successful. The Chinese had a passion for these elaborate clocks and automata, and the Emperor's collection of clocks and mechanical curiosities was outstanding. In the 1930s, during the Sino–Japanese war, Simon Harcourt-Smith was given the enviable task of cataloguing the collection. At that time he was able to report that 'the passage of the hours was marked by the fluttering of enamelled wings, and a gushing of glass fountains, and a spinning of paste stars while from a thousand concealed and whirring orchestras the

Gavottes and Minuets of London society rose strangely into the Chinese air'.

Plate 55 – An ebonised bracket clock by Recordon and Dupont, *c.* 1795. Recordon was Breguet's agent in England, and Recordon and Dupont took over Josia Emery's business in 1795. The painted dial bears Turkish numerals and has a strike/silent lever and a pendulum regulation dial in the arch. The painted dial was known in the late eighteenth century as a 'japanned' dial, as opposed to an enamelled one. The elaborate dome top and the generous use of cast brass mounts is characteristic of clocks made for the Near East. The arched shape to the base, however, is quite unique.

Tortoiseshell veneered cases were among the most elaborate and successful, profusely mounted with gilt metal and surmouted by a hemispherical dome and flambeau finials.

Lantern clocks were also exported to Turkey throughout the eighteenth century. They were fitted with arched dials, and a raised chapter ring and spandrels, as on a longcase clock. The side frets and doors were often decorated with engraved crescent moons.

Plate 56 – The bell top bracket clock was the standard form throughout the century, subject to the expected changes of detail. This ebonised example of *c.* 1780 has a rare Bilston enamelled dial. The enamel is fired onto a moulded copper sheet, and to prevent the surface cracking the dial is screwed to a heavy brass false dial plate. The back plate of the movement is elaborately engraved.

By the late eighteenth century, clocks were not intended to be carried from room to room. The bracket clock would have a set position in the room and no doubt there would be a clock in nearly every room. Consequently the rear of the clock would never be seen and so there was little point in covering the back plate with beautiful and expensive engraving.

Plate 58a – The fusée movement from a bracket clock by J. H. Tyrer, London, *c.* 1830. It is interesting to compare this with the bracket clock movement by James Blackborow of a century before. The early movement strives to keep the back plate quite uncluttered by parts of the mechanism so that we can see the engraving at its best. The late movement has its back plate mounted with heavy securing brackets, a bridge and spring for the striking hammer, a spring for the strike/silent mechanism and a massive pendulum-securing bracket. The only engraving is the maker's signature in the centre of the plate.

Provincial Clockmaking

So far we have covered the more unusual clocks of the eighteenth century, made by makers of repute working in London. By 1700 a number of provincial towns had become quite important regional centres of clockmaking. The leading makers in these towns were usually those who had served their apprenticeship in London and their work is very close to that of London, both in quality and style. It is quite natural that these makers would want to keep in step with changing London fashions and it was no doubt a good selling point if they could advertise their clocks as being in the latest London style. Gradually, as the eighteenth century progressed, provincial centres no longer followed London styles but produced clocks of a distinct character. It is possible with a little study to distinguish, for example, between a longcase made in Bristol and one made in Liverpool or between cases from Wigan and Halifax. The same cannot be said of provincial bracket clocks which, being much less common, tend to follow the London styles much more closely.

Plate 58b – It must not be assumed that clocks made in provincial towns were inferior to London-made clocks. This clock from the Whitehurst workshop is in the style associated with his name. It has a circular, engraved and silvered dial. The mahogany case of fine proportions has an imposing swan neck top and finely carved mouldings, a feature which could possibly be traced back to Chippendale's designs.

Other important centres of clockmaking include Newcastle-upon-Tyne, Liverpool, Manchester, Wigan, Halifax, York and Bristol. Scotland also produced some fine makers. The balloon top longcase clock is a type associated with Edinburgh and Glasgow in the early nineteenth century, where the hood follows the circular form of the dial.

Plate 58b – A fine example of a Scottish longcase clock, this is unusual in that the trunk is built in the form of a fluted Greek Doric column. The maker, James Muirhead of 90 Buchanan Street, Glasgow, was watchmaker to the Queen.

With the popularity of the circular dial it is not surprising that oval dials were introduced in order to accommodate moon phases. To know the phase of the moon was of some importance when travelling at night, and few cared to journey through the countryside when there was no moon. The dial could also be used to show the state of the tide, since the tides are dependent on the moon.

Plate 59a – This clock has a universal tidal dial on which one of the movable pointers is adjusted to the date of the lunar month, while the other is made to point at the appropriate hour on the thin band of numerals seen on the moon disk itself. Once these hands have been adjusted for the port in question the hour of high tide can be read off. This clock of about 1800 has a painted iron dial and is signed Jas. Gowland of Blyth, a coal mining and exporting town on the Northumberland coast. The style of the case could be loosely described as Sheraton.

The Regency

During the early nineteenth century many so-called clockmakers were becoming simply repairers and retailers. At the most they finished and assembled parts produced by factories, and the local cabinet-maker or specialised case maker supplied him with the case.

The painted dials of many of the clocks were fitted to cast iron false plates and were made by Birmingham factories. It is quite likely that some clockmakers ordered their dials from these factories but it is also possible that others would order complete movements or even finished clocks from them. In this case the firms would buy in the movements from other makers in or around Birmingham. The painted decoration on these dials sometimes exhibits very competent brushwork. Some examples are signed and dated on the reverse by the artist.

The simple forms of Regency clocks with their sparsely applied ornament lent themselves admirably to large-scale production, for which cases could be made in batches and then sold to the firms making the movements. Consequently identical cases house movements by many makers.

Plate 61a – One of the most popular low-priced clocks was the spring-driven fusée dial clock. This example, *c* 1800, has a flat wooden dial, painted and signed Alcock and Wright. However the movement was supplied to them by the well-known manufacturers to the trade, Handley and Moore. John Thwaites (later to become Thwaites and Reed) and Robson also supplied fine movements of every kind to London and provincial clockmakers. They also supplied completed clocks together with cases.

Plate 59b – An example of an attempt to produce a cheaper 8-day clock. The good-quality striking movement is enclosed in zinc dust covers. The dial is 20 cm (8 in) wide and signed Taylor and Son. The clock hangs on the wall. The lack of a wooden case kept the price down but also made it a less imposing piece of furniture, which may account for the scarcity of these clocks. Whitehurst and Son of Derby are known to have made some very similar clocks often with circular painted dials.

Plate 61b – A 'drop dial' clock complete with carved 'ears' beneath the dial, which is of painted iron. Regency examples often have delicate brass and ebony, or mother-of-pearl inlay round the dial or on the trunk. This clock by Barwise is of about 1830.

Large weight-driven wall clocks with the pendulum and weights enclosed within the trunk had been made from the early eighteenth century when they were normally lacquered. Such clocks were probably made for assembly rooms, entrance halls of public buildings or any large room where nothing too splendid was required. The dials are very legible, being black with gilt numerals and brass hands, or white with black numerals. Nineteenth-century clocks of this type were encased in mahogany or rosewood and the dial was usually protected by a glass in a brass or wooden bezel.

In London, in the nineteenth century, there was a general decline in the output of longcase clocks. Of those which have survived a considerable number are regulators or striking clocks with regulator escapements. Some of these precision clocks were made for clock and watch repairers and retailers so they could check the clocks in their charge, consequently the cases are very plain and severe in design. There was also a demand for a precision clock for domestic use.

Plate 60a – A fine example of a domestic regulator of the 1830s in an elaborate mahogany and ebony moulded gothic style case ordered, no doubt, to fit in with the gothic decoration of the owner's house. The movement is not of special quality but is massively built. It has a Graham dead beat escapement, maintaining power and a wooden rod pendulum.

Plate 60b – Another domestic clock, again with a dead beat escapement. This clock, however, also strikes the hours and half-hours on a bell. The case is very much in the eighteenth-century style, although the full arch dial is typical of Regency clocks, especially bracket clocks. The zinc dial is painted with roses and forget-me-nots. Both the dial and back plate are signed French, Royal Exchange, London, and the clock dates to *c.* 1820.

If an English clock strikes the half-hour it is usually by a single stroke on the bell. This is most confusing, as a clock will strike one three times in succession between half-past twelve and half-past one.

Benjamin Lewis Vulliamy was one of the leading clockmakers in the early nineteenth century. Like his father and grandfather before him he was clockmaker to the monarch until his death in 1854. He appears to have worked through a great range of cases of French designs, from neoclassical themes in porcelain and marble back to the Louis XIV style, richly ornamented in tortoiseshell marquetry in the manner of Boulle, and mounted in ormolu. He also used the more conventional Regency cases.

Another influential figure was Thomas Hope. His *Household Furniture and Interior Decoration* was the most important design book of the period in England. Unlike its predecessors it was not a pattern-book but an illustrated description of his London home in Portland Place. The rooms were decorated in the Antiquarian Grecian, Roman and Egyptian styles as well as the exotic Chinese and Turkish. His designs were strongly influenced by those of the French Directoire and Empire periods. Hope made no secret of his source of inspiration and referred to his friendship with Charles Percier and Pierre Fontaine, the masters of the Empire style in France. Two design books quickly followed Hope's publication, George Smith's in 1808 and Richard Brown's in 1820.

Plate 62 – This clock, *c*. 1810, is very close in feeling to the designs of Thomas Hope. It includes such architectural features as the classical pediment and Grecian akroter surmounting tapering pedestals. The carving and brass inlay is crisp and neat. The enamelled dial is signed on the reverse by the enameller, Richard Symes. The movement fits tightly into the circular top and is by Desbois and Wheeler of Gray's Inn Passage, London.

Plate 63 – A chamfer top bracket clock by D & W Morice of Cornhill, London, displaying a particularly refined and severe treatment of a classic Regency form. The enamelled dials of Regency clocks are perhaps the most legible of all clock dials.

Plate 64 – This clock made by Viner and Company of London *c*. 1830 is an example of the Gothic revival, a theme which appears as early as Chippendale's *Director*. The Gothic of the eighteenth century is a rustic gothic, in contrast to the hard, uncompromising interpretation of the style this clock displays. Standing about 56 cm (22 in) high it has enamelled dials with Breguet-style hands and a gilt engine-turned surround. The quarter-chiming movement is of massive proportions with a back plate plain except for the maker's name. Cases of identical design to this were made in various sizes, the smallest being little larger than a carriage clock.

Plate 65 – This modest-looking clock is a rare example of a mantel regulator. It has a dead beat escapement, with a large seconds dial, maintaining power and a wooden rod pendulum. The small keyhole within the figure XII is for regulating the pendulum. The silvered brass dial is signed James Tupman, London.

The Victorian Era

The mid-nineteenth century saw dramatic changes in the clock- and watch-making industries in America, Germany and Switzerland. Mechanisation was the only way to provide low-priced articles which everyone could afford. Clocks such as those of the Tupmans and others could only be afforded by the wealthy and professional and business men. The English trade never interested itself in producing decorative clocks for farmworkers or mill and factory workers.

In 1843 the British watch company was founded under the chairmanship of John Barwise. It was the brainchild of the Swiss P. F. Ingold and was to make watches by machine tools. Unfortunately the opposition of Clerkenwell and Coventry, the centres of the British craft, killed the scheme before it was able to prove itself. Ingold subsequently took his ideas to America where they were soon adopted.

John Bennett of 65, Cheapside, was another man who advocated new methods of production to compete with foreign imports. His ideas were most unpopular and he was widely criticised for selling foreign products in his shop. a practice which nearly all retailers were eventually forced to adopt, including such famous names as Dent, Vulliamy, Barraud and Lund, and Frodsham. In 1883 Sir Edmund Beckett warned, in his book *Clocks, Watches and Bells*, that 'Although labour is dearer in America than here this machinery enables them to undersell English watches as the Swiss also do with cheaper labour and more organisation though with less use of machines; and if our English makers do not bestir themselves they will lose the trade in all but the best watches as they have already lost that of both cheap and ornamental clocks'. The English trade had already been hit very badly by the factory-made imports of America, Germany and France.

In fig. 25 we see an engraving of Benson's much advertised steam factory on Ludgate Hill. This was one of the few such factories of the late nineteenth century. In the background is the steam-engine with its huge flywheel driving lathes, vertical drills and other machinery. This was not like factory production in America, since it was really only a streamlining of the old clockmakers' craft. No new methods had been introduced in England such as rolled and stamped-out brass. The main workshop here was for the production of turret clocks, while upstairs watchmakers are finishing and assembling watches.

One very successful quality ornamental clock made in nineteenth-century England as well as in France was the skeleton clock. As the

164

BENSON'S CLOCK FACTORY.

25. THE ENGRAVING OF BENSON'S FAMOUS STEAM FACTORY ON LUDGATE HILL IN THE 1890s

name implies this has heavy plates cut into decorative shapes allowing all the wheels to be seen. The movement is mounted on a heavy wooden or marble base and displayed beneath a glass shade. Sometimes the opportunity was taken to show off a complicated escapement, while others were made with nests of bells chiming the quarter-hours, but mostly they were timepieces or simply struck the hour on one bell or a gong.

Plate 66 – This skeleton clock is made in the form of Lichfield Cathedral. It has a dead beat escapement and a mercury pendulum for temperature compensation. The dial is also cut out in a Gothic style to reveal the striking lifting pieces on the front plate. As a result,

9839b.—Registered Design.

26. LONGCASE CLOCK
MODELLED ON 'BIG BEN'
WHICH RETAILED IN THE
1890s FOR £110

27. THE 'ELIZABETHAN'. A
QUARTER–CHIMING
LONGCASE CLOCK FROM
THE CATALOGUE OF
S. SMITH AND SON, *c.* 1900

it is, like most skeleton clocks, almost impossible to see the position of the hands.

In the late Victorian period there was a revival in the popularity of carved furniture, inspired by Ruskin's ideals. Ruskin, who had considerable influence upon popular taste in art and design, hated machine work and believed that the beauty of Gothic architecture resulted from the pleasure enjoyed by the workmen engaged in its construction. He and Pugin were the leaders of the nineteenth-century Gothic revival. Pugin had been employed by Barry to design all the Gothic detail and fittings for the present Houses of Parliament after the old Palace of Westminster was destroyed by fire in 1834. Perhaps the ultimate in Gothic design cases is that advertised in the 1890s and seen in fig. 26. It is a longcase clock made as a miniature of the great clock tower at Westminster.

Other heavily-carved styles appeared at this time variously known as Elizabethan, Louis XIV, Chippendale and Louis XV, none of which bear any resemblance to the styles which are supposed to have been their inspiration. They are all typically late Victorian, of good quality but of heavy design and badly proportioned. Some of these cases contain fine quality English fusée movements of immense weight, but similar clocks were imported from Germany and contain much lighter German movements without fusées.

7   *U.S.A.*

Clockmaking in the Pioneering Days

In the past collectors and historians have dismissed American clocks as inferior to the contemporary European products. As such they were not considered worthy of further investigation until recent years when their true importance in American history was understood. Even today few but the Americans themselves who show any appreciation of their products of the latter part of the nineteenth century.

In the seventeenth and eighteenth centuries clocks were modelled closely on European products. This was only natural, for many clockmakers in the early days received their training in Europe before they arrived in America. Many of these pioneering craftsmen not only made clocks but also provided other services related to their skill as metalworkers. Among these would undoubtedly be that of bellfounder and locksmith, as well as the essentials of gunsmithing and blacksmithing.

Domestic clocks in the early eighteenth century were an expensive item, the raw materials probably accounting for a large proportion of the price of the article. As might be expected, the spring-driven clock was made only in very small numbers, for the making of the coiled spring and the fusée posed considerable difficulties then. In fact, springs had to be imported until 1830 when they were first manufactured in America. By the late eighteenth century many tools and some clock parts were imported, but it is unlikely that this would have occurred to any great extent at the beginning of the century.

Between 1700 and 1740 the clock trade grew rapidly and many specialist craftsmen produced tall clocks, which certainly equalled the work of most provincial clockmakers in England. Case and movement design showed little sign of departing from English tradition. Mahogany was the most popular wood for casemaking, though cherry and walnut were occasionally used. Some cases were veneered; others were lacquered and decorated with gilt *chinoiserie* designs.

Plate 67a – A mid-eighteenth century tall clock by Isaac Doolittle who completed his apprenticeship in 1742 and in the same year opened a shop on Chapel Street, New Haven. He died in 1800 aged 79. The case is of solid mahogany with ogee feet and an elaborate swan neck cresting with three finials. The brass dial is very similar to contemporary London-made dials, and is signed on the segment-shaped plaque in the lower half of the dial centre. The brass movement is of 8-day duration and strikes the hours.

A National Style Evolves

From the mid-eighteenth century a truly American style of cabinet-making began to evolve which was also reflected in clock case designs. Although tall clock cases of this period are somewhat similar to those of, say, Liverpool or Birmingham in England, the American cases are unique in a number of respects. The block front, in particular, distinguishes the finer American tall clocks from the products of any other country. As can be seen from the drawing the block front

28. THE BLOCK FRONT

consists of a shallow bowed front to the trunk door which is topped with a carved voluted shell motif. The arched hoods are usually surmounted with a scrolled pediment of more exaggerated proportions than is usual on English clocks. It is uncommon to find brass mounts of any sort on these cases but there is correspondingly greater use of carved ornamentation.

The capabilities of American craftsmen are demonstrated in the work of David Rittenhouse of Philadelphia (1732–96), who was the most celebrated maker of his day. He was chiefly a scientist and astronomer making scientific instruments as well as clocks. His masterpiece is a magnificent astronomical chiming tall clock housed with the Drexel Institute of Technology, Philadelphia. This clock is of superlative quality and is contained in a beautifully carved Chippendale-style mahogany case.

Plate 67b – A tall clock made by Thomas Harland of Norwich, Connecticut, *c.* 1790. The solid cherry wood case is a magnificent example of the cabinet work associated with the Norwich area. The arch topped hood has a decorative fret work design known as 'whale's tails', and three carved wooden finials. The 8-day brass movement has an engraved silvered brass dial with the moon's phases in the arch.

Thomas Harland settled in America from England in 1773, and opened a shop in Norwich in that year. Baillie's *Watchmakers and Clockmakers of the World* records that he left London for America so he may have been trained in London. Harland is said to have used early forms of mass production methods in his business. One of his numerous apprentices was Daniel Burnap who in his turn took on as an apprentice Eli Terry, the father of American mass-produced clockmaking.

Post-Revolution Federal America
The Revolution somewhat disrupted the clock trade and many clock-makers started making bullets and guns. After the Revolution materials were scarce and therefore expensive. The price of brass towards the end of the century made the tall clock un-economical, and a few makers eventually turned to wood as an

alternative material for making, not only the clock plates, but also the wheels. The clearest way to illustrate this progress in the trade in the following decades is to trace the career of Eli Terry.

Terry was born in 1772 and apprenticed to Daniel Burnap of East Windsor, Connecticut. In 1793 he started in business on his own at Plymouth. Terry's importance in clockmaking history is due not only to his inventiveness but also to the fact that he was an astute business-man. He invented and perfected the wooden movement. Apart from the change in materials and the proportions of the parts, the con-struction of the movements remained basically unchanged.

Plate 67c – A tall clock by Eli Terry in a solid cherry wood case. The style of the case owes not a little to current London designs, with quarter columns in the trunk corners and a pagoda top to the hood. The case contains a 30-hour pull-wind wood movement. The dial is also of wood with a facing of printed and hand-coloured paper. Terry's name is in the calendar dial. The hands are of cast pewter.

Terry made both brass and wood movements but had discontinued the former by about 1800. He realised that there was a huge potential market for a reasonably priced clock and so he slowly began intro-ducing more streamlined methods of production. In 1800 he was using water-power to drive his saws and other equipment. By 1807, according to Jerome, he was producing 200 clocks a year. This was a revolution in production methods, since each clock was no longer made to order, but it was practicable to make the goods and then afterwards think about promoting sales. Chauncey Jerome, in *History of the U.S. Clock Business*, tells how people ridiculed Terry. 'The foolish man they said had begun to make 200 clocks; one said "he would never live long enough to make them" and another that "he would nor could possibly sell so many".' At first each movement was sold without a case, and the customer had to case it himself. Or it could be hung on the wall, and it was then known as a 'wag on the wall', a term applied to any wall clock the weights and pendulum of which are not encased.

Following Terry's success an increasing number of makers pro-duced wooden clocks in large numbers using primitive machinery. This increased competition and inevitably put many small concerns out of business, for the price of clocks had been more than halved by the new techniques.

In 1814 Terry 'invented' a shelf clock known as the pillar and scroll clock. In American horology new case designs as well as mechanical ones were regarded as inventions. This style of case was very popular in Connecticut between about 1818 to 1830. The weight-driven movements were normally of wood, and the weights are suspended on cords which ran over pulleys at the top of the box-like case in order to gain the maximum drop.

Plate 68 – A pillar and scroll clock make by Ephraim Downes for George Mitchell of Bristol, Connecticut. The wooden weight-driven movement is of thirty hours duration. Downes was a wood movement manufacturer in Bristol and supplied clocks to George Mitchell who was a prominent merchant. According to Kenneth D. Roberts in *Eli Terry and the Connecticut shelf clock*, Downes made 3,002 clocks for Mitchell between March 1826 and February 1828.

Terry was by no means the first to introduce a new design. Simon Willard (1753–1848) of Grafton, Massachusetts, was a maker who continued to use brass for his movements in which he took great pride. He made a 30-hour wall clock which developed into the Massachusetts shelf clock. In order to save brass his wall movements were circular. The design of these weight-driven wall clocks was not unlike a bracket clock standing on a large wall bracket which housed the weight and pendulum. The step from this wall clock to the shelf clock variety was a very small one.

Plate 69a – One of Simon Willard's later banjo clocks, made in Roxbury, Massachusetts, in the 1820s. The case is faced with simple curved section mouldings forming panels filled with delicately painted glass panels. The waist is flanked by long brass scrolls which give the impression that they are supporting the dial.

Plate 69b – A lyre clock made by Samuel Abbot of Montpelier, Vermont, and so inscribed on the dial. This piece is dated 1810 and has an 8-day brass weight-driven movement. The lyre clock is a development from the banjo type. This is a typical example with vigorously carved lyre-shaped scrolls and leaves forming the trunk.

In the late 1790s Simon Willard produced a new clock design, known today as the banjo clock. It was not patented until 1802 and was always known as the 'Improved Patent Timepiece'. From about 1802 Simon Willard abandoned the production of other clocks to concentrate on the banjo clock which was immediately successful. He is believed to have made some four thousand of these clocks. The brass movements were well-made, and almost invariably they were timepieces only and did not strike. Some alarm clocks were also made.

The banjo and lyre clocks are without doubt two of the most beautiful of American clocks. The finest development of the banjo clock was the girandole, where the lower part of the clock was circular rather than rectangular and supported on a carved and gilded bracket of acanthus leaves. The whole design had an extra touch of grace and quality. The glass panels were often painted with scenes from classical mythology and there was an increased use of gilt for the mouldings. However the trend during the early nineteenth century was towards simplicity and economy. This can be seen especially in the decline of style and beauty of the later lyre clocks.

Plate 70a – A Massachusetts shelf clock by Aaron Willard of Boston made c. 1800. The mahogany case is finely veneered and the upper section follows the outline of the kidney-shaped dial. The brass weight-driven movement is of 8-day duration.

The Massachusetts shelf clock was made between the late 1780s to about 1830 and vary stylistically considerably over this period. Eighteenth-century examples are often made to look like belltop or archtop bracket clocks on a large base or stand. Later examples unite the two parts and the base often contains a painted glass panel to match the decoration around the dial.

American makers were now seeking cheapness of production but there were also some inventive and scientific minds at work, notably Joseph Ives. It was he who had 'invented', or introduced to American clockmaking, roller pinions for wooden movements. His most important contribution was the introduction of rolled brass which was to be a great step forward in production methods. Before this was introduced he had experimented with iron-plated movements using cast brass wheels and later still, in 1859, with tin-plate movements. The coiled spring was not used in mass-produced American clocks till about 1850, but about 1825 Ives introduced his wagon spring clock.

Plate 70b – An early wagon spring clock by Joseph Ives, made between 1823 and 1830 at Brooklyn, Long Island, New York. It has the early style movement with cut and filed wrought sheet brass plates. Later movements had plates of riveted strips of brass, the so-called 'ladder' type movement. The movement has roller pinions as invented by Ives and the wagon spring is mounted in the bottom section of the case.

Another invention which this time led the world was Aaron Crane's torsion clock. Instead of using a swinging pendulum to control the rate of the clock, he devised a balance suspended from the movement by a wire which twisted first one way and then the other. This principle was later used very successfully by the Germans. Crane's clocks were made with eight-day or one month's duration and sometimes, as with German torsion clocks, a year, and were also an early example of the use of a coiled spring for their going power. These clocks utilised a fusée.

Plate 71 – The principle of the wagon spring clock was used as early as 1680 in France, but it is most unlikely that Joseph Ives was aware of its earlier application. Its action is quite simple. A laminated spring, similar to a wagon spring, is securely bolted to the bottom of the case. The ends are attached indirectly through a lever system to the barrels of the two trains of wheels so that on winding the clock, the ends of the spring are pulled up under tension. The lever system serves to amplify the movement of the spring. This clock was made by Birge and Fuller of Bristol, c. 1845. It is just over two foot high.

Dr Benjamin Franklin, the well-known American philosopher, was also responsible for a particular clock design. He was born in Boston, Massachusetts, in 1706 and visited London several times after 1750. When in London he became a close friend of James Ferguson who designed many astronomical and tidal clocks. It is thought that the horological work of Ferguson inspired Franklin to design a clock which could be simply and economically constructed.

Plate 72 a and b – A clock made in America to Dr Franklin's design. There are only three wheels in the train: a great wheel which carries the winding pulley, an intermediate wheel of 120 teeth and an escape wheel of 30 teeth which, with its seconds pendulum, shows true seconds on the dial in the arch. To the great wheel arbor is fixed the single hand from which both hours and minutes can be easily read. This hand goes round once every 4 hours. The design of this clock dispenses with motion work behind the dial. The plates of the movement are of wrought iron and the clock is hung on the wall and has no case. The movement is protected from dirt and dust by a tin cover fixed to the back of the painted cast iron dial.

Mass-produced Brass Clocks
In 1837 the great monetary panic and subsequent depression for a short time brought clockmaking to a standstill, and indeed many wondered if the business would ever recover. During this time Chauncey Jerome of Bristol, Connecticut, who had earlier worked for Terry, designed the 30-hour O.G. shelf clock.

This clock had a rolled brass 30-hour weight-driven movement, and can be considered to be a descendant of the pillar and scroll clock. Its simplicity and cheapness revived the industry and was soon copied by many factories. The way the clocks were made in the Jerome factory is interesting. All the pine for the case was cut into the required width on a circular saw, the lengths were then run over the planing machine and then through the O.G. cutter, which formed the shape of the front of the case. The veneer was glued onto these lengths which were clamped together, one shape fitting into another, for the glue to set. The O.G. shape was then sanded on shaped wheels onto which sandpaper had been pasted. The lengths were then ready for varnishing and mitreing to the correct size. At the height of production Jerome had the materials for 10,000 of these cases in the works at any one time. The case cost 50 cents. The dials were punched out of thin sheets of zinc and the numerals printed on and twelve to fifteen hundred could be printed in a day. The designs on the glass doors were also printed and then coloured by hand. The complete clock cost about two dollars. Jerome believed that he had the most advanced factories in America for clock production.

Plate 72c – A 30-hour O.G. clock in a mahogany veneered case produced by the Waterbury Clock Co. of Waterbury, Connecticut. The painted zinc dial is decorated with a printed blue design in the spandrels. Quite often the graining was faked onto US clocks and varnished. Slightly larger O.G. cases were made to house 8-day movements.

Plate 72d – A rosewood veneered 8-day column shelf clock by Seth Thomas who had a factory at Plymouth Hollow. Thomas was one of Jerome's big competitors and Plymouth Hollow was renamed Thomaston in his honour in 1865. This clock was made after this since it contains a label giving his address as Thomaston. Both the 30-hour O.G. and the column clocks were suitable as either wall or shelf clocks. This example stands 32 inches high (81 cms).

The coiled spring allowed clocks to be made very much smaller and opened the door to a rush of new designs. At the same time, the American exhibits at the Great Exhibition at Crystal Palace in 1851 boosted demand. Elias Ingraham was an important designer of cases and it was he who introduced the Gothic 'Steeple' clock shown in plate 71.

Plate 73a – Ingraham's original steeple clock design had free-standing pillars at the corners of the case. The clock illustrated here, by Jerome of New Haven, is a simplified version veneered in mahogany. It strikes the hours and has an alarm mechanism. The alarm setting disk is in the centre of the dial while the alarm mechanism is a separate movement screwed to the back of the case, below the clock movement proper.

It is interesting to compare this steeple clock design and other designs with contemporary or earlier English bracket clock designs. The steeple clock can be compared with the Gothic style clock in plate 64, the English lancet top became the American beehive or Tudor clock, the arch top became the American rounded top and the four glass bracket clock design evolved into the cheapest of American shelf clocks seen in plate 73b.

Plate 73b – This clock must have been one of the lowest priced models of all. It stands nine inches high and has a brass 30-hour movement. Notice the novel idea of incorporating the maker's initials in the design of the hands. The maker is, of course, Seth Thomas.

It was not only English designs which inspired the designers of American clocks. Almost every popular type of European clock was eventually copied in an attempt to capture an even wider market. Cheap imitations of the Vienna wall regulator were so popular in Holland that they helped kill the Dutch clockmaking industry in the late nineteenth century.

The catalogue plates shows two of the 500 models made by the Ansonia Clock Co. by 1914. Their catalogue for that year is a

29. THE 'ENVOY'. A FOUR-GLASS MANTEL CLOCK FROM THE ANSONIA CLOCK COMPANY CATALOGUE OF 1914

30. DIANA BALL SWING. A
MYSTERY SWINGING BALL
CLOCK FROM THE ANSONIA
CLOCK COMPANY
CATALOGUE OF 1914

book of some 140 pages from which a customer could choose a clock costing from 2 dollars to 300 dollars.

Plate 73c – The very popular French marble clock was copied in America although marble was rarely used in its construction. The American factories imitated marble with enamelled iron or, as here, with painted wood. It must be remembered that the movements were of stamped-out rolled brass and bear little resemblance to the fine quality French ones.

178

Plate 73d – A few makers introduced the fusée into one or two of their models. This illustration shows a fusée movement in a steeple clock as advertised by Jerome around 1850. The movement is the standard one with added brackets to take the spring barrels. The fusée itself takes the place of the normal open coiled spring on the great wheel arbor. The gut line is clearly visible. The fusées are very badly shaped, with hardly any variation in their diameter from one end to the other. It seems likely that American makers thought that a fusée clock would sell better in England where the fusée was so highly regarded.

During the last thirty years of the nineteenth century American factories produced a range of imaginative novelty clocks. Some of the most sought after today are the blinking eye clocks. They consist of painted cast iron figures where the clock dial forms the body of a musical instrument. A well known pair is Topsey and Sambo. Topsey, a dancer, holds in her hand a tambourine, while Sambo plays the banjo.

Fig. 31 shows an old photograph taken in the early 1900s of a country clock and watch repairer's shop. There must have been many such small businesses throughout Europe which specialised in selling the cheaper clocks of America and the Black Forest area of Germany. Here we see Mr Lloyd in front of his shop in the high street of Llanfyllin in Montgomery, Wales. In the window are displayed a range of spring-driven shelf clocks. On the back of the bottom shelf is a marble French clock and a Black Forest cuckoo clock.

Plate 74a – A clock made by the Ansonia Clock Co. in imitation of the French style. Notice especially the visible Brocot-type escapement and the paper dial which gives the impression of enamel very convincingly. The 'marble' base is enamelled iron, while the 'ormolu' figure and mounts are finished with what the catalogue describes as a Japanese Bronze Finish.

Plate 74b – An example of the late nineteenth-century drop dial wall clock in a walnut case with satinwood inlaid lines. Wall clock cases of this sort were marketed in England where they were very popular. Compared with the cases of English fusée wall clocks it is

31. COUNTRY CLOCK SHOP OF THE EARLY 1900S SELLING THE CHEAPER
AMERICAN AND BLACK FOREST PRODUCTS

flimsy and poorly finished. The movement of this clock is by the
New Haven Clock Co., and the name, W. Harris of Knighton, on
the dial is that of the retailer who had a shop in Broad Street in 1887.

Plate 74c – An American clock of unusually fine quality. The
heavy solid brass case is inspired by French four glass clocks. The dial
is enamelled and the movement, which is circular in shape, is signed
by the Ansonia Clock Co., New York. The springs are encased within
brass drums and are mounted between separate plates, so that the
springs can be replaced without dismantling the whole movement.

180

The pin pallet watch-like escapement is also mounted separately on the back plate. The clock strikes the hours on a coiled gong.

The list of clocks seems as endless as the materials with which the cases were made. Bracket or mantle and wall clock cases were often made of papier mâché inset with mother-of-pearl and painted with flowers. Nineteenth-century American clocks were of lesser quality than English clocks of that period, and although handsome when new, time did not treat them kindly. They were, however, serviceable and their low cost made them available to many who could not afford clocks of higher quality.

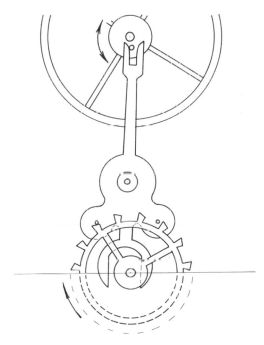

32. A PIN PALLET ESCAPEMENT USED ON SOME CHEAP NINETEENTH-CENTURY AMERICAN CLOCKS

8

Japan

The Japanese Calendar and System of Time Measurement

To understand antique Japanese clocks it is necessary to have a knowledge of the Japanese system of time reckoning. In Europe the period of the day and night is divided into twenty-four equal hours. Until 1873 the Japanese divided this same period into twelve 'hours'. Daylight was divided into six hours and so was the period of darkness. Thus, in midsummer, the daylight hours were very much longer than the hours of darkness. Japanese clocks were devised using several methods to allow for the changing length of the hours. It is interesting to note that the period of daylight was considered to include both the dawn and twilight. Using the stars as a gauge, dawn commenced when the stars were no longer visible and similarly twilight ended as the stars appeared. The hours were known as 'toki' which was divided into ten 'buns' which in turn, for greater accuracy were divided into ten 'rin'.

The twelve hours were numbered nine-four twice over in descending order with the number nine, with its supposedly magical properties, denoting the fixed moments of midday and midnight. Associated with each hour of the day and night was, as well as the numeral, one of the twelve Chinese signs of the zodiac. Many clock dials display both the numerals and the zodiac signs. The half hours were often sounded by the clock with one stroke on the bell after the uneven numbered hours and with two strokes after the evenly numbered ones.

The following chart shows the information given by most Japanese clocks. The hours and zodiac signs are, of course, denoted by Japanese characters and not by the Arabic numerals given here.

hrs.	½ hrs.	zodiac		hrs.	½ hrs.	zodiac	
6		Hare	Dawn	6		Cock	Dusk
	2				2		
5		Dragon		5		Dog	
	1				1		
4		Serpent		4		Boar	
	2				2		
9		Horse	Midday	9		Rat	Midnight
	1				1		
8		Goat		8		Bull	
	2				2		
7		Ape		7		Tiger	
	1				1		

The Introduction of the Mechanical Clock

Mechanical clocks appear to have been introduced into Japan by European traders. It was not until 1542 that the Portuguese discovered Japan and, like all the European seafaring nations, their chief aim was to develop trade. The Portuguese were followed by the Spanish and later by the Dutch who opened a trading station in Japan in 1605. In 1613 the English East India Company followed suit, but the Dutch competition was too great and the company abandoned the venture after some ten years.

Among the first clocks to reach Japan would have been those brought as gifts by the Jesuit missionaries who, because of their close connections with Rome, would no doubt have had Italian clocks. Spain and Portugal were not clockmaking centres and from examination of early Japanese clocks it appears that they used Dutch models. Certainly they are very closely based on European weight-driven clocks At first, no doubt, the Japanese regarded European clocks as curiosities and little more than elaborate toys since the European system of hours and minutes bore no relation to their own method of measuring time. Among the missionaries who arrived in Japan there may well have been trained clockmakers who could pass on their skills to the local craftsmen, for as well as spreading the Gospel, the Jesuits always contributed other skills to the community among which they worked. The Japanese were particularly skilled metalworkers and even without outside guidance, combined with the extraordinary ease with which they were, and still are, able to reproduce foreign articles, the production of a clock would not have posed too great a problem.

However, very few people in Japan needed timepieces since society was ordered very much as it had been in medieval Europe. Clocks were always a luxury item enjoyed only by the very wealthy. Indeed they are so scarce in Japan today that many Japanese do not know of the existence of antique clocks in their country. The scarcity of examples makes their study and dating very difficult, although some landmarks in their development can be found.

The Japanese Lantern Clock

The so-called Japanese lantern clocks appear to have been the first clocks to be made in Japan and were very close in construction to Dutch weight-driven chamber clocks. Small examples could be hung on the wall but it was more usual for them to be placed on a stand on the floor. Since it was customary to sit on the floor the stands are no more than 18–24 in (45–60 cm) in height. It is quite possible that the enclosed pyramidal stands are the earliest style made of decorated lacquered wood. Later stands supported the clock on four legs and were made of lacquered wood, with the legs sometimes carved into the form of trees. Occasionally the stands were of blue and white porcelain, but few of these have survived. As well as having the movement enclosed by tightly fitting doors at the sides the movement is usually given added protection from dust by a glazed hood which matches the stand decoratively. The short drop which the weight is allowed means that many of these lantern clocks require winding as much as twice a day.

Plate 75a – Japanese print depicting a courtier attending an old man seated on the floor reading. Behind the figures stands a lantern clock, with a single foliot balance, supported on a wooden stand. This clock does not have matching glazed hood to protect it.

Plate 75b – Another contemporary Japanese record of a lantern clock, a painting on a silk scroll by Nishikawa Sukenobu (1671–1751). The clock which the lady is winding has a single foliot balance and a fixed dial with a single hand.

Lantern clocks were made as early as the seventeenth century when they were made of iron. It is extremely rare to find any Japanese clock signed by its maker. Eighteenth-century movements are normally of brass and their cases may also be of brass, often beautifully engraved with chrysanthemums in the asymmetric compositions which the western world has come to admire so much. The clock on a stand would be placed fairly centrally within the room where all its sides could be seen. Some cases are of plain silvered copper.

Lantern clocks were almost invariably controlled by a foliot even into the nineteenth century. Some have two foliot balances, one for use during the day and the other at night, the striking mechanism effects the changeover from the one to the other. Such clocks have a fixed dial and hour numerals with a single hand which makes one revolution a day. The weights on the foliots have to be adjusted every two weeks as the length of the day and night alters.

Plate 75c – A lantern clock on a stand not unlike that seen in the print in plate 75a. The matching hood of hardwood, oak or sycamore, is beautifully made and finished. The side and rear windows are fitted with delicate brass fretwork of flowers. This clock also has its original weights of unusual and decorative form. The movement is controlled by a double foliot and has a dial which rotates past a fixed pointer. The 4-poster movement of brass is fitted with four extra decorative turned pillars at the corners. An unusual feature of this clock is its striking action. The last two strokes of the hour are sounded in quick succession to indicate that it has stopped striking. This is achieved by an extra hammer lifted by pins on the countwheel. This sytem of striking imitates the way in which the hours were sounded in the temples by hand.

If a clock had a single foliot it would require a dial with adjustable numerals as seen in plate 76. Between the hour numerals are half-hour divisions, all of which are a friction tight fit. Each plate has an extension which protrudes behind the dial, and serves as a lifting pin to release the striking mechanism.

The foliot on a lantern clock is a most important part of its visual appearance and it may be for this reason that the less imposing balance wheel or pendulum was not used. It is believed that decorative turning in metal was not practised in Japan until the 1830s. If this is correct all the clocks with fancy turned corner pillars can be assumed to be later. This includes some lantern clocks and the great majority of spring-driven table clocks and pillar wall clocks.

Spring-driven Bracket Clocks
The construction of the bracket or 'pillow' clock is based on that of the lantern clock, except that it is spring-driven and it is wider than it is tall. This means that the fusée is placed beside the spring barrel and not above it as in comparable European clocks. The balance wheel is the most common regulator employed in bracket clocks.

Plate 76 a and b – Two views of the same clock. The upper picture shows the clock in its perfectly fitting wooden case, about 6 inches high. Both the front and the rear panels of the case run in grooves in the sides and can slide out. The finish of the woodwork and the metal work of Japanese clocks is usually of the highest standard and this clock is no exception. The front and back plates are finely engraved. The dial has only hour numerals and consequently only strikes the hours. The numerals are, of course, adjustable. The balance wheel which is encased within the shallow drum, mounted on the top plate has provision for regulation.

The lower picture shows the clock out of its case and seen from the rear. The back plate is engraved similarly to the front one. The notched count-wheel for the striking can be seen. The going train fusée set up ratchet can be seen to the left, while the going barrel ratchet for the striking train is to the right-hand side.

Plate 77 – This interesting clock does not have a balance, but uses a short bob pendulum with a verge escapement. It, too, has a wooden case very like the preceding example, and the back plate is also engraved in a similar manner. Only the going train uses a fusée. The front plate of this clock is very beautifully decorated with cloisonné enamel which was a technique introduced into Japan in the late 1830s. The shallow angular bell is also a nineteenth-century feature. Earlier bells are deeper and almost hemispherical in shape. The drawer in the base contains the winding key. The apertures above the dial are for the calendar. The pierced brass 'fence' around the base of this clock is quite unusual and very effective. The use of fretted brass was a favourite method of decorating clock cases and plates.

Occasionally spring-driven clocks were made with a musical box contained within the base which would be released by the clock mechanism. This idea was probably inspired by European imports as were the few Japanese clocks made to play tunes on a nest of bells.

The Pillar Wall Clock

The pillar clock is the second type of weight-driven clock made in Japan. They are also known as 'foot rule' clocks, many of them being of that length. They can also be found as large as four feet in length. This form of clock may well have been produced as a cheaper form of timepiece for the less well off, many of them being exceedingly plain and simple.

The pillar clock has been likened to a pencil box and a longcase clock. It is simply a long box hung from a nail on the wall, on top of which is mounted an ordinary weight-driven timepiece mechanism of diminutive size. The trunk has a slot cut down its front through which shows a pointer attached to the driving weight. This pointer registers against the hour numerals as it descends. Needless to say, these clocks are of one-day duration although they often have 13-hour numerals so that there is at least an hour in which to re-wind the clock. The key is housed in a small drawer at the base of the trunk.

Plate 78a – This very simple type of pillar clock has the strap form of movement screwed to the back board. This is an early pillar clock, possibly of the eighteenth century. The movement is made wholly of iron and is controlled by a tiny foliot with adjustable weights. The clock is wound by the miniature cranked handle on the front plate.

The hinged wooden hood is here seen opened. The adjustable hour plates can be seen down the front of the wooden trunk, reading from top to bottom 6, 5, 4, 9, 8, 7 twice over.

Plate 78b – A very much more sophisticated and beautiful example of a pillar clock, with the dial in the form of a graduated scale. The table on the trunk has the twelve months across the top. Midwinter is on the left and midsummer on the right, where the night hours are very short, and back from right to left to complete the year. The pointer on the descending bar has to be set by hand to the appropriate month or half month. The hour scale is down the left-hand side of the table with the corresponding zodiac signs to the right. With this form of dial the only adjustments required are the half-monthly ones of the hour pointer.

The balance wheel of this clock is contained within the shallow drum above the movement and fine regulation can be made by means of two small adjustable weights. The balance is fitted with a hair spring. This clock is about 16 inches high. The most striking feature of this clock is the beautifully fretted and engraved front plate, and also the decorative pillars at the corners.

It is quite usual for pillar clocks to have decorative corner pillars or half-pillars but it must be remembered that they are only decorative and do not serve a functional purpose. Since there is no dial on the front plate of the movement this area can be used to display the engraver's skill to great effect. The shape of such engraved and pierced plates bears no relation to its function but is determined by the twists and curls of the leaves and flowers of the design. In this respect the front plate of a pillar clock can be compared with the backcock of an eighteenth-century European watch.

Striking pillar clocks are as ingenious as they are rare. To incorporate a weight-driven striking train in a pillar clock would have required a radical change in its proportions and also a great increase in its weight. These problems were both overcome by constructing a spring-driven striking mechanism within the driving weight of the going train. The striking part enclosed in its brass box was therefore a substitute for the usual lead weight of the clock. At the hour the striking mechanism was released in the same way as on any other clock – by the small inward projections on the reverse of each movable hour plate. Large clocks were also sometimes provided with half-hour plates.

Plate 79 – This small spring-driven clock is constructed within an inrō. The inrō was a small box made in very many shapes and sizes, usually with several compartments which fit tightly together, and was used to carry small items required during the day, serving much the same purpose as a pocket. It was hung from the girdle and was secured by means of the netsuke. An inrō containing a clock such as the one illustrated is therefore the equivalent of the European pocket watch of the period.

The inrō is made of brass and has the remains of polychrome skin or leather covering. The netsuke is of a grotesque face in bronze and silver with an ivory surround. The matching toggle or ojime is signed in silver.

The spring-driven fusée movement fills its case and has a balance-controlled verge escapement. A single figure on the rotating dial, the numerals of which are adjustable, shows through a hole in the case.

The revolution of 1866 opened Japan to western influences in very many areas of life, including the adoption of the western calendar and system of time measurement in 1873. Unless they could be converted, all the clocks we have discussed became obsolete at this time. Most of them were disposed of to dealers in Japanese art and curios, who apparently found a ready market among European and American travellers and collectors. This explains why today these clocks are more common in Europe than they are in Japan. Some of the ones found today will have been converted to the western form of striking the hours from 1–12. The clocks could still be used today for telling the time so long as the numerals were equally spaced and the half-hour numerals were registered as hour divisions.

9 China

The ancient civilisation of China has produced many wonderful things which have been the envy of Europe. Porcelain, for instance, was first made in China perhaps around the year AD 800, and yet it was not until the sixteenth century that a reasonably satisfactory copy was produced in Europe. Lacquered decoration on wood has been practised in China since at least the seventh century BC. In the seventeenth century, when the East India Companies began importing it from China, it was immediately copied in Holland and England.

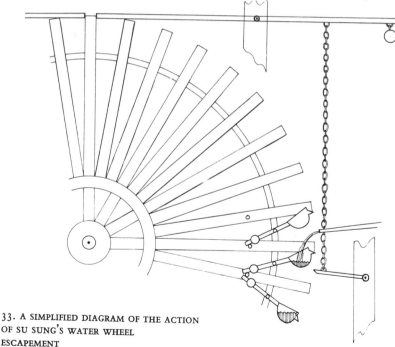

33. A SIMPLIFIED DIAGRAM OF THE ACTION
OF SU SUNG'S WATER WHEEL
ESCAPEMENT

It is seldom realised that a certain Su Sung developed a clock with a form of mechanical-cum-hydraulic escapement as early as around 1090. It used running water to regulate the clockwork of toothed wooden wheels. A later waterwheel had, instead of the usual vanes or troughs, weighted see-saws with buckets on the lighter ends. It was not until the bucket was full of water that it tipped and in doing so released a brake which allowed the whole wheel to turn until the next bucket was in position (see fig. 33). This crude form of escapement could have been of great importance if it had been developed further. Unfortunately it appears that it was an isolated example of one man's ingenuity, the principles of which were lost in the following centuries.

The Introduction of Mechanical Clocks to China

In the sixteenth century, when the first European traders arrived in the country, China's culture had remained virtually unchangd for very many centuries; other cultures were regarded as inferior and contacts with other countries were always tentative and guarded. Foreigners were not allowed freely into the country since China's rulers did not want the way of life disrupted by alien ideas. Permission to enter the country had to be granted by the mandarin of the region in question and was only granted if the foreigner was going to be of special value to the community. China was willing to take what she needed from other nations, but jealously guarded her own assets.

The secret of porcelain production was an example. The export of porcelain in the seventeenth and eighteenth centuries provided a source of great revenue and those who were engaged in its production were formed into monastic-like communities sworn to secrecy and threatened with terrible tortures if caught divulging information. The story goes that one method of punishment was for the culprit to be covered in a mass of porcelain and slowly cooked in a kiln.

The Chinese took a great interest in the mechanical clocks which arrived with the Europeans in the sixteenth century. The Jesuit missionaries used this interest as a way of gaining entry into the country. In 1582 they approached the Viceroy of Kwantung and Kwangsi to inform him that they would like to present him with gifts, among which was a clock which struck the hours. Eventually the missionaries reached the imperial court and presented the Emperor himself with two clocks. The first was a large iron weight-driven chamber clock, the second a small gilt bronze spring-driven table clock. Before very long the Jesuits were instructing four eunuchs of the court in the making of clocks – a superb opportunity of prolonging their stay and gaining a permanent foothold in China.

It must be remembered that the Chinese never considered European clocks as being useful time-measuring instruments, since they had a very different system of hours, somewhat similar to that of the Japanese. Mechanical clocks were considered simply as elaborate toys or curiosities. The term eventually used to describe them was 'self-ringing bell'. Consequently those clocks which contained elaborate chiming musical or automata movements were especially prized.

Having begun trading activities with China the Europeans found difficulty in producing goods to interest the Chinese in exchange for the silks, spices, tea, lacquered objects and porcelain which poured into European ports. It was mainly a one-way traffic and the result was a vast flow of gold and silver bullion to the 'Celestial Empire'. Clocks were one of the few items which were constantly in demand in China and it is not surprising that during the eighteenth century a particular type of clock evolved which was especially made for the Chinese market.

In 1769 Father Mathieu de Benton wrote 'I have been appointed by the Emperor as clock-maker but I should rather say that I am here as machinist because the Emperor expects me to produce not really clocks but curious machines and automata'. Another contemporary writer commented that 'one should bring to Peking especially those play things which European boys use to amuse themselves. Such objects will be received here with much greater interest than scientific instruments'. The kind of toys to which he referred were probably such things as glass bottles containing little wooden mills worked by the falling of sand, rather like a sand glass. Such toys could be bought for a penny or so in Europe.

Clocks with enamelled dials which showed off to great advantage the movement of a central seconds-hand were very popular in China, as were clocks with any form of automata or musical movement. In order to avoid damage to the enamel dial or the central seconds-hand the winding squares were normally made to protrude through the back plate. Often a revolving stand was provided to facilitate turning the clock when it required winding. As well as wooden-cased clocks, gilt metal ones were frequently made for China. Often parts of the case were enamelled and decorated with split pearls and paste brilliants. In 1788 the order books of Thwaites of Clerkenwell include, for Barraud of Cornhill, 'For the China Markett. A pair of small four tune clocks with seconds in the centre, the Chime Barrill in the heade with 3 in. enamelled plates and gold hands and with a Ballance instead of Pendulums fitted into enamelled cases'. A large order follows in 1790 for '6 Pair of Plain Spring Clocks. 3 Pair of them to convex glasses and 3 to wind up behind and made in every respect suitable to the East India Trade'.

In the late eighteenth century the Chinese began to produce clocks of their own which were copies of European models. The quality of many of them is inferior to the European ones of a similar nature and it would appear that they were seldom as complicated. However, in 1800, J. Barrow was able to report that the Chinese 'now fabricate in Canton, as well as in London and at a third of the expense all those ingenious pieces of mechanism which at one time were sent to China in such quantities from the repositories of Coxe and Merlin'. This suggests that there was by this time a noticeable reduction in the import of clocks from Europe. Clocks made in China often bear on the back plate, a signature intended to be a copy of an English or Austrian name. Because the engraver did not understand European writing, he produced a quite unintelligible result.

Plate 80 A fine quality drum-shaped table clock of brass. The case is signed on the base from where it is wound. The sides are decorated with a cast and pierced design which incorporates the Pa Chi-Hsiang or eight Buddhist symbols of the vase, the conch shell, the state umbrella, the canopy, the lotus, the flaming wheel of the law, the fish and the endless knot. The dial, which is of about 6 inches in diameter, is fitted with a single hand and points to an outer enamelled ring which displays the twelve signs of the Chinese hours. The inner ring shows the twenty-four hours of European time. The spring-driven movement uses a fusée and is controlled by a balance wheel and verge escapement. The clock also has an alarm mechanism.

Glossary

Arbor A shaft or spindle

Balance The balance, in the form of a wheel, controls the going of a clock or watch

Balance staff The arbor on which the balance is mounted

Bezel A ring, usually of brass, which surrounds the dial and is used to hold the glass

Chapters The hour numerals on a dial

Cock Bracket or bridge screwed to a clock plate in which an arbor is pivoted

Collet Brass collar used to fit a wheel to its arbor

Contrate or Bevelled wheel Wheel with its teeth cut at right angles to the plane of the wheel and used to transmit motion through 90°

Dead beat A dead beat escapement is one where no recoil is imparted to the escape wheel

Detent Locking device

Ebauche Unfinished or 'rough' movement

Escapement Link between the going train and the pendulum or balance. It is through the escapement that the impulse is given to the pendulum or balance

Fly Fan-like governor used to regulate the speed of the striking train

Foliot Bar balance used with the verge escapement in early clocks

Fusée See p. 11

Gathering pallet A single-leafed pinion, used in rack striking, which gathers the teeth of the rack, one at a time

Going barrel Mainspring barrel which incorporates the great wheel

The motion is transmitted directly from the spring to the great wheel without using a fusée

Going train That train of wheels from which the hands are drived

Impulse face Any part of an escapement which receives an impulse from the escape wheel

Lantern pinion Pinion, with pins, held between two metal disks, which act as the leaves or teeth

Motion work The wheels and pinions, mounted behind the dial, which drive the hands of a clock, normally giving a 12:1 reduction ratio

Pallet The parts of an escapement upon which the escape wheel acts. On some escapements one part may be locking and another for receiving an impulse

Pinion A wheel with few teeth. The teeth, or leaves, are normally cut from the same piece of metal as its arbor

Recoil A recoil escapement is one where the escape wheel is made to recoil by the pallets

Set-up The amount by which a spring remains wound when the clock is run down

Train A number of wheels and pinions geared to one another

Bibliography

Basserman, Jordan, *The Book of Old Clocks and Watches* (Allen & Unwin, 1964)

Battison, Edwin A. and Kane, Patricia E., *The American Clock 1725–1865*. Greenwich, Conn: New York Graphic Society, Ltd., 1973.

Britten, F. J., *Watch & Clockmakers Handbook* (E. & F. N. Spon, 1946)

Cescinsky and Webster, *English Domestic Clocks* (Hamlyn, 1969)

Drummond, Robertson, *The Evolution of Clockwork* (S.R. Publishers Ltd., 1931)

Edey, Winthrop, *French Clocks* (Studio Vista, 1967)

Hoopes, Penrose R., *Connecticut Clockmakers of the Eighteenth Century*. Hartford, E. V. Mitchell, 1930 (Reprinted 1974 by Dover Books)

Jerome, Chauncey, *History of the American Clock Business for the past Sixty Years*. New Haven: F. C. Dayton, 1860 (Reprinted by Adams Brown Co., Exeter, N.H.)

Lloyd, H. Alan, *The Collector's Dictionary of Clocks* (Country Life, 1964)

Palmer, Brooks, *The Book of American Clocks* (Macmillan, 1972)

Roberts, Kenneth D., *The Contributions of Joseph Ives to Connecticut Clock Technology*, 1810–1862. Bristol, Conn.: The American Clock & Watch Museum, 1970.

Roberts, Kenneth D., *Eli Terry and the Connecticut Shelf Clock*. Bristol, Conn.: Ken Roberts Publishing Co., 1973.

Symonds, R. W., *A Book of English Clocks* (Penguin, 1947)

Tyler, E. J., *European Clocks* (Ward Lock, 1968)

Ward, F. A. B., *Time Measurement* (H.M.S.O., 1966)

Acknowledgments

The author and publishers wish to thank the following for allowing the reproduction of the illustrations in this book:

Mr M. Aalders, 13b; the American Clock and Watch Museum, Bristol, Conn., U.S.A., 67–70 (photographed by Edward Goodrich); the Antique Porcelain Co., London, 31, 53; the British Museum, London, 4, 71 (photos by courtesy of Weidenfeld and Nicolson); Aubrey Brocklehurst Antique Clocks, London, 6, 10, 11b; Adrian Burchall, Antique Clocks, Bristol, 12c, 55, 63, 65; Mrs S. Burchall, 36; Camerer Cuss & Co., London, 3b, 11a, 39, 46; the Clock Clinic, London, 21, 22, 34b; the Clockmakers Company Museum, London, 3a (photo by courtesy of Weidenfeld and Nicolson); Mr G Eadington, 72c; Bartholomew Flaggett Antiques, London, 38, 66, 72a, 72b; the Holburne of Menstrie Museum, Bath, 32, 48a, 51; Johann Klein Antique Clocks, London, 8, 23b, 24, 45a, 60a; Malletts, London, 54; the Netherlands Gold, Silver and Clock Museum, Utrecht, 9, 18, 19, 35 (Museum photographs); Perio Antiques, London, 12a, 12b, 13a, 13c, 40a, 40b, 73, 74b, 74c; the Science Museum, London, 1, 2, 15, 16, 20, 43, 44, 75b, 76, 78b, 79, and plates 75c, 77, 78a, 80 (from the collection of the late P. L. Harrison, Esq.); Mrs J. Simpson, 59a; Strike One Ltd, London, 34a, 52; the Victoria and Albert Museum, London, 5, 17, (Museum photo), 23a, 25, 26, 28, 29, 30, 45b, 48b, 50; the Wallace Collection, London, 27, 33 (Museum photographs); Mr R. C. Woofinden, 42; Mr J. Woollard, 47.

All photographs by Bob Loosemore, except where otherwise stated.

Clock and Watch Collections

ENGLAND
Bury St Edmunds Gershom-Parkington Memorial Collection of Time Measurement Instruments, Angel Corner, Bury St Edmunds
Cambridge Fitzwilliam Museum, Trumpington St., Cambridge CB2 1RB
Lincoln Usher Gallery, Lindum Rd., Lincoln
Liverpool City of Liverpool Museum, William Brown St., Liverpool L3 8EN
London British Museum, Great Russell St., WC1B 3DG
Clockmakers' Company Museum, the Guildhall, EC2
National Maritime Museum, Greenwich, SE10
Science Museum, Exhibition Rd., South Kensington, SW7
Victoria and Albert Museum, South Kensington, SW7
Oxford Ashmolean Museum of Art and Archaeology, Beaumont St., Oxford
Museum of the History of Science, Broad St., Oxford OX1 3AZ

AUSTRIA
Vienna Clock Museum
Kunsthistorisches Museum

DENMARK
Aarhus Danish Urmuseum
Copenhagen National Museum
Rosenborg Castle Museum

FRANCE

Besancon Musée des Beaux Arts
Paris Conservatoire des Arts et Métiers
  Louvre
  Musée des Arts Decoratifs
Toulouse Musée Paul Dupuy
  Musée Saint Raymond

GERMANY

Augsburg City Museum
Baden Wurttemberg Collection Landesgewerbeamt
Furtwangen Clock Museum
Munich Bavarian National Museum
Nuremburg Germanisches National Museum
Schwenningen Collections of the Mauthe & Kienzle Factories

HOLLAND

Amsterdam Rijksmuseum
Groningen Groningen-Museum
Leiden Dutch Science Museum
Utrecht Netherlands Gold, Silver and Clock Museum

SWEDEN

Stockholm Nordliches Museum
  Stadsmuseum

SWITZERLAND

Basel Kirchgarten Museum
Geneva Musée d'Horologerie
La Chaux de Fonds Musée d'Horologerie
Le Locle Musée d'Horologerie
Neuchatel Musée Historique

U.S.A.

San Francisco California Academy of Sciences, Golden Gate Park, San Francisco, 94118

COLORADO
Denver Hagans Clock Manor Museum, Bergen Park, Evergreen, Denver, 80439

CONNECTICUT
Bristol American Clock and Watch Museum, Inc, 100 Maple St., Bristol, 06010

ILLINOIS
Chicago Adler Planetarium and Astronomical Museum, 1300 S. Lakeshore Drive, Chicago, 60605
Springfield Illinois State Museum, Spring & Edwards Sts., Springfield, 62706

MASSACHUSETTS
Sturbridge Old Sturbridge Village, Sturbridge, 01566

NEW YORK
New York James Arthur Collection, New York University, Washington Square Metropolitan Museum of Art, Fifth Ave. at 82nd St., 10028

OHIO
Cincinnati Taft Museum, 316 Pike St., 45202

PENNSYLVANIA
Columbia National Association of Watch and Clock Collectors, 514 Poplar St., 17512

VERMONT
Shelburne Shelburne Museum, Shelburne, 05482

WASHINGTON D.C. Smithsonian Institution, 1000 Jefferson Drive S.W., 20560

Index

Watches in Colour

Watches in Colour

RICHARD GOOD

Contents

1

The Beginnings of the Watch

Watches developed from small clocks. The exact moment at which they can be described as a watch must, by the very nature of things, be uncertain.

By definition a watch must be able to be worn or carried on the person. What shape or how small must the timepiece be before it is reasonable to carry it about? Who can say?

When documentary evidence is all that one has to go on then this must be accepted as a guide. With this in mind, it is probable that watchmaking began in Italy. In November 1462, Bartolomeo Manfredi wrote to the Marquess Lodovico Gonzana Modena that he had begun to assemble a small watch similar to that owned by the Duke of Modena, and that he was determined to perfect it. The term that he employed is specific because in Italian 'orologetto' does not mean a small clock but definitely a watch. This point is agreed by both ancient and modern dictionaries.

The clocks that undoubtedly led to the watch were the tambour or drum clocks. Here the dial was horizontal and had no protective cover. Although weighing half a pound such clocks began to be carried, either suspended from the neck or placed in a leather pouch, which nobles and gentlemen wore at the waist. They were unreliable as sooner or later the hand would catch, stopping the clock. These small clocks had lips at the top and bottom for aesthetic reasons and when the idea arose of adding a cover to protect the hand, the upper part of the case band was left smooth and the cover edge appeared as the lip. Unfortunately, no early Italian watches have survived, a great misfortune for the horological historian.

One of the earliest paintings in which a watch appears is by Hans Eworth. It is a portrait dated 1563 of Lord Darnley, later to be the husband of Mary, Queen of Scots. He is shown wearing what appears to be a gold and blue enamel circular watch on a cord around his neck. We learn from her will that the Queen of Scots left to Lord Darnley – 'One watch garnished with ten diamonds, two rubies and a cord of gold.'

Early watches were undoubtedly costly items. They were extremely difficult to make and must have taxed the ability of the finest available craftsmen. Every tooth of each wheel had to be marked out and filed by hand. The craftsman himself usually had to make the files that he used. Mainsprings were particularly difficult to make and soon became the province of specialists.

Wherever watchmaking began, it is almost certain that Nuremberg was the great centre of watchmaking in the early years of the 16th century. Later in France in about 1525, other centres came into being notably at Dijon, Rouen, Blois and Paris. The watches made in Germany and France were very similar, the main difference being in the fitting of the striking arrangement. German watches had the 'nags head' method of striking, whereas the French system had 'warning'. All striking of this period was of the count wheel variety.

Religious strife led to the exodus of French Huguenot watchmakers. They settled in various places, one being Geneva where they helped to found the centre that was eventually to become so well known. In the last two decades of the 16th century more French craftsmen left France for London and stimulated the watchmaking industry there. Only a small number of craftsmen were needed to form a centre of watch production. They needed to take little with them but their skill and could set up anywhere, providing that the necessary supply of metals and the know-how to work them already existed.

Watches – The Train and Escapement

All the wheelwork in mechanical watches is powered by a coiled spring, usually contained in a barrel. The inner end of the spring is attached to an arbor and the outer end attached to the wall of the barrel. When the arbor or the barrel is turned, a ratchet prevents the spring from immediately unwinding again. The only way it can unwind and thus expend the energy that has been put into it, is to turn the train of gears to which its output end is connected. This may be the barrel or the arbor according to the design.

In an ordinary watch the first of the gears to be turned is the centre wheel, which is mounted on a pinion. This centre wheel usually carries the minute hand. The last of the gears in the train is the escapement wheel. By reason of the high ratio between the barrel and the escape wheel, only a small portion of the power of the mainspring reaches it. If the rate of rotation of this escape wheel can be accurately controlled, then so will the speed of rotation of the rest of the gear train. Thus, the hand will rotate at the correct speed and indicate the right time. Further gearing can be employed to achieve any other rate of rotation required, once in twelve hours, once a minute, once a year or what you will.

The mechanism that controls the rate of rotation of the escape wheel is the escapement. This comprises all the elements that follow and includes the escape wheel. The most important is the balance; the foliot will be discussed later.

The balance wheel is pivoted on an axis and is constructed so that the major portion of its weight lies in its rim. This is to make maximum use of its inertial properties. In most of the early watches, where there was a balance, this had no spring, but after about 1650 balance springs were fitted, which gave the balance a specific rate of oscillation. One end of the spring was attached to the piece that supported and located the balance and the other to the balance axis, or staff, as it is known. If the balance is turned through a certain angle it will immediately be urged back to its rest position by the spring. However, the inertia of the balance will cause it to pass the rest position and, but for inevitable frictional losses, it would oscillate for ever. As the energy is given to the spring through coiling, it is transferred to energy contained in the balance because of its motion. It is the energy contained in the escape wheel that is used to make up the frictional losses that occur at the balance.

If the balance oscillations could be made free of factors that upset their uniformity, a perfect timekeeper would result. Unfortunately, this is not possible and the following are those factors that upset timekeeping:

1. The fact that the impulse cannot be given exactly at the rest position of the balance and spring assembly.

2. Changes in the balance losses that need to be made good due to changes in temperature, changes in oil viscosity and changes in position of the timekeeper.

3. Changes in the motive power itself.

4. Changes in temperature that affect the balance and spring itself by altering the moment of inertia of the balance and the strength of the balance spring.

Escapement Types

It is evident that some escapements must give better results than others. There are two basic types of escapements. The first, the frictional rest type and the second, the detached escapement.

The frictional rest type operates in such a way that once a tooth of the escape wheel has finished impulsing the balance the following tooth rests on some part of the balance or its axis. Evidently this cannot be a good type of escapement since the balance is never free from interference.

The detached escapement is one in which after a tooth of the escape wheel has finished giving impulse, the following tooth is arrested by some part, other than the balance, and kept away from the balance until the next time it is necessary for the balance to release the escape wheel. This way the inference to the balance can be kept as far as is possible around the desirable position, when most of the energy of the system is in the moving balance.

Endless thought and experiment has been put into the attainment of the perfect escapement, balance and spring. The answer is still being sought, but is likely to become purely academic due to the advent of the electronic watch.

What made portable timepieces possible then, was the invention of the mainspring as a source of power. Previously the falling of a weight had supplied power to most mechanical clocks but obviously this was not suitable for a portable timekeeper.

It is probable that locksmiths pioneered the development of the mainspring, a ribbon of hardened and tempered steel, which provides power by releasing the energy that has been put into it to deform it. Such springs were very difficult to make at this early stage of the engineering art. Indeed, even today, they are still the province of specialists, for although some present-day craftsmen make every other part of a watch, not one would contemplate manufacturing his own mainsprings.

The mainspring, however, has one unfortunate characteristic that presents a great problem; that is, when fully wound it gives a greater force than when it is run down. This was a tremendous disadvantage in early watches, since their controlling element, the foliot or balance, depended on a constant source of power for its ability to keep any sort of time at all. To help somewhat, stop work was used to prevent the worst condition which occurred when the spring was fully wound. The stop work ensured that the watch could only be wound at the most to within about one turn of fully wound, although sometimes only two turns of the mainspring output were utilised, these being around the half-wound condition. It is here that the output of a spring is at its most uniform.

Two devices were developed to overcome the difficulty, one was called the stackfreed and the other the fusee. The stackfreed (Fig. 1) consisted of a stiff blade spring (A), which bore against a cam (B), that was geared to the barrel arbor (C). This spring resisted the force of the mainspring to a greater or lesser degree so as to help to equalise the spring output.

The earliest datable stackfreed watch is in a tambour case and is in the Louvre, Paris. It was made by Viet Schauffer of Munich in 1554. It is probable that the stackfreed was only introduced a few years before this date. Watches usually went for about twelve to fourteen hours so that they needed to be wound twice a day. Stop work remained and was an integral part of the stackfreed, the tooth that was uncut forming the stop. In later stackfreeds the cam against which the blade spring acted was made of brass and screwed to the stop wheel. It could thus be removed to alter its shape without altering the set-up of the stop work.

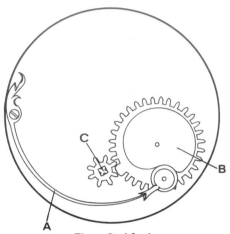

Fig. 1 Stackfreed.

A stackfreed watch with an English name does exist, although it is not certain that the signature is genuine. The name on the dial is G. Smith and there are also the initials GS on the movement. The stackfreed cam works for 270° of its rotation. It retards the main-spring for 20°, acts frictionally for a further 50° and then actively assists the mainspring for the remaining 200°. The retarding part of the cam covers 70° but some of this is prevented from acting due to the stop work. The cam is mounted on a stop wheel having twenty-six teeth which meshes with a pinion of eight leaves, thus allowing an effective three and a quarter turns of the mainspring. It is not possible to say that the style indicates anything other than the fact that it might have been made in Germany or the Netherlands. The watch also has hog's bristle regulation which is to be discussed later. All of the other extant stackfreeds are thought to have been made in Germany, Switzerland or the Netherlands. The stackfreed was a very crude device and did not last for long.

The fusee, however, which is in effect a pulley of varying diameter, was a sophisticated and elegant answer to the problem of the varying

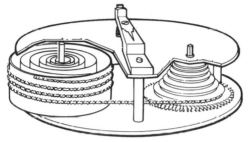

Fig. 2 Fusee.

power of the mainspring, so much so that it is still in use to this day. As can be seen from Fig. 2, the mainspring when fully wound works on the smallest diameter. In the figure, however, it is run down and is on the largest diameter of the continuous spiral groove machined on the fusee. As the mainspring runs down, then, it works on an increasing radius so as to offset its loss of power.

2
The Foliot and the Verge Escapement

As already described, the escapement in a watch or clock is that part that transforms the rotation of the train of gears into the reciprocating motion required by the controlling part of the mechanism. The first mechanical escapement was the verge, which was probably used to begin with as a type of alarm ringing device in monasteries although both its origin and its date of invention are obscure.

Two paddle-shaped pieces, known as flags, are mounted on a shaft that runs across the escape wheel, which has upright standing

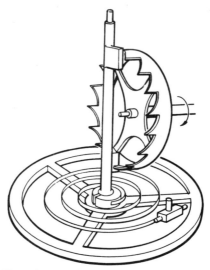

Fig. 3 Verge with crown wheel, balance and spring.

teeth. There are usually an odd number of teeth in the escape wheel. Due to the obvious resemblance, the escape wheel is known as a crown wheel (see Fig. 3). The flags mesh with the teeth so that one or the other is always in contact with a tooth. Thus, as the wheel turns, the flags, and thus the shaft, move first one way and then the other. The speed at which the wheel rotates depends upon the force applied to it and the inertial resistance of the shaft. This inertial resistance is increased by mounting a bar or a balance wheel on the shaft. In early clocks the bar, or foliot as it is called, often carried small weights that could be moved along it, so as to change the timekeeping, but this was not applicable to watches. Instead, the foliot ended in two fixed weights. The balance wheel has an advantage over the foliot in watches in as much as it is easier to 'poise'; that is, to make adjustments so that when it runs on edge no heavy point exists around its periphery to further upset timekeeping. Because of this only very early watches have a foliot, or bar balance.

The Hog's Bristle

Some control of the timekeeping of clocks with foliots was possible by moving the weights on the arm, so that they came nearer to or further away from its centre of rotation, thus altering the moment of inertia. This method of regulation was not practicable in watches.

In some early watches the balance arm was made to bank against a hog's bristle, as in the 'English' stackfreed watch already mentioned. By altering the position of the bristle and thus the angle at which the arm first touched it, a degree of adjustment is possible.

Watches were also regulated by altering the set-up of the mainspring, first by setting up the mainspring through a ratchet and ratchet wheel on the barrel arbor (see Plate 4). A later arrangement where the arbor that engages with the mainspring has a wheel mounted upon it, that can be turned by means of a worm, is shown in Plate 11c. The end of this worm was squared and if the watch went fast over a period, as it so often did, then it could be slowed by setting the mainspring up slightly, using the winding key. This system had dangers, for if the mainspring is set up too far, the fusee stop work could become inoperative and the gut line or chain broken.

Stop work is absolutely essential with a fusee, since the full force that is able to be applied by the winding key must never be directly felt by the gut line or chain. If this is allowed to happen then the line can be broken. The line can overcome the resistance of the mainspring, of course, because this is a design requirement and the amount of the resistance is known. Therefore, there must be a device to limit the amount of winding so that this ceases before the mainspring is

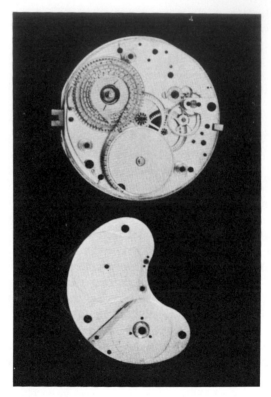

Fig. 4 Reverse fusee and stopwork. The beak of the piece on top of the fusee catches on the notched end of the spring on the top plate when this is pushed up by the chain. This happens as the last groove of the fusee is filled by the chain.

fully wound. This is accomplished by a hook that is pushed into the way of a projection on the fusee by the line, as it fills the last groove on the fusee. A version is shown in Fig. 4, and is associated with a reverse fusee.

Stop work is also applied to the going barrel, that is the ordinary barrel that drives the wheelwork directly, by means of a gear on its periphery. However, this is not required for the same reason, as the mainspring and its hooks are able to take the force applied by winding with a normal key when the mainspring is fully wound. Here stop work, if fitted, is used to eliminate the very high torque given by the mainspring when fully wound. Accordingly, further winding is prevented when there is still about half a turn to a turn (or even more) of winding to go, before the fully wound condition is reached. Stop work that accomplishes this is shown in Plates 44 and 47. It also prevents the mainspring from running down fully, although there is no great virtue in this.

At the middle of the 17th century the watch as a timekeeper was a poor affair, having errors of up to half an hour a day. Some radical improvement, a step forward, like that which occurred when the clock was transformed by the pendulum, was also required for the watch.

However, let us take pause here to examine the decorative aspects of the watch before, during and after this step – the invention of the balance spring – took place.

3 *National Styles*

The Movement

The difference in striking trains between early German and French watches has already been noted. When English watches appeared at the end of the 16th century they followed the French system of striking. German watches often had an alarum in preference to striking-work. Sometimes this alarum mechanism was separate and could be attached at will.

Early plate pillars were plain and square or round section. The top plate was pinned to secure it, a practice which continued well into the 19th century. Even very early watches had one screw. The stackfreed spring was usually secured by a screw and so was the set-up ratchet in a fusee watch (see Plate 9).

By the end of the 16th century national styles began to develop. German watches developed slowly. Iron frames and the stackfreed continued in use throughout the first quarter of the 17th century, when the Thirty Years War (1618–48) so crippled Germany that she ceased to be a factor in the horological field. This left France supreme, although her position was to be challenged by the British in the last quarter of the century.

By 1600 the movement was a beautiful item, although its time-keeping had not noticeably improved. Errors of a quarter of an hour a day were commonplace. Since timekeeping was so bad, attention was drawn away from it by lavish decoration, both of the case and the movement, and by adding complications such as calendar and astronomical work.

In French watches the balance cock was enlarged and was pierced and engraved. It was pinned to the plate. Pierced and engraved parts were also used to cover the locking plate of the striking train, alarum stop work and the set-up ratchet. The maker's name also began to be engraved on the plate.

In Britain, the balance cock was given floral-type decoration and for a little while after 1600 a border was engraved around the top-plate edge. After about 1620, the balance cock began to be secured by a screw instead of being pinned. As the century went on the shape changed from oval to circular and covered the balance completely. Pillars became more decorative. The Egyptian type was the commonest and after 1600 the tulip shape began to appear as did other types of decoration between the movement plates. A three-wheel train and twice-a-day winding remained the rule until about 1675. During the third quarter of the 17th century, thin watches appeared. The gut line also gave way to the fusee chain, although this is rarely found before 1670.

As to the escapement, there was no serious rival to the verge, so that, apart from the decorative aspects of watches, the period from the invention of the watch to the introduction of the balance spring was a period of stagnation. However, from the collector's stand-point and the external appearance of the watch, it is indeed a very interesting period.

Clock and Watchmakers' Guilds had existed abroad from early in the 16th century, but nothing much in this direction was achieved in Britain until 1631, when the Worshipful Company of Clock-makers was founded. David Ramsey was its first Master. From this time onward the quality of British watchmaking improved until, by 1675 at the time of the development of the balance spring, the British makers were able to take the lead from the French.

After the introduction of the balance spring it soon became difficult to make a weak enough mainspring to cope with a three-wheel train so another wheel was introduced, making a going period of twenty-six hours virtually universal. Some makers, both French and English – Tompion was one – thought they could dispense with the fusee, but soon found it necessary to return to using it with the verge escapement. The set-up regulator that the owner needed to manipulate was, however, found to be unnecessary but was retained for the convenience of the maker and repairer.

The application of the pendulum to clocks made a great impression on people and when the balance spring came into use this fact was still fresh in their minds. The new watches often sold better if there was a pendulum connotation. In France, watches were made with solid cocks and a simulated pendulum bob that could be seen swinging through an annular slot in this cock (see Plate 21). It was in fact no more than a disc on the balance arm. With English watches the balance was placed between the back plate and the dial, and this 'bob' appeared through a slot in the dial. This practice, however, did not last much after 1690.

Soon after the introduction of the balance spring, the decoration of the English watch movement became fairly standardised. The cock changed from the floreate pattern to an arabesque pattern, at first bold, but becoming increasingly fussy. The table covering the balance was circular and later was to have a solid rim. The foot was not so regular in shape, but by 1690 both foot and table had acquired a well-delineated rim, that of the foot following the plate edge. After about 1680 most clocks had a mask engraved where the table joins the foot; prior to 1685 this mask was small. This mask did not disappear until the middle of the 19th century where verge watches were concerned. Up to about 1740 the pattern of the decoration on the cock was symmetrical, but as the rococo style took over it became asymmetrical.

The French seldom used any pillar other than the Egyptian type in the *Oignons* and plain baluster pillars in their later thin watches, where the movement did not hinge out of the case. The cursive script of the English maker's name became less bold after 1680 and soon after 1690 appeared more and more often in plain capitals, as it almost always did in France. Dust caps over English movements are not often found before 1725 and rarely before 1715. After 1725 however, they became the rule for watches of any quality. Usually of gilt brass, they were, however, sometimes made of silver.

After 1725 the cock became more and more solid and engraved instead of pierced. When compensation balances were introduced, the table of the balance cock ceased to be circular and became wedge-shaped. Sometimes these cocks were solid and engraved, but pierced cocks (including Arnold's) continued up to the end of the century. Verge watches, however, continued to have circular tables until the mid-19th century.

The Case, Dial and Hands

Up to 1650, it is easier to date a watch by the style and decoration than it is by the mechanism. Plain metal cases are the only ones known before 1600. Gold and silver cases were made, records show this, but none survive; only gilt brass cases are extant.

Fig. 5 This German mid-16th century watch has a tambour case and movement with stackfreed and foliot type balance.

Since so many watches were clock-watches or alarums most cases had to be pierced to let out the sound. Also the lid had to be pierced to avoid the necessity of raising it to tell the time (see Fig. 5). These cases were usually cast. Most watches were shaped like boot polish tins. The bell was fixed to the bottom and the movement was hinged and swung out of the front for winding. Winding from the front, or through a hole in the back and bell, did not come until the second half of the 17th century. After casting, the case was usually chiselled in quite high relief. As the 17th century came to an end the chiselling became less deep, and engraving began to take its place. During the last quarter of the 17th century the cover began to be domed and the sides slightly convex, instead of straight. Some cases were octagonal but in general cases were circular (see Fig. 6).

Initially the dial was almost always engraved gilt metal. The applied silver chapter ring does not really appear until after 1600.

Twenty-four-hour dials were used in Italy and Germany. The first twelve hours were marked in Roman numerals, the second in Arabic. IIII was used for aesthetic reasons, not IV, and the Arabic 2 was Z (see Plate 1). After 1600 when English watches appeared these had the normal 2, but the German watches continued with the Z for another two decades or so. The centre of the dial usually had a star-shaped pattern.

Fig. 6 This watch has a dial with enamelled cartouches and a strong single hand.

The single hands were of steel or iron and strongly made to resist the forces put upon them (see Fig. 6) during hand setting, since they were pushed round by the finger. The only exception to the ferrous metal hand is found in enamelled watches where the hand is gilt metal. The pendant was usually fixed, drilled through from back to front and fitted with a loose ring (see Plate 1).

During the 16th century cases were made in a great variety of shapes, styles and decoration. In the first half of the 17th century the pair case appeared. The arrival of expensive and delicate cases made a second protective case, in which to keep the watch when not in use, a sensible idea. At first these were made of leather, but with the introduction of pockets it became usual to also wear the outer case. By the middle of the 17th century outer cases were an integral part of the watch and not meant to be separated from it.

The dial side of the outer case was open and the outer case itself soon became decorated. By 1670 the anomalous position was then

Fig. 7 This watch has an early gut fusee, Egyptian pillars, and pierced band to the case.

achieved when the inner case became completely plain and the outer sometimes so decorated that, if delicate, it was itself protected with a third case. From 1680 onwards the ordinary English watch had two plain cases, the outer to prevent the ingress of dirt through the winding hole. This resulted in a thick watch. The French, however, did not follow this system but had a single case, the watch being wound through the dial. This has not been a good thing for posterity since so many French watches have damaged dials as a result.

Around 1600 the form watch appeared, the case in the form of a skull, a book, a dog, crucifix, bird, flower bud, etc. (see Plates 2, 3, 7 and 18 and Figs. 8a and 8b). The traditional round, octagonal and increasingly oval watches continued to be made throughout the first quarter of the 17th century. Straight sides to the case increasingly gave way to the convex side, and in British watches particularly the whole case became like a somewhat flattened egg, a shape no doubt conducive to comfortable wear in the pocket. These cases were not

Fig. 8a The front of the watch shown in Plate 18.

Fig. 8b The movement of the watch shown in Plate 18.

decorated and were to become known as 'Puritan' watches by the middle of the century, by which time the dial also had become plain and the case almost invariably silver. Glass covers had also appeared during the second quarter of the 17th century. Gilt brass remained the usual metal, but silver and, to a lesser extent, gold cases also appeared.

French watches began to take on the elongated oval or the octagonal shape and this style was followed by the Swiss watches that began to appear. After the third quarter of the 17th century German watches virtually disappeared. True minute hands are seldom found before 1680.

During the third quarter of the 17th century the watch began to assume the form it was to retain for the next century. The matt surface silver or gold dial began to appear and the figures of the chapter ring grew longer. By 1675 they had become so long as to overwhelm the dial (see Plate 19). Hands became simpler, sometimes being quite plain; most had tails although many are found without. The pendant ring began to change from its original position, lying at right angles to the case, and moved to its present position lying in the same plane as the case. This probably followed the introduction of waistcoats into England by Charles II.

The balance spring brought about great changes in the English watch when it became generally introduced in 1675. The emphasis moved from exterior decoration to the aspects connected with timekeeping ability and the commonest case was a plain pair case. During the third quarter of the century watches had become much thinner but changed once the emphasis was on timekeeping. The French watch became especially thick and earned for itself the name of 'oignon' (onion). The commonest French case was a single gilt-brass case, decorated in a similar way to the case with the hour numerals on enamel cartouches (see Fig. 6). There was sometimes a narrow ring inside the hour plaque with the hours and half-hours marked on it. Minute hands were unusual and did not become universal until after 1700. When there is a minute hand there is sometimes another chapter ring outside the numerals with minute marks. Hands continued to be pushed about with the finger and even after 1700 may be found to have no motion work, so that they have to be set separately. Winding is through a hole in the dial, sometimes through the hand centre.

Back to English watches. When cases were of gold these were hallmarked and of twenty-two carat gold. Silver cases were seldom hallmarked before 1740. Watchmakers began to number the movements and the case makers to use their initials. Repoussé cases made their appearance, but before 1715 this decoration appears as radial fluting Repoussé scenes and figures do not appear much until 1725. The great period for repoussé cases lasted from then until 1750, after which it again declined in favour until by 1770 such cases were rarely found (see Plate 27).

Christopher Pinchbeck discovered an alloy of three parts zinc and four of copper that bears his name. The secret of its composition was kept from the time of its discovery in 1720 until the end of the century. The industrial spy was not yet a breed to be reckoned with – or so it would appear.

Shagreen-covered cases came into fashion and the popularity of pinwork on leather, horn and shell continued (see Plate 31). Tortoise-shell was also used and was often inlaid with silver or gold strips. The shape of the decoration is cut out of the shell and the shell then heated and the strips are pressed in.

Pendants continued to be loose rings until about 1690 then the hinged stirrup type became almost universal. The case hinges also changed from the earlier square-ended type to the curved ends that merge more into the case rim.

Dials

Dials became standardised after 1700, after a very interesting period during which makers experimented with the best way of telling the minutes as well as the hours.

The concentric minute and hour hand had appeared by 1680 but was not universally accepted. These other methods were tried:

1. The wandering-hour dial (see Plate 23).
2. The differential dial.
3. The six-hour dial (see Plate 24).

They all try to tell the time by means of a single indicator. These types of dial are discussed where they appear with the appropriate watches.

A strange thing about the wandering-hour dials is that nearly all of them have a royal connection, such as a royal portrait on the dial, or the royal arms engraved on the cock, or both. Also many have the fluted repoussé case which is rare at this time. As one example bears a portrait of Queen Anne it is evident that this type of dial continued to be made well after the turn of the century. Seconds dials are occasionally found at a very early date in the normal modern position.

Hands

The hands are either 'beetle and poker' (see Fig. 9) or else the hour hand sometimes 'tulip'. The tulip hand did not survive long after 1715, but the beetle and poker went on until after 1800.

Dials were silver or gold with a matt ground and champlevé hour and minute numerals. The maker's name, when it appeared, was usually on a polished cartouche in the centre area of the dial. Enamel dials are not common before 1725 on English watches, when Graham adopted them as his standard dial.

For the next fifty years after Graham invented the cylinder

Fig. 9 This watch movement has an enamelled dial with beetle and poker hands. It is also centre seconds.

escapement in about 1725, another period of little change occurred. Both Continental and British watches hardly altered during this time.

Dials did change slowly. The old concentric circles gradually disappeared as did the minute marks, no longer needed as people began to read the time at a glance. By the end of the century the minute marks had virtually disappeared.

Engine turning began to appear from 1770 onward, probably because of the influence of Breguet. This was to be often associated with enamelling – the combination known as basse-taille enamelling.

A new school of precision makers came into being; Arnold and Earnshaw in England and Breguet in France. These makers stamped the watch of the time with surety. Elegant severity became the keynote in England. So much was timekeeping in mind that Emery sometimes used the clock-type dial that had previously been applied to regulators. Here, the minute circle occupied the whole dial with the minute hand on its own at the centre of the watch. Subsidiary dials at twelve and six o'clock were for hours and seconds. Emery used a special spade hand (see Fig. 10). This arrangement was much copied for the next forty years. Both Arnold and Emery, in common with other first-class makers, used the consular case in which the front and back meet in such a way that no band is visible, although in common watches, the pair case remained in vogue until the end of the century.

Soon after 1800 a plain matt gold dial with raised and polished numerals became fashionable in England, for watches with cylinder and duplex escapements. Serpentine hands often went with these dials. On the Continent, painted enamel dials of poor quality became common. Often they were allied to simple automata such as a revolving windmill (see Plate 22).

During the 1830–40s the period of heavy decoration began. Heavy cast and engraved watch cases with four-colour gold dials were impressive indeed and felt as good as they looked. Without the superb workmanship that went into them they could have seemed merely vulgar.

Automata movements were often repeaters, where the figures

28

Fig. 10 This watch shows the spade hands peculiar to Josiah Emery.

moved when the watch was made to strike (see Plates 35, 39, 41). Sometimes, these figures were engaged in pleasurable but far from innocent pastimes. Form watches came back into fashion in Switzerland soon after 1800 and have continued to be made ever since.

4 *Breguet and his Influence*

The man who really changed styles on the Continent was Breguet. He set up on his own in 1782 and at once established a new style of restrained elegance. His eye for proportion was unfailing but throughout his work he also had function firmly in mind.

One of his most elegant watches was the 'souscription', although it was his cheapest. This had a flat-sided band with plain rim bezels. Both back and glass were almost flat. The body and back were usually silver, the bezels and pendant ring gold. The back might be either plain or engine turned (see Plate 30).

His fashionable watches were almost always engine turned and were often quite thin. The case was not remarkable, having a narrow rounded band and curved bezels. Breguet did not make much use of enamelling, mainly reserving enamelled cases for his montres à tact (see Plate 46) and for watches for the Turkish market.

For his complicated watches, Breguet used the consular type of case where there was effectively no band. The sides of the case might be nearly flat or curved. Breguet mainly used red gold like most other Continental makers of this period. Inside the back cover there should be a 'B' with the watch and case number. There were French hallmarks at this time, but they are difficult to interpret and date.

Dials were of enamel, gold or silver. The enamel dials usually had Arabic numerals. Roman numerals on an enamel dial were rare in Breguet's lifetime. The signature appears below the 6 position in capital letters; either 'Breguet' or 'Breguet et Fils' after about 1807, but not invariably. The seconds dial is not a separate piece, for enamel dials were not in vogue in Breguet's lifetime. The seconds dial appears anywhere on a Breguet dial, its position was dictated by the movement design. This indifference to symmetry in the dial sets Breguet apart from most other makers. Breguet did not vary his hand design to any extent either so much so that his type of hand bears his name to this day. These hands can be seen in Plate 36; they are also called 'moon hands'. Metal dials are signed in the same way as the enamel dials. The numerals are Roman and the chapter ring plain. The dial centre is patterned with simple engine turning and, if present, the seconds dial is sunk. Soon after Breguet returned to Paris after the Revolution he discovered that his work was being copied and his signature forged. The result was his 'secret signature' intended to protect him and his customers. Put on both enamel and silver dials, although not invariably, the signature was engraved with a diamond point from a master plate using a pantograph. The name Breguet was usually followed by the watch number and is positioned just below the 12 above the fixing screw. On metal dials the signature appears twice, to the right and left and just below the 12.

After Breguet

From 1820 onwards little happened to the outward form of the watch. It is as if everything that happened within the watch prevented anything from happening to the outside. The only changes that took place were mainly connected with the change in winding methods.

There were one or two exceptions, the lady's watch of 1840 for instance. There were a few fashions, false Gothic, then false Greek, followed after the opening of the Suez Canal by false Egyptian styles. After about 1880 there was a return to the Renaissance style, somewhat modified by the revival of the Louis XV style.

In the late 1800s a new style was developed. This was Art Nouveau. The movement which did so much to popularise Art Nouveau was fostered by the enthusiasms and beliefs of the Arts and Crafts Society at whose head was the talented William Morris. The society was worried about what they felt to be the erosion of standards of craftsmanship by the increase of machine production methods. They achieved only a limited success and the only really important effect of the movement was the introduction into England of the Art Nouveau style from the Continent.

The greatest exponents of the style among the European jewellers were Georg Jensen in Copenhagen and Lalique in Paris. The Art Nouveau style was described by its followers as a return to naturalism. Chief among the motifs were flowers, the tulip and daffodil, but the female form and head were also often depicted. The representations were lively and sensual and characterised by a flowing grace that soon imprints itself on the eye as the signature of the styles.

For a while the movement and interest in it faded, but there has been for some years a greatly renewed interest that has resulted in the best examples of Art Nouveau being treated as if they were truly antique, that is conforming to the artificial requirement of being more than one hundred years old. Art Nouveau, although it affected clocks more, did have a corresponding effect on watches, as can be seen clearly by the illustrations in the book of the 1900 Paris Exhibition.

1 A gilt metal alarum watch pre-balance spring and verge escapement. Probably German, dating from the third quarter of the 16th century.

2   A silver gilt fritillary watch, *c.* 1620, with gut fusee, by Daniel Van Pilcom of Amsterdam.

3   A silver skull watch, *c.* 1620, by J. C. Vvolf, with verge escapement and pre-balance spring.

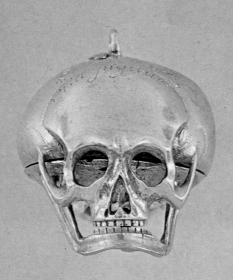

4   A Swiss astronomical watch, *c.* 1620, with verge escapement and pre-balance spring, by Gaspard Girod of Geneva.

5　A French verge watch pre-balance spring, *c.* 1620. It is in an elaborately enamelled and jewelled case.

6 A Swiss verge watch pre-balance spring, by J. Sermand of Geneva (1595-1651).
The crystal case has an enamelled rim and bezel.

7 A French crucifix verge watch pre-balance spring by O. Tinelly, 1630-35. The case is embossed silver and gilt.

8 This enamelled gold-cased verge watch pre-balance spring was made by D. Bouquet of London. The case is probably Swiss and the watch dates from 1630-40.

9   This tiny French verge watch with pre-balance spring was made by A. Bretonneau of Paris, 1638-43. The enamelled gold case measures only 22½mm by 20mm.

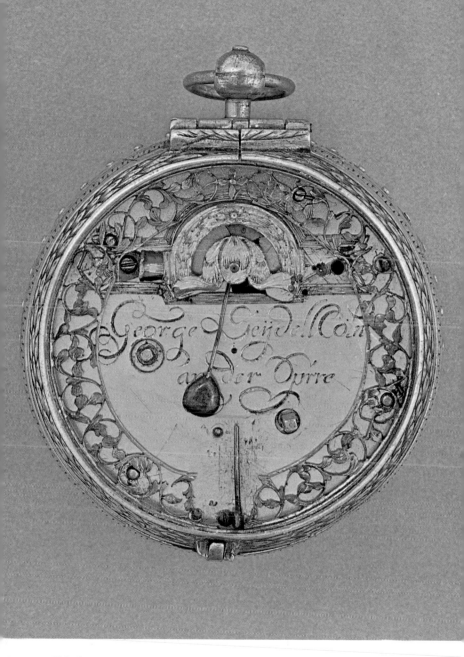

10 This German astronomical verge watch has a pendulum balance with a straight
hairspring. It was made by George Seydell in the mid-17th century, and has a
silver case.

11a   An English verge watch pre-balance spring.

11b The gold and enamelled case for the watch shown opposite was probably made in Geneva.

11c Its movement was made by Isaac Pluvier of London, 1641-65. Note the pinned balance cock and worm set-up.

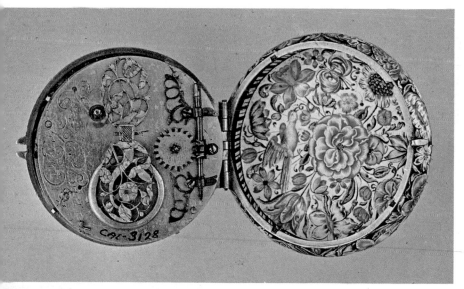

12　A Swiss verge watch, *c.* 1684, by Estienne Ester. The enamelled back shows
Venus and Adonis.

13　This French verge watch was made by B. Foucher, 1630-40. The enamelling is
attributed to Jean or Henri Toutin and shows scenes of the Amazons.

14 *Opposite*. Beautiful miniatures in enamel from the edge of a French watch case.

15 This Swiss clock watch with alarm was made by Jean Baptiste Duboule of Geneva (1615-94), who was also responsible for its engraving.

16 This pre-hairspring German verge watch was made for the Turkish market and thus has Arabic numerals. It dates from *c.* 1680 and has a gilt finish case.

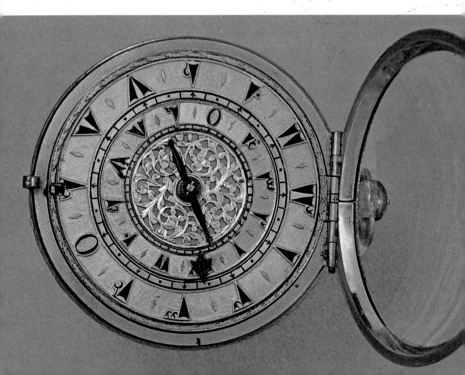

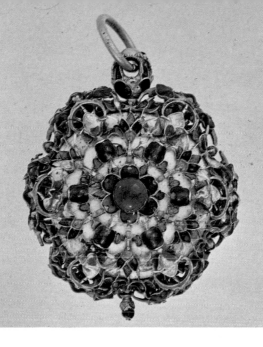

17 A French verge watch made by L. Vautyer in the 17th century. The case is enamelled with raised and pierced gold and enamel decoration.

18   A 17th century German pre-balance watch with fusee and chain. The case is made of rock crystal.

19   An English pair cased alarm watch made in the last third of the 17th century by Tompion.

20 A large French watch, *c.* 1680, by Fardoil of Paris. The silver case is pierced and engraved. The dial is made of gilt brass and the hand of blued steel.

21   The movement of the watch in Plate 20, showing the pendulum cock.

22   Although inscribed 'Barraud, London', this verge watch is Swiss. The sails of the windmill revolve. The pair cases are gilt metal set with paste and enamelled. The watch dates from 1756-94.

23 An English verge watch, dating from the late 17th century, with balance spring and wandering hours dial. It is inscribed 'Jos Windmills 0717'. The pair cases are silver, the outer being engraved with the arms of King William III.

24   An English verge watch, *c.* 1700, by Stammer, with a double six hour dial. This was an attempt to achieve an accurate indication of the minutes with only one hand.

25a   An English double dialled watch, *c.* 1770, by David Pons.

25b   *Opposite.* The 24 hour dial also carries the signs of the zodiac.

25c   The movement has a cylinder escapement.

26   Cased as a chronometer, this is nevertheless really a large and complicated astronomical watch. It is English, *c.* 1780 and was made by Margetts.

27   A Dutch watch, *c.* 1710. The beautiful gold repoussé case illustrates 'The Last Supper'.

28   This English gold watch case, dated 1774, is enamelled with a portrait by Henry Spicer.

29   An English spring detent chronometer. The gold case is hallmarked and dated
      1780. The hands are also gold and the dial enamel. This watch has a half quarter
      dumb repeater.

30   A French cylinder 'souscription' watch made in a silver case, by the incomparable Breguet in 1798. An 'inexpensive' line, these watches were ordered and made in batches. The barrel is at the centre.

31   *Top.* An early enamel dial with cartouches. The case is piqué.

32   *Middle.* This watch is unusual as it bears a portrait inside the front cover.

33   *Bottom.* A superbly enamelled case.

34 This Swiss musical watch, dating from the early 19th century, strikes on five
bells. The case is gold and has a beautifully pierced and engraved cuvette. The
watch is decorated with split pearls and enamelled.

35   This is a Swiss quarter repeater watch with automata, dated 1800-25. Two cupids
ring bells and at the bottom two figures operate a grinding wheel. The watch has
a cylinder escapement and the case is gold.

36b *Left.* The back of the watch shown below. The gold case is decorated all over with grains, filigree and amethysts.

36a *Right.* A Swiss verge watch, *c.* 1810. The movement is inscribed 'Fx. Pernetti à Geneve 13601'. The dial is gold with the numerals on oval plaques.

37 Breguet's testimony to Arnold, 1808. He fitted his 'tourbillon' with spring detent escapement to an Arnold watch.

38 Another Breguet watch, *c*. 1810, with one of his experimental escapements. It is a repeater with a vertical wheel natural lift escapement. Only the movement of this watch now exists.

39   A Swiss repeater watch with automata, made by Meuron and Co., 1800-25. The
case is gold and the dial has coloured gold figures and foliage.

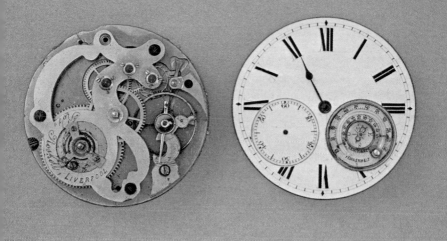

40 This club tooth lever watch, *c.* 1836, is inscribed 'Robert Roskell', but is in fact Swiss. The dial has a thermometer and a compass fitted into it.

41 This is a French cylinder watch with repeating dated 1812-25. The figures stike real bells.

42 Two cylinder watches. The top one is plain and delicate; the bottom one is decorated with enamelling and engraved and has a shaped case.

43 *Top Opposite*. This is a musical quarter striking clock watch, *c.* 1815, by Courvoisier.

44 *Bottom Opposite*. A French independent seconds watch, *c.* 1815.

45b *Left*. The back of the silver watch shown below. The large seconds beating balance nearly covers the top plate.

45a *Right*. This watch, *c.* 1815, is inscribed 'Ls George and Co., Berlin'. It is a quarter repeater with a Pouzait type lever escapement. The small upper dial shows the day and date.

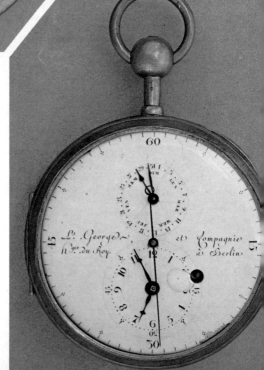

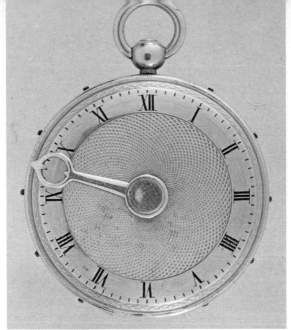

46 'A tact' gold watch by Breguet, *c.* 1820, with a cylinder escapement.

47 An English clock watch by French, Royal Exchange with a duplex escapement.

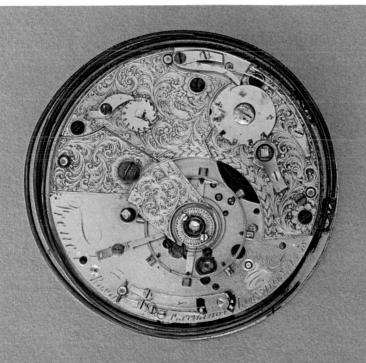

48 A very flat French cylinder watch. It has niello on gold decoration and digital display.

49 An English watch, *c.* 1820, with Massey type lever escapement and 'Liverpool jewelling'.

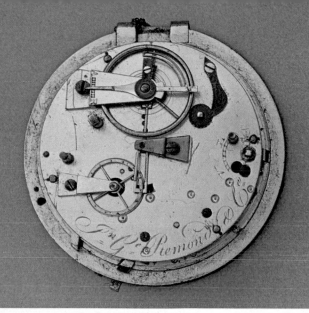

50 A Swiss watch, *c.* 1830, with Tavan pinwheel lever escapement and compensation curb.

51 An English watch, 1828-32, with a ratchet tooth lever escapement. It has a three arm bimetal balance.

52 A magnificent tourbillon with chronometer escapement. It is inscribed 'Hunt and Roskell, London', but is probably Swiss. The top illustration shows the movement.

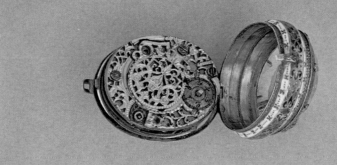

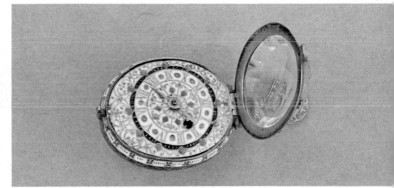

54 A Viennese reproduction watch, *c.* 1840. It is a copy of a 1650 style watch. It has a crystal front and back with enamelled bands. The illustration below shows its single hand.

55 An English club tooth lever watch, *c.* 1846, by E. J. Dent. It is marked 'compound movement' and is an early example of a split seconds watch.

ball watch
h an enam-
d case and
ain.

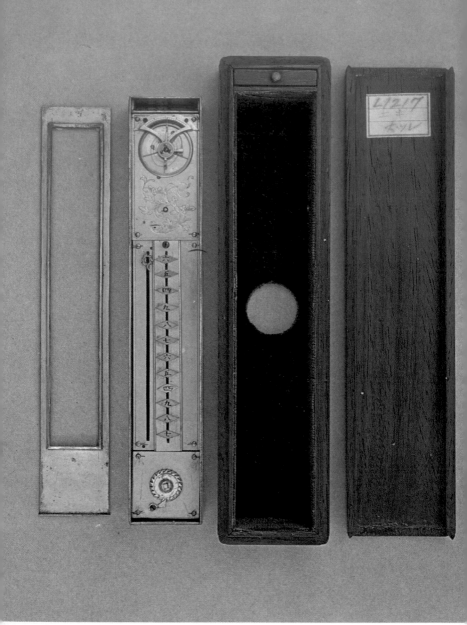

56 This is Japanese and is described as a paperweight or doctor's clock, but it is really a watch. The case is brass, while the outer case is made of shitan wood. It probably dates from the 19th century.

57 This is a Japanese inro watch of the mid-19th century. It has a verge escapement. The watch strikes and the bell can be seen through the aperture at the top. It was carried on the girdle.

58 This Japanese watch, with verge escapement, probably dates from the 19th century. It strikes on the Japanese system. The case is silver and the gilded metal dial has moveable steel characters.

59   The movement of this Swiss cylinder watch, *c.* 1860, is all made of steel. The style of the movement is Bovet. The dial is enamel and the case silver.

60 Often sold in pairs, these Swiss Bovet watches were decorated all over, both case and movement. This silver gilt case is enamelled and decorated with split pearls.

61 The movement of the watch shown opposite. It is enamelled and engraved. The escapement is Chinese duplex and the watch was made *c.* 1860.

62　The Swiss 'Roskopf' watch, *c.* 1870. This was the first watch to be made for the working man. It has a pin lever escapement and is keyless, with a rocking bar system.

63 Made by an American in Switzerland in 1876, the movement of this watch is inscribed 'Albert H. Potter and Co., Geneva'. The escapement is pivoted detent.

64 An early American full plate lever watch, *c.* 1880.

65 A Swiss one minute tourbillon with lever escapement, 1880.

66 An American rarity, 1887. This watch has a worm gear in the train.

67 A German watch, c. 1880, with an English name.

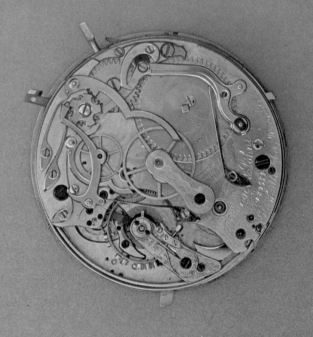

68 This German movement was made by A. Lange and Son who also made the watch shown in Plate 67. It has a club tooth lever escapement and is a half quarter repeater and chronograph.

69　This American watch, *c.* 1888, by Waltham, has a crystal top plate and balance cock. It has a lever escapement. The case is later.

70 An English watch movement, *c.* 1890, by Frodsham. It is 8 day and has two barrels. The escapement is English lever.

71 A French movement, *c.* 1890. The bars make the word 'Paris'.

72 This Roskopf watch is later than that shown in Plate 62. It has acquired the form it was to take for decades.

73 A flat Swiss lever watch with engraved movement.

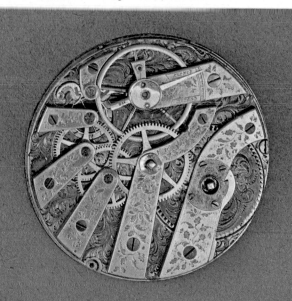

74 A Swiss tourbillon, *c.* 1920, by Fureur. It has a lever escapement and a going barrel. The case is silver.

75 This early 20th century English Karrusel watch is by Yeomans. It has centre seconds and a going barrel.

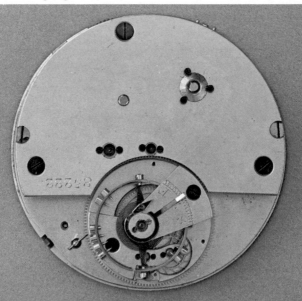

76 A superlative quality American watch, 1918, by Elgin. It is beautifully damascened and has up and down work.

77 An early 20th century tiny Swiss minute repeater. It measures 27mm in diameter.

78 A modern Swiss wrist watch, *c.* 1950, by Mathey-Tissot. It shows the day, date, month and phases of the moon and is a chronograph with a minute recorder.

79 The first successful self-winding wrist watch, *c.* 1930. It was designed by Harwood, an Englishman.

80 A self-winding watch prototype made by the author and P. W. Amis in 1957. It has a shock-protected weight.

81 The first successful electric watch, 1957, made in the U.S.A. by the Hamilton Watch Co.

84a *Below*. A remarkable design feat - a self-winding chronograph with date work. Made by the Hamilton Watch Co. in 1970.

82 *Above*. The first truly electronic watch. The balance and spring has given way to the tuning fork. American made, it was designed by a Swiss in 1963.

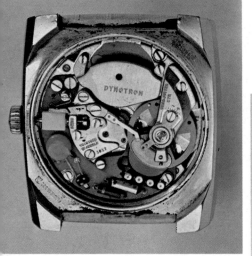

84b *Below*. The chronograph work of the watch above can be lifted off as a complete unit, thus facilitating repair.

83 *Above*. This Swiss watch, made in 1967, was one of the last battery watches with a balance and spring. There were no contacts.

85 and 86 (*over*). These are modern examples of colour used in watches. These matching watches, earrings and rings were made by the prestigious firm of Patek Philippe of Geneva in 1977. Those above are decorated with diamonds, onyx and malachite. Those shown over the page have diamonds and lapis lazuli.

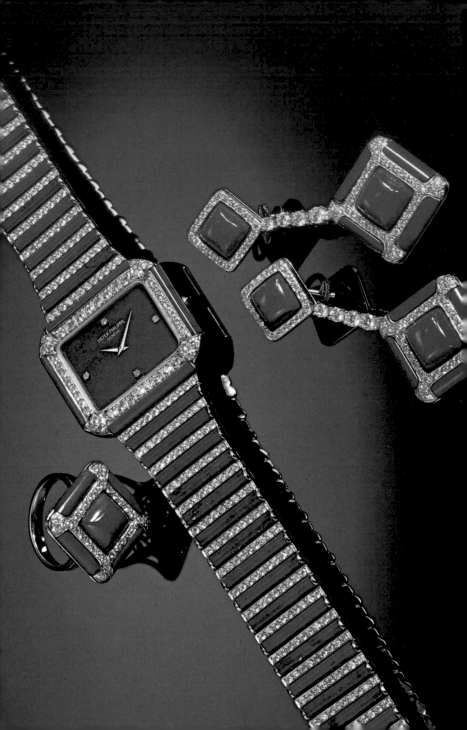

5   *The Decoration of the Case*

These are by: (1) engraving, (2) chiselling, (3) casting, (4) repoussé work, (5) engine turning, (6) presswork, (7) piercing.

Of course, more than one of these techniques could be employed at the same time and frequently were. Surfaces could also be enamelled although this will be dealt with separately. Cases could also be covered in fish skin, tortoise-shell, inlaid as in damascening work and, of course, set with precious and semi-precious stones.

The movement itself can also be treated in many of the above ways although decoration is found less frequently than on the case. The movement could also be damascened, a process which has nothing to do with the inlaying type of damascening but consists of a type of engine turning. This was frequently used on the better later American watches (see Plate 76).

To return to watch cases, however, some were first cast and then worked upon by chiselling to crisp up the relief and also by engraving for fine detail (see Fig. 5). Chiselling is done with a hammer and punch whereas engraving is done with a graver which is pushed by hand. Many shapes of graver are used to produce different effects. Pierced work can also be cast in. Chiselling and engraving are often combined as in champlevé engraving, where the background is chiselled back to a ground level and then engraved with fine grooves, or some other pattern, to give it a dark appearance. The foreground can also be finished by engraving. The pockets so formed can be enamelled or filled with niello. Repoussé, an ancient art, is done by punching up the pattern from behind. (See Plate 27. The dial of the watch in this repoussé case is shown in Fig. 11.)

*Fig. 11 Typical Dutch dial. This is the front of the
watch whose outer case is shown in Plate 27.*

Enamelled Cases

Enamelled cases are a subject on their own, and of course appeal to
many people who have no thought at all as to the mechanism they
house. Enamel is a glass composed of silica, red lead and potash.
When used without colouring it is a transparent flux called 'fondant',
but it is usual for it to be coloured. It is coloured variously by the
addition of the appropriate metal oxide and may be hard or soft
according to its composition. Hard enamel can only be applied to
metals with a high melting point but retains its surface and colour
indefinitely. It can, however, be cracked and chipped easily. Soft
enamel which does not crack or chip is unfortunately easily scratched.

Enamel decoration takes six forms:

1. Plain enamel (fondant).
2. Painting on enamel.
3. Painting in enamel.
4. Basse-taille.
5. Cloisonné.
6. Champlevé.

1. Fondant is hardly ever found on its own.

2. Painting on enamel was evolved in about 1630 by Jean Tontin, a French goldsmith (1578–1644). A plain enamel ground is laid down and the painting done with coloured enamels which are then fired. The whole is then covered with another layer of fondant and again fired. This is also the process used in making enamel dials.

The early painted enamel cases were splendid, but after about 1660 the quality deteriorated and colours were less brilliant. The favourite subject then became women in various stages of undress being ogled by old men or satyrs. The Haut family were the most renowned artists of this style (see Fig. 12). A magnificent example of

Fig. 12 Enamelling in the style of the Haut Family.

English enamelling is shown in Plate 28; the signatures inside this case are shown in Fig. 13.

Fig. 13 Signatures inside the case shown in Plate 28.

The Geneva school continued throughout the 18th century, while the Blois school declined. Latterly Swiss artists have specialised in scenes known as 'gallant'. Not to put too fine a point on it they are pornographic and were often associated with the automata already mentioned.

3. Painting in enamel was developed during the 16th century, after which it is seldom found. It found its simplest expression on watch cases and some of these are the most beautiful enamelled cases to be found. Small blobs of enamel are deposited on the case, usually in a floral pattern. After firing the blobs remain in relief (see Plate 8).

4. Basse-taille is a layer of transparent coloured enamel over a chiselled or engine turned gold ground. Some cases in which the enamelling is over chiselling survive from before 1650, but in the main basse-taille did not become fashionable until after 1780. Most surviving examples are Swiss. (See Fig. 14 which is the back of the watch shown in Plate 34.)

5. Cloisonné is enamelling in which the outline of the pattern is formed of thin wires, usually gold, soldered to the metal ground

and then filled with coloured enamels. The whole is then ground and polished to a uniform surface.

6. Champlevé, the earliest form of enamelling, is most frequently met with and was used extensively on dials as well as cases. Here the pattern is hollowed out and then filled with enamel.

Fig. 14a The back of the watch shown in Plate 34.

Fig. 14b A view of the back of the watch shown in Plate 34. Note the beautiful cuvette.

Fig. 14c Dial of watch shown in Plate 34.

Niello is a specialised form of champlevé most frequently done on silver but also on gold. Here the filling is black, this being an alloy of silver, lead, copper and sulphides (see Plate 48).

Under certain circumstances champlevé may be difficult to distinguish from cloisonné. It is interesting that brass and copper need to be enamelled on both sides or the metal would distort in the firing process. Gold is the only metal that need only be enamelled on the one side.

Rock Crystal Cases

Early examples of rock crystal cases are to be found such as the case reproduced in Plate 54. Usually the case is facetted, but not invariably. The case consists of two parts, the main part, which is hollowed out of a single piece of crystal, and the lid. Usually each part was mounted in a bezel and these hinged together. In the 17th century, the cases of small watches were hollowed out of precious or semi-precious stones such as amethyst. Again, cases were set with slabs of cornelian or agate.

The work of lapidaries was seldom used in the 18th century but during the early 19th century Swiss watches were often decorated with brilliants or split pearls, often associated with enamelling (see Fig. 15).

Having dwelt at some length on the decorative aspects of watches, some technical points responsible for these aspects have been noted. However, the main purpose of a watch is to tell the time and we must now take up the story of the changes that transformed the crude and inaccurate instrument that was the watch of the 17th century into the accurate machine that it had become by the end of the 18th century.

Fig. 15 The front of the watch shown in Plates 60 and 61.

6

Mechanical Considerations

If a spring is used to control the beats of a balance, then in theory at least, such an assembly is isochronous, that is, it will perform a swing of a large arc in the same time as a swing of a small arc. Therefore, it will not matter if the source of power is not uniform. It was 1675 before this was realised, apparently independently, by Christian Huyghens, the Dutch Mathematician, and the London Physicist, Dr. Robert Hooke.

However, although theory suggested that the balance spring could make timekeeping perfect, this was unfortunately only under mathematical and not true-life conditions. In fact, although the balance spring enabled a radical improvement in timekeeping to take place, it revealed the shortcomings of the verge escapement in no uncertain fashion. For the best results, the loss in balance swing due to friction of the pivots and the fanning of the air, should be made good by an impulse of zero duration given exactly at the mid-point of the balance swing. This is when all the energy of the moving system is stored in the balance momentum and not as stress in the spring. For the rest of the swing of the balance it should be undisturbed. The results of any disturbance on the timekeeping abilities of the balance and spring become worse, as they occur nearer to the point of maximum swing. The verge escapement interferes with the balance for all of its swing and the conditions at maximum swing are especially bad, since at this time the balance is forcing the escape wheel to recoil against the full force of the motive power.

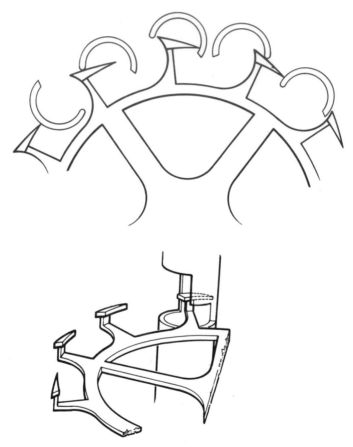

Fig. 16 Cylinder escapement.

The Cylinder Escapement

Around 1726 an effective improvement on the verge, the cylinder escapement was produced by George Graham. It is shown in Fig. 16. The cylinder escapement is a 'dead beat' escapement, that is there is no recoil of the escape wheel during the escapement action. It is fitting that Graham should have designed this escapement, for he also designed the dead beat escapement for clocks which reigned supreme for two centuries as the escapement for precision clocks.

The cylinder escapement is what is known as a frictional rest escapement, that is, the escape wheel teeth are in contact with the balance during supplementary arc. (Supplementary arc is that portion of the arc over and above that minimum required for the action of impulse to take place.) The best escapements had wheels of steel and cylinders of ruby.

The reason why the cylinder escapement was an improvement on the verge escapement is that no longer did the balance have to recoil the train at the end of its swing. It is true that the balance was still in contact with the escapement for the whole of its swing, but under much improved conditions. The impulse was given over a much smaller angle of travel of the balance, therefore getting a little nearer to the ideal of a sharp blow about the zero position. At any other time, the only disturbance was caused by the friction between the escape wheel tooth tip and the polished surfaces of the cylinder.

Not only was the cylinder escapement an improvement on the verge but it also enabled slimmer movements to be made. The escape wheel of the cylinder escapement was placed in the same plane as the plates and not at right angles to them as in the verge. As a result, the cylinder escapement was called the horizontal escapement when Graham introduced it. After 1726, Graham used the cylinder escapement almost exclusively and following him Thomas Mudge used it frequently. Thomas Mudge was Graham's apprentice and was renowned for the beauty of his workmanship and his inventiveness.

About 150 years before the invention of the balance spring it was realised that if a ship carried an accurate timekeeper, then a comparison of local time, (as found by observation), with a standard time at a known place could establish how far a ship was east or west of this place. Since it was already possible to determine the latitude of a ship by observation, this additional determination of longitude would pin-point the position of a ship on the face of the globe. When the pendulum was first invented, there was hope that this might prove to be the answer, but the problem of insulating the pendulum from the influence of the motion of a ship at sea was too great to be overcome at that time.

Finding the position of a ship at sea was of vital importance, since any long voyage incurred risks of shipwreck that were so high, that the safe arrival of any ship was a mere gamble. Fortunes were lost every year and it was a matter of great concern to all the major maritime nations. So much so that in 1714, on the advice of Isaac Newton, the British Government offered a prize of £20,000 to any person who could produce a time-keeping device that would be accurate and remain accurate at sea. This was a vast sum of money worth probably a million pounds sterling today, and it inspired some of the finest clock and watchmakers of the day to compete. It inspired a lot of other aspirants too, so many that a Board of Longitude was set up to consider their many and varied claims.

The maximum prize was only to be awarded if the timekeeper could ascertain longitude to half a degree. Since this was over a period of six weeks, it could mean an accrued error of no more than two minutes in six weeks, or an average of about three seconds a day! When one realises that the average watch of the time had errors of minutes a day it is evident that something radical had to occur if a portable timekeeper was to be devised that could keep time to three seconds a day.

John Harrison, after three attempts with clocks eventually succeeded in winning the prize with what was in fact a large watch. He modified the verge escapement (see Fig. 17), fitted a constant force device in the gear train to eliminate errors from the mainspring, fusee and gears, and solved the problem of temperature compensation. He also used jewels in his movement. This was possible because of the invention in 1704 of a method of piercing and cutting stones, so that they could be used as pivot bearings in clocks and watches. Such jewel bearings eventually appeared in English watches as early as 1750, but the great A. L. Breguet appears to have been the first to use jewel

Fig. 17 John Harrison's modified verge escapement.

bearings on the Continent. The purpose of jewels was, of course, to reduce friction and wear, and without them no fine adjustments would be of a lasting nature.

Regulating the Balance and Spring and Temperature Compensation

If the length of the balance spring is changed, then the timekeeping of the balance and spring assembly also changes. Making the spring longer makes the watch go slow, making it shorter, fast. The easiest way of effectively changing the length of the balance spring was to pass it between pins that were near to its outer end, and make these pins moveable. By using this method the old way of regulating the watch by altering the set-up of the mainspring was discontinued.

Barrow is reputed to be the first to invent the balance spring regulator. He took the worm that was once used to alter the mainspring set-up and instead made it move the pins that embraced the balance spring. For this purpose, the part of the balance spring traversed by the pins must be straight, otherwise the body of the spring would be moved as the pins traversed it.

Tompion invented a type of regulator whose pins moved concentrically with the spring centre, so that they more nearly followed the natural spiral of the spring. The pins were carried by a geared segment driven by a pinion, that carried a square for the winding key. The pinion was covered by a divided dial to assist in making accurate changes. This form of regulator omitted the balance spring that lay beneath the balance.

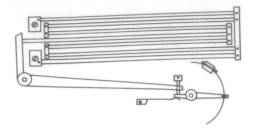

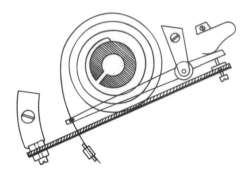

Fig. 18 Top:
Berthoud's type of
temperature
compensation using
a 'grid iron'.
Bottom:
temperature
compensation with
single bimetal strip.

Fig. 19 '*Sugar tongs*' *compensation curb.*

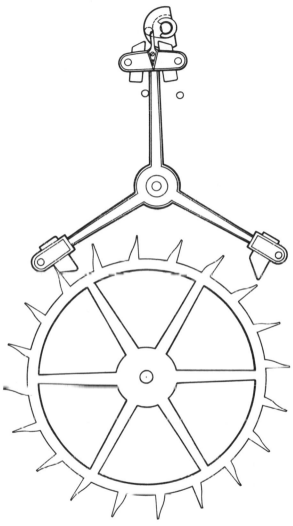

Fig. 20 Mudge's lever escapement laid out in a straight line.

Maintaining Power

During winding early watches (and clocks) in the main stopped since the act of winding robbed the train of its power. The watch was not then accurate enough for this to worry anyone. Once the way was clear to improve the timekeeping of a watch sufficiently it became important for the watch not to stop each time it was wound. John Harrison invented a device called maintaining power that kept the watch going whilst it was wound and was so good that it is still in use today.

Temperature Compensation

If a brass balance has a steel balance spring and no form of temperature compensation it will display timekeeping changes of *six minutes a day* for a change in temperature from 30°F ($-1\cdot1$°C) to 90°F (32·2°C). Harrison solved the problem of these changes by using a compensation curb. If these pins can also be moved by a compensation device whose position changes with changes of temperature, then when this device is correctly adjusted the rate of the watch can be made to stay reasonably constant, although temperature changes occur. An early and a later type of compensation device is shown in Fig. 18.

Harrison's curb pins were moved by bimetallic strips made from brass and steel riveted together. The differing coefficients of expansion of the two metals cause a strip constructed of them to take on more or less of a curve with changes of temperature. The portion of the spring along which the curb pins move has to be shaped to fit in with the way in which these pins move. Another version known as the 'sugar tongs' has limbs that affect the separation (see Fig. 19).

Mudge's Lever Escapement

Thomas Mudge, already mentioned, one of the great men of horology, produced in the middle of the 18th century, an escapement that was to be the single most important escapement ever, the lever escapement. Figure 20 shows the escapement in detail, although it is rearranged to show how closely it resembles the English lever escapement which held favour for so many years and which appeared in what are probably some of the finest watches ever to be made.

7

The Emergence of the Precision Watch

Despite the discoveries of both Harrison and Mudge no real improvements had occurred in the common watch by the third quarter of the 18th century. They were still almost identical to the watches produced by Graham fifty years earlier. However, there were exceptions to this – Breguet in France and Earnshaw and Arnold in England.

Breguet was probably the most brilliant horologist of his and indeed any time. He had extraordinary ability and some of his improvements are still in use today. Breguet established his business in 1775. At that time John Arnold was probably the best-known watchmaker in Europe and Breguet and Arnold enjoyed a firm friendship, cemented during Breguet's visits to London. So great was their mutual regard that each sent the other his son for instruction. Plate 37 shows a watch that commemorates their friendship.

John Arnold was established by 1764 and in this year presented to George III a watch with ruby cylinder and repeating mechanism. Its size was little more than $\frac{1}{2}$ in (13 mm) in diameter. Such a watch would be an item of note even today; at the time it marked Arnold as a craftsman of exceptional ability. Added to this he was a man of great intelligence, who appreciated the fundamentals of horology.

John Arnold was responsible for the helical balance spring that has been used in almost every marine chronometer from that day to this. He patented this spring in 1776 and Plate 29 shows a watch made in 1779 containing such a spring. At the same time he patented a balance, which itself incorporated the temperature compensation device, thus setting the pattern for two centuries. In the previous year

John Harrison had suggested the temperature compensation balance as an alternative to the compensation curb; also Le Roy in France had made one.

Whether or not Arnold takes the full credit for the chronometer or detent escapement is arguable, since Ferdinand Berthoud devised a spring detent escapement and Thomas Earnshaw was a counter claimant. Whether this is so or not seems relatively unimportant now. Certainly, the escapement is the most beautiful in its simplicity and elegance and approaches the ideal. It is shown in Figs. 21a and 21b.

In one grand step the escapement moved from being a relatively crude to a very sophisticated device. For the first time, if one ignores Mudge's lever escapement, the balance was free for the major part of its swing, and impulse and unlocking occurred over a relatively small angle.

The results were immediate, Arnold made a watch which throughout a year of testing kept within an error of three seconds a day. But, Arnold's escapement, however good, was still inferior to Earnshaw's, an escapement similar in principle but having the added attribute

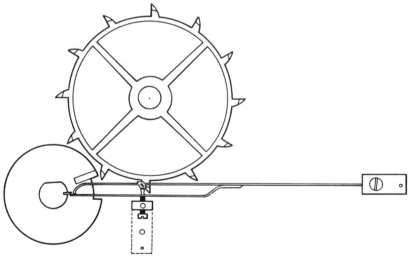

Fig. 21a Arnold's spring detent escapement. (Escape wheel revolves clockwise in the drawing.)

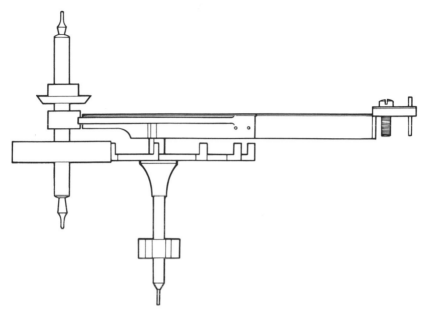

Fig. 21b Arnold's escapement – edge view.

that it did not require oiling at the escape wheel teeth (see Figs. 22a and 22b).

Arnold also improved his helical balance springs by curving the ends into a smaller radius than the main body of the spring. By correctly curving these spring ends, Arnold was able to both reduce the effects of the side thrusts on the balance pivots consequent upon the uneven dilation of the spring, and also to utilise a remaining thrust to minimise the errors due to the escapement.

Thus in Arnold's lifetime an enormous leap forward was taken in producing accurate and reliable watches, simple and elegant in design and construction. This also meant that they could be made in quantity and at a price that ensured their proliferation. This enabled the Royal Navy, upon which England depended for her survival, to navigate accurately anywhere on the face of the globe. The contribution this made to both England's supremacy in horology and her accumulating wealth is difficult to overestimate.

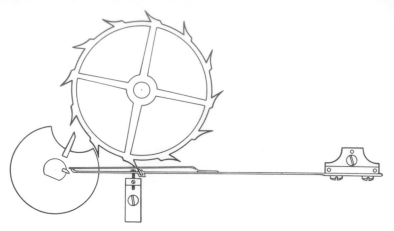

Fig. 22a Earnshaw's type of detent escapement. (Escape wheel revolves anti-clockwise in the drawing.)

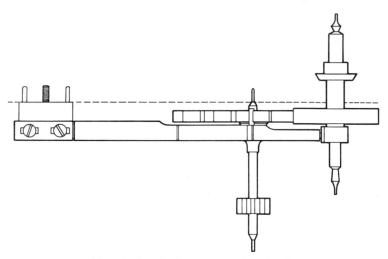

Fig. 22b Earnshaw's escapement from the edge.

The Temperature Compensation Balance

Although the devices that affected temperature compensation of the balance and spring assembly by moving the curb pins were to continue to be used for many years, the compensation balance was the proper answer to the problem. Many and varied were the types that were used.

Many of these need not be discussed here, since they were only used in marine chronometers. The main type of balance used has two, three or four arms made of bimetallic strips. These carried weights or screws, which could be moved nearer to or further away from the free end of the bimetallic strips, so as to afford a degree of adjustment. Early watches often had segment weights, but screws eventually became almost universal. Sometimes, even when all of the holes at the free end of the strip were full of screws, the degree of compensation was not sufficient. As a result, one sometimes sees the brass screws at the end replaced by gold or even platinum screws. When extremely accurate watches are being made, that are to be compensated for middle temperature error, the Guillaume balance is used with a steel spring.

This will be discussed in the section on Guillaume as will the so-called 'self compensating balance spring'.

8

Breguet
As Mechanic

Abraham Louis Breguet, mentioned already, was probably the most remarkable horologist ever to live. His vast range of accomplishments could have taken up this entire book. All of his work had a distinctive character and often contained technical innovations.

His inventions include the following:

1. The tourbillon, where the entire balance and escapement revolves to eliminate the positional errors that occur when the watch is on edge.

2. A Montre 'à tact', which is a watch with a touch piece at the edge of the case which indicates the time. A hand at the back of the case is turned, until it is felt to contact the internal mechanism, when its position can be felt relative to the hour pieces. This meant that the time could be ascertained in the dark or by a blind person.

3. Shock-proof bearings for the balance pivots called 'parachute'.

4. A Ratchet winding key to prevent attempts to wind in the wrong direction.

There were also many improvements relating to clocks, to say nothing of a marriage between watches and clocks, where the clock sets the watch to time and regulates it in accordance with the errors so corrected. In later developments of this, the clock winds the watch each day and sets it to time, although no regulation is done.

When Breguet came on the scene on the Continent little had happened there as regards the watch for fifty years. Jean Antoine Lepine, it is true, had invented an entirely new design of watch. He was born in 1720 at Challex, France, a district near to Geneva. This district supplied ebauche to Geneva during the 18th century. At the age of twenty-four Lepine left for Paris, where he soon made his mark. In his design he discarded the fusee and used the going barrel. The top plate and its supporting pillars were also discarded and replaced by separate bridges and cocks. This meant that thinner calibres could be made and after several improvements the manufacture of the Lepine calibre expanded greatly from 1795 onwards. Lepine used both the cylinder and the virgule escapement. Some early development work had been done by Ferdinand Berthoud and Le Roy to produce a precision timekeeper but this had had no impact upon the common watch.

In England everyone was well catered for. Arnold and Earnshaw were producing precision watches but most French watches were still using the verge and the virgule. Neither can keep good time, although the verge has the merit of being reliable and needing little attention for long periods.

No individual makers had given serious thought to improving the timekeeping qualities of the ordinary watch and the precision watch was still virtually unknown on the Continent. In England, it is true the industry had been given an enormous fillip by the gigantic prize offered by the government to produce an accurate portable time-keeper. Only minor prizes were offered in France by the Académie des Sciences out of an endowment left them by De Meslay.

Someone was needed to inspire the French industry to make the contribution that their position in the horological world merited and this task was left to Breguet. A man of genius, imagination and industry, nothing was ever to be quite the same again after him.

The movements of his early watches give little indication, however, of what was to follow, although he did give up the verge in favour of the cylinder escapement. However, he was to spend thirty years in his search for the perfection in his escapements. This is one reason for the variety of his work. The other, is his evident love of complexity. His Marie Antoinette watch was a triumph of the time (see pages 150 and 151).

However, Breguet's achievements were not only in the field of technical innovation, for he brought his own unmistakeable brand of elegance to the current Continental vogue for flat watches. This desire for less bulky and more elegant watches was virtually ignored by the English. Technical excellence was the criterion that governed the designs of the best English makers, who saw no need to sacrifice their principles to the fashions on the Continent. However, this was really the beginning of that inflexibility that was ultimately to destroy the English watchmaking industry, for in the end, the advances made on all fronts in horology made the flatter mass-produced watch a truly excellent product.

9

The Lever and Duplex Escapements

Although the lever was eventually to become the dominant watch escapement, its merits were generally unrecognised during the time that the chronometer was being developed. This is understandable since it is, in fact, a more difficult escapement to manufacture and its best geometry had not been established.

However, Mudge's patron, Count Von Bruhle, was very keen to have some watches made incorporating Mudge's escapement and managed to persuade Josiah Emery to undertake the task. Emery, a Swiss-born watchmaker, resident in London, was a very able man but was reluctant to start the work, saying it was too difficult.

Nevertheless, he produced his first lever watch in 1782, although his lever escapement was not just a copy of Mudge's. He incorporated improvements relating to the proportions and also employed a compensation balance. This watch proved superior in wear, both to Mudge's original watch and to the chronometer in general. Although not a superior timekeeper to the chronometer, it was not so inclined to stop during wear.

Emery continued to make these watches making nearly forty until his death in 1797. He continued to make improvements in the escapement, but these related more to ease of manufacture than to fundamental improvements.

Others used the lever escapement, such as Grant, Pendleton, Perigal and Dutton, but none incorporated what is called 'draw'. Without draw, the lever tended to rub on the balance roller when the watch was moved roughly or knocked. Alterations in the geometry of the pallets could overcome this problem, by biasing the lever towards the stops that limited its movement. Even though this was appreciated by many makers, they were reluctant to incorporate the change, since the force that kept the lever against the banking pins had to be overcome each time unlocking occurred, thus wasting some of the available power.

It was a man named John Leroux, who first introduced a recoil to the escape wheel as unlocking occurred, the recoil that thus gave draw.

The Duplex Escapement

However, about this time (1782) the duplex escapement was introduced into England and this was taken up as the alternative escapement to the chronometer for the precision watch (see Fig. 23).

This escapement was probably French, but its origins are obscure, its invention having been claimed by Robert Hooke, Pierre Le Roy, J. B. Dutertre, Thomas Tryer and others. Hooke may have possibly had the basic idea, but it is probable that J. B. Dutertre devised it in its early form in about 1725, although Le Roy perfected it in about 1750. The French makers dropped it because it really needed a fusee to give good results. Thomas Tryer took out a patent for it in England in 1782 and for some time it was known as Tryer's escapement. As in the chronometer, the escape wheel delivers impulse directly to the balance. One set of teeth perform this function whilst another set of teeth perform the locking function. These locking teeth are long pointed teeth, which intersect with the balance staff or a small roller mounted upon it and pass through a notch in the same when impulse is to be delivered. Thus the escapement is a frictional rest type, that is, the wheel is always rubbing on the balance. It is theoretically superior to the lever escapement without draw, in that the rubbing is consistent instead of intermittent and variable.

Furthermore, like the chronometer, the duplex escapement does not have to be oiled at the impulse teeth, and because of this it was considered for some time to be a serious rival to the chronometer. However, it had to be made with great care to function reliably for long periods and still needs oil at the locking teeth.

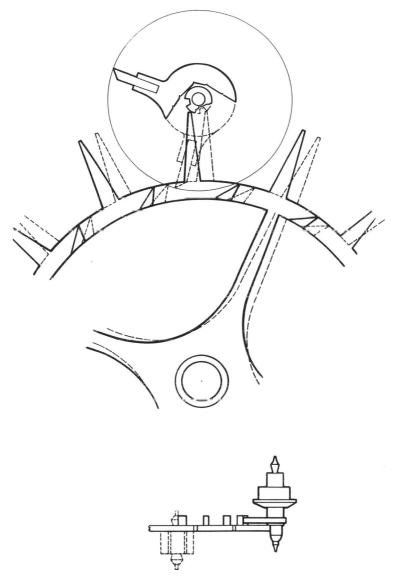

Fig. 23 Duplex escapement. (Wheel revolves clockwise in the drawing.)

As time passed the influence of Breguet's work on the Continent began to affect styles, even in English watches, and watches became thinner. For technical reasons, the duplex was not as suitable for thin watches as the lever and the development of the rack lever, in an improved form by Peter Litherland in 1792, helped at last to get the lever escapement under way (see Fig. 24).

Fig. 24 Rack lever escapement.

No safety action was needed for this escapement, since the connection between the lever and the balance was affected by gearing. The lever end carried a segment of a gear, and a pinion was incorporated into the balance staff. Since these gears were always in mesh, no derangement was possible.

Tools were made by the industry to overcome the difficulties of manufacture, and many Liverpool makers began to turn out rack lever watches on a semi-mass production basis. In 1815 Edward Massey, a Liverpool maker, introduced a detached version of the escapement which, after fairly minor variations, became the English lever escapement for the remainder of the 19th century.

Breguet had also been working on the lever escapement on the Continent, often including incredible refinements. However, he had a curious 'blind spot' with regard to the necessity for draw in the escapement and still made no provision for this necessary modification, fully accepted by English makers by 1820.

In its final form the lever escapement was to approach the chronometer in accuracy and to exceed it in reliability where watches were concerned.

The Club-tooth Lever

The English lever escapement was characterised by the feature that all of the lift was on the pallets. This meant that only the tip of the wheel tooth slid along the pallet impulse face to give impulse to the lever (see Fig. 25).

However, at an early stage experiments had been made with a lever escapement that had divided lift, that is with half the impulse face on the pallets and half on the escape-wheel teeth. This meant that the tooth did not terminate with a tip but with a suitably angled impulse plane. First, the corner of the wheel tooth slid down the pallet impulse face, then, when it reached the end of the pallet face, the corner of the pallet slid along the escape-wheel tooth impulse face. The benefits of this arrangement were twofold. Firstly, the thickness of the tooth tip is utilised to give impulse action and does not represent wasted motion, as in an escapement with all the lift on the pallets. Secondly, the oil tended to remain where it should be for a longer period.

Although first designed in England the club-toothed lever (see Fig. 26) did not find much favour with English makers, although the Dent watch in Plate 55 had this type of escapement. It came into more general use in the 20th century, but this coincided with the death of the English watchmaking industry and it was left to the Swiss and the Americans to make it almost the universal escapement. The best of the late Swiss watches had escapements that were paired to the bone to achieve lightness. The escape wheel was recessed, so that only the boss and the tips of the teeth were at full thickness. The pallets were very delicate too. There was a phase when poising pieces were added

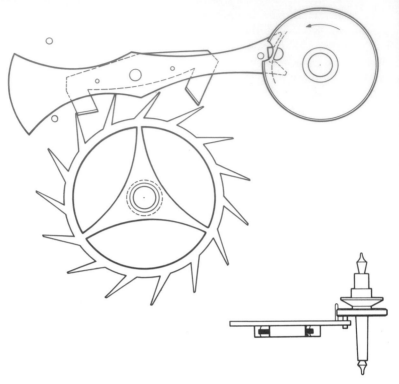

Fig. 25 English or ratchet tooth lever escapement. (Escape wheel revolves clockwise in the drawing.) In the edge view the dark portions are jewels.

to the pallets, in the mistaken belief that it was more important to try to poise the pallets than to make them as light as possible. For the same reason it was a mistake to make the escape wheel or the pallets of gold.

The best American watches had endstones of diamond throughout the escapement. Although a nice refinement, except with heavy balances, this is not really justifiable. Even then, if the ruby endstones are correctly cut with respect to the optical axis they will, in general, stand even the working conditions of a marine chronometer, where a large and heavy balance has small pivots with possibly a small radius of curvature at the pivot end.

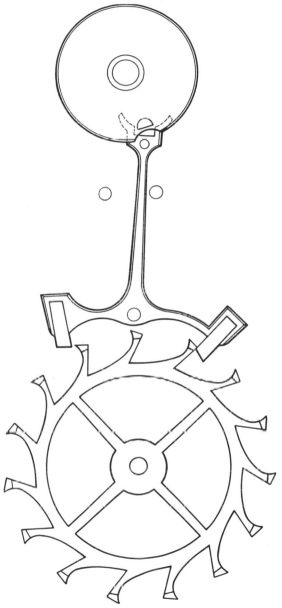

Fig. 26 Club tooth lever escapement. (Escape wheel revolves clockwise.)

10 *Keyless Winding*

One of the first attempts to overcome the need for a separate key to wind a watch was mentioned in 1752 by Pierre Caron, afterwards to become famous as Beaumarchais, the dramatist. His father, also a watchmaker, had made a watch for Madame de Pompadour which fitted into a finger ring. It was 9 mm in diameter and he wrote of it: 'To render this ring more commodious I have contrived instead of a key, a circle round the dial carrying a little projecting hook. By drawing this hook two thirds round the dial the ring is re-wound, and it goes for thirty hours.'

However, in 1820 Thomas Prest, who was John Arnold's foreman, took out Patent 4501 for 'a new and additional movement applied to a watch to enable it to be wound up by the pendant knob, without any detached key or winder'. The pendant button was mounted on a shaft, which also carried a pinion. This pinion, through a short train of gears, turned a wheel mounted on the barrel arbor. Unfortunately, this system was only applicable to going barrel watches and since the fusee was considered virtually essential by English makers the mechanism was not generally taken up. However, the idea was to be the pattern in the future.

Another early form of keyless winding was pump winding. The patent of the year 1793, taken out by Robert Leslie and numbered 1790, reads:

'A method of winding up a watch by the pendant. On the square where the key should go is a ratch; the pendant being alternately moved in and out, turns this ratch by means of two clicks on either end of a fork fastened to the pendant.'

Edward Massey took out another patent in 1824 and Viner also used a rack keyless mechanism with pump action. However, with all the foregoing types a key was still needed to set the hands, so that they were not truly keyless. The first watch that could be wound and set through the pendant appears to have been made by Louis Audemars of Le Brassus in 1838. He was followed by Adolphe Nicole in 1844, who took out a patent in England, No. 10348.

It was the work of Adrien Philippe (1815–94) which led to the watch that is both wound and set by means of the button, without the need to push or pull any other piece to set hands. He first offered his watches to the makers in Paris in 1842, but met with little encouragement. However, it was at the Exhibition of 1844, when his invention won him his first medal, that his work was appreciated by the Comte de Patek. A few months after the Comte offered him a partnership in his firm at Geneva, and thus was born one of the most illustrious watchmaking companies in the world, that of Patek Phillipe. This firm, one of the finest in the world, is still going strong with an unrivalled reputation. Two of their watches are shown in Plates 85 and 86.

11 Guillaume and the Balance Spring

It is strange that modern horology owes an enormous amount to Dr. Charles-Edouard Guillaume, a man who was not a horologist but a physicist. However, he came from a horological family and a horological district. He was born in Fleurier in the upper valley of the Swiss Jura Mountains, a region that also gave birth to Berthoud and Breguet.

After graduating from the Polytechnicum at Zurich and serving as an artillery officer, he joined the Bureau International des Poids et Mesures. Here he studied the mercury thermometer in great depth. In 1891 he began to research the characteristics of nickel from the point of its use as an alternative to the costly metals such as platinum and iridium used at that time as the standard lengths.

About 1895, the observations of the Director, J. R. Benoit, drew attention to certain alloys of iron and nickel, and after years of experiment Guillaume determined the constituents of an alloy which virtually remained constant in length despite the normal changes in temperature. Subsequently called Invar, this alloy was composed of 35·6 per cent nickel with iron. This has been used for pendulum rods ever since. Next, Guillaume turned his attention to balance-spring material and eventually developed Elinvar. This was another nickel–iron alloy, but with a considerable amount of chromium and a little tungsten and carbon, to obtain better mechanical properties, with 1 per cent or 2 per cent manganese added to assist in the working of the material. Used for balance springs it greatly eased the problems of temperature compensation, for it was possible to get results good enough for average usage without the need for a bimetallic balance.

A further development was Ni Span C, which together with Isoval and Nivarox, constitute the three types of balance-spring material in use today. All have fairly similar constituents and all are basically improvements of Elinvar, without departing to a major extent from the original. This is not to say that they are not vastly improved as compared with Elinvar, they are. Elinvar was soft and did not give a good balance action, all other things being equal.

Guillaume died in 1938, after being given many honours, one being the Nobel Prize in 1920, he also gained the gold medal of the British Horological Institute.

12 *The English Watch Reaches its Peak*

At the end of the 19th century the English watch still had an un-rivalled position in the world. Great firms like Dent and Frodsham, Nicole Nielsen, Jurgensen, S. Smiths etc., turned out the finest of work (see Figs. 27a and 27b). Unfortunately, however, the English were satisfied with their way of working and did not feel the need to modernise their methods and employ an ever increasing number of machines, as did the Swiss and Americans. The result of this was that the industry became depressed and firm after firm went out of business. By the time the Second World War arrived, the industry was so depleted that it could not be successfully revived, even for the minimum requirements of the war effort. Lives had to be risked to obtain watches from Switzerland. After the war, an effort was made to revive the industry by setting up a National College of Horology. This produced about a hundred highly skilled technicians, designers and managers, before it was finally closed for lack of support from industry.

For a while S. Smith and Sons contrived to manufacture watches, but except for one or two of the less expensive variety, their efforts eventually ceased. Plate 80 shows the first prototype of a self-winding watch developed in Smith's own laboratories designed by P. W. Amis and made by hand by the author in collaboration with P. W. Amis.

Today and Tomorrow: A Revival of the English Watchmaking Tradition

Some individual craftsmen are beginning to make watches again. One such is a year watch made by Antony Randall, a young English

Fig. 27a Front view of triple complicated tourbillon, made by Nicole Nielsen for S. Smith and Sons. It is a split second chronograph, perpetual calendar, minute repeater.

Fig. 27b Movement of the triple complicated tourbillon. The tourbillon carriage is unusual in that it drives the chronograph work from the edge of the carriage.

watchmaker, trained in a Swiss school. Year watches are exceedingly rare, only one other example being extant. To make a watch that only needs to be wound once a year is a testing problem, solved only with the greatest difficulty.

Another superb craftsman is George Daniels. His latest master-piece is a one-minute tourbillon, somewhat in the style of Breguet, with a constant force device in the train. He has also designed a type of Robin escapement with two escape wheels, giving impulse to the balance in both directions. This has all the advantages of the lever escapement and the chronometer rolled into one. It is in fact the last logical step in the evolution of escapements, the only thing that is surprising is that it had to wait until 1977 to be invented. The escapement has its roots in Breguet's 'escappement naturelle', not surprisingly, since Daniels is considered to be the world expert on Breguet.

Watchmaking in Other Countries

Swiss Watchmaking

The history of watchmaking in Switzerland begins in Geneva. How it started is not so certain, but is probably due in part to the influx of Huguenots, and also no doubt to the sorties of native Swiss into the established centres of watchmaking. By 1556 there are no less than fifty-two notary acts in Geneva relating to watchmakers during the 16th century, the oldest dating from 1556.

Apart from the magnificent enamelling done in Geneva, there is nothing in the early Swiss watches to make them outstanding. Nor did Switzerland have the outstanding figures, like those who blazed a trail in France and England. Technical innovation was never the strong point of the Swiss, and cannot be said to be so even today. The enormous talent of the Swiss has lain instead in, (1) their attention to detail, (2) their ability since the middle of the last century to produce watches cheaply by machinery, (3) their ability to produce these special purpose machines – to an accuracy unequalled elsewhere – and (4) their extreme specialisation.

Another feature that cannot be too strongly praised is their supremacy in complicated work, mainly situated in Valle de Joux. So successful were they in this field that it was common for ebauche to be sent from England to be fitted with complications, especially repeating work, thence to return to England for the rest of the watch to be finished. There was equally a flow of balance springs from England to Switzerland, until the latter years of the 19th century.

This is not to say that Switzerland did not have her own superb makers, she did. One of my favourite watches, shown in Plate 52, was almost certainly made by Houriet (Jacques Frédéric), 1743–1830, who was the founder of precision watchmaking in Neuchâtel. This is the magnificent tourbillon signed Hunt and Roskell. Abram-Louis Perrelet (1729–1826) is another famous name and his contribution to the invention of the self-winding watch is not disputed. Other famous names are Sylvain Mairet (1805-90), Louis Richard (1812–75), Ulysse Nardin (1823–76) and Frédéric-Louis Favre-Bulle (1770–1849).

Whether or not Breguet should be claimed by them is always a sore point with the Swiss. He was born in Switzerland and spent part of his working life there, when France was torn by the Revolution. However, he was trained in Paris and spent all his life there except for a period in England and the time in Switzerland already mentioned. Ferdinand Berthoud was also a Swiss. He was born in 1727 at Plancemont, over Couvert in the Canton of Neuchâtel and died in Paris in 1807. He left Switzerland for Paris when he was eighteen.

Jean-Moyse Pouzait was another famous Swiss maker. He invented the independent centre seconds watch in 1776 and also a lever escapement in 1786 that bears his name. There was also Henry-Louis Jaquet-Droz (1752–91), who was famous for his magnificent automata, among which were many watches with complications such as singing birds.

Antoine Tavan, although born in France in 1749, did most of his work in Geveva, having gone there once his apprenticeship was over. He is best remembered for his escapement models of which there were ten, three of the escapements being his own design. He was also a famous chronometer maker.

The Beginnings of Mechanical Manufacture in Switzerland

The beginning of the 19th century saw the beginnings of mechanical manufacture. About 1820 Humbert et Darier set up a factory for the production, by the use of machines, of rough movements and wheels and pinions. In 1854 Ritor, an ebauche maker of Geneva, conceived the idea of the die set, a two-pillar block in which the punch and die of a press tool were mounted. The use of a shaving tool, through which the relatively rough blank from the press tool was passed, originated it is thought from Ingold, a famous engineer. Ingold specialised in tooling for the watch industry and it is he who is credited with introducing watch-duplicating machinery in the U.S.A.

By 1875 the decorative chamfers on bridge and cock edges were also being put on by means of a press. The Swiss were further stimulated by the work being done in America in the way of mass-production. On attending the Exhibition of Philadelphia in America in 1877, the Swiss went directly back to Switzerland to introduce the new methods which they had seen. There was opposition to the new idea of 'mass-production', as there was in every industry in every country, with the exception of America, where skilled labour was in short supply. It is to the credit of the Swiss watch industry, (and the reason that they remained active while the industry in England dwindled to vanishing point) that they faced up to the facts and accepted the machine with all its ultimate benefits.

Within the space of half a century the industry was transformed. Ultimately, machines became so sophisticated and specialised that, despite the fact that the machine-tool industry was a separate entity with its own profits to make, they were controlled and not allowed to export key watchmaking machines.

Switzerland was particularly suited to the production of watches. The long cold winters meant that for six months of the year farmers could turn to another occupation. With few raw material resources, a labour intensive product was particularly suitable. It is probably also true that the national temperament is tailor-made for such work, for I think few would argue that the Swiss people are patient and painstaking.

In the 1930s all manufacturing countries were under threat. Many watch companies, as in every other sphere, contributed to their own downfall by embarking on a murderous price war. But for the action of some far-sighted men in Switzerland the whole watch industry could have foundered. These men co-operated and drew up a statute of sound trading. The Swiss Government approved and an autocratic organisation was set up. As they had over the matter of introducing machinery, the industry saw sense and were persuaded to sell only at economic prices. The prices of all the components that were made by specialists were negotiated a year ahead. Prices were related to the cost of production and there was no price cutting. It meant rigid control, but it saved the Swiss industry from ruin. With a monopoly of world markets this system was satisfactory, but when serious competition came from Japan and Russia, then cost became a factor outside Swiss control. In 1965, when the old statute ran out, competition was already so fierce that it was not renewed.

Things have now changed to the extent that Swiss firms will actually set up complete factories abroad, with ready designed and tooled calibres, so that the whole difficult process of producing watches can be started with the minimum of labour pains. Now, day after day, automatic lathes produce parts correct to a thousandth part of a millimetre. Parts not only go together without fitting, but are actually put together by machines. The skills have not disappeared, however, they have been shifted from one branch of the industry to another. The toolmaker of today regularly performs miracles. The making of checking and measuring equipment is an enormous industry in its own right. Press tools have become so sophisticated that components come from them better finished than they could be by hand. Diamond tools facet parts to a mirror finish, doing in a second what once took minutes. Hard plating produces durable finishes that last a lifetime.

It is probably now true to say that, apart from the attentions of a skilled adjuster, there is little to choose between the finest machine-made watch and one finished completely by hand fitting. In fact, if one allows for component selection it is possible that the machine-made watch could be better. Such is progress!

American Watches

Naturally enough, the first American watches were made by immigrant craftsmen from England, later joined by watchmakers from Switzerland and Holland. Early watchmakers, however, had a difficult time without the necessary support from specialists in their field. However, the first men in the field were not to be discouraged and a slow growth resulted in the setting up of the first watchmaking factory by Luther Goddard in 1809. Before he retired in 1817 no less than 500 watches had been turned out. This is a considerable number and probably means that movements in the 'rough' were obtained from England.

The first attempt to make a completely American watch was made by James and Henry Pitkin of Hartford, Connecticut, in 1838. Although this business foundered in 1841, this was not primarily due to technical difficulties, thus showing that an all-American watch could be a successful undertaking.

Only ten years were to pass before the setting up of the American Horologe Company. This was the result of the coming together of two brilliant men, Aaron Dennison and Edward Howard. Both men had ideas of producing watches by automatic machines which produced interchangeable components.

The first watches were produced by them in 1853 under the name of the Warren Manufacturing Company. The watches were full plate of the English style and sold for forty dollars. A year later the firm moved to Waltham, where under the name of The Boston Watch Company, some ninety men produced thirty watches a week.

However, the dream of producing all the parts in the factory caused endless difficulties and by 1856 Dennison and Howard split up. Dennison stayed as work's manager when a watch-case manufacturing firm bought the foundering company. In 1870 Dennison left the firm of Tracer Barker and Co., which eventually became the Waltham Watch Co. He came to England, where he founded the famous case-making company that still bears his name.

Howard, however, was not disposed to give up and by 1861 he had renamed his company the Howard Clock and Watch Co. In 1881 Howard retired, living on until 1904. He was the man who established the American precision watch.

The first watches produced by the Howard Watch Company were full plate and had uncompensated balances with flat springs. This was followed by a much superior design, as advanced as any of the time, which was three-quarter plate and had a patent barrel, designed to prevent damage to the gear train should the mainspring break. The barrel was stationary and the arbor was both rotated during winding and gave power to the train via the winding ratchet. To ensure that the watch did not stop during winding, maintaining power had to be employed. This was followed by a keyless watch, also employing a safety barrel and was jewelled in the English style.

Superb watches were to be made in America by Waltham, Hamilton and Elgin, comparing favourably with the best made anywhere and at any time. Waltham's finest watch was the 'Riverside Maximus'. It was fully jewelled, with diamond end stones fitted to the escapement and had beautifully damascened nickel silver plates. The train wheels were a low carat gold.

Elgin was to produce a deck watch fitted in a small chronometer-type case, complete with gimbals that were really superb (see Plate 76). It was free sprung with a guillaume balance and performed at least as well as many a marine chronometer, although probably not capable of keeping its rate for a comparable length of time.

Hamilton was to finally produce what is probably to be the finest portable mechanical timekeeper ever to be made. This was a marine chronometer, produced entirely by mass-production methods, which was developed and produced in an exceptionally short space of time. W. O. Bennett was the man who masterminded this operation, the same man who later backed the Bulova tuning-fork watch, 'The Accutron'.

Although the American watch cannot claim to have been better than either the English or the Swiss watch at any time, America certainly showed the way with respect to production techniques.

As already mentioned, at the Philadelphia Exhibition in 1876, the Swiss were greatly impressed and their methods of production were reorganised as a result. At the turn of the 19th century, production lines existed in America where raw material was fed in at one end and a finished plate came out of the other. Safety precautions were incorporated into the line, whereby if a tap or drill broke, an indication appeared and the line stopped.

Although American watches were made by the most modern of methods, the output of the Swiss was never equalled. The degree of specialisation achieved by the Swiss was never matched elsewhere.

At the heyday of output, for instance, just four factories produced almost all the escape wheels for the Swiss industry. The day came eventually, when the famous American names were put to watches imported from Switzerland and for a while it looked as if watch production in America would cease. The only reason that this did not finally occur was because of the electronic watch which favoured a return to American manufacture.

To add to the troubles of the American watch the Japanese watch industry, helped in its recovery after the war like the rest of the Japanese industry, began to present a strong threat to the watch producers of all other nations.

Watchmaking in Germany

The earliest known clockmakers' guild was founded in Annaberg in Saxony in 1543 but although the German watch industry was among the first, watches virtually ceased to be made during the Thirty Years War (1618–48) and the once vigorous industry lost out to the French.

What there was of the industry in the early 1800s was concentrated around Friedburg by Ausburg, Pforzheim, Silberberg in Schlesien, the Black Forest, Ruhla in the Turinger Wald and Glashütte, a mountain village thirty miles from Dresden. Until 1845 this village, with about a thousand inhabitants, existed mainly by farming and was very poor. However, a great man was to come forward who was to transform the lives of those who lived in Glashütte – Ferdinand Adolph Lange. Ferdinand Adolph Lange was a remarkable man. Born in Dresden on 18 February 1815 he went to Paris in 1840 where he worked for five years for the chronometer-maker Winnerl. Lange studied the watch industry in France and Switzerland and on his return to Sachen he began negotiations with the government to start a watch industry in the poverty stricken area of Glashütte. He was successful and in 1845 with a 30,000 Reichsmark loan, he started the production of watches with about twenty to thirty workers. These men were unused to such work and progress was slow. It took two years before the first watches were produced. Lange's first watches were pin pallet, first with steel pins, later jewelled.

These types were made during the period 1845–51. He also adopted the metric system of measurement. It was another thirty years before France and Switzerland followed suit.

However, during this period the characteristic Lange escapement was developed with its club-toothed, gold-coloured escape wheel. The enclosed pallets are also gold coloured and jewelled, with the impulse face of the entry pallet concave and the exit convex. Banking was provided by a pin on the underside of the pallet frame, near the entry pallet, working in a hole in the front plate. The ruby impulse pin was set directly into a strengthened part of the balance arm and the polished steel safety roller mounted on the staff. The two arm bimetallic balance had compensation screws and quarter screws. The latter were given the necessary friction in their tapped holes by a method unique to Glashütte watches. The rims were finely slit through the quarter screw holes, the slit reaching the hole on either side. This gave a slight spring, if the tapped hole was correctly matched to the thread on the quarter screws. These balances were made by Griesbach in Glashütte. The balance springs were steel. The fastening of the barrel ratchet wheel to the arbor, by means of an offset screw, is also characteristic.

The Lange factory flourished. Lange took training very seriously and designed and made the tools that made the watches. A case factory was also established in Glashütte to make gold and silver cases. Chronographs were produced from 1863 onwards and in 1866 he was granted an American patent for a repeating watch. Lange died in 1875 after thirty years of hard and successful work. His two sons, Richard and Emile, carried on his work. In 1885 Richard developed the first of the Company's self-winding watches, but it was not until 1892 that the first marine chronometer was made in the Lange factory. One of these marines, No. 795, took second place in the 1934 Hamburg trials.

After 1870 the higher grade Lange watches were made with removable barrels. The top plate was slotted and a bush used to locate the top end of the arbor. Removing two screws allowed the removal of the bush. In 1866 Lange patented a setting mechanism which allowed stem operation without disturbing the hands. Keyless wound watches are, however, later in date.

Lange watches are difficult to date, but one point to remember is that from the beginning of 1888 the German government required that gold cases be marked 14K or 18K on both the case and the bow. The Lange factory produced some exceptional watches. A number of tourbillons were made which are today snapped up at high prices in the unlikely event that one comes up for sale.

Fig. 28 English keyless watch with Glashütte escapement. (Recased by the owner.)

Watches were also produced with constant force escapements, others had three or four complications.

It is interesting that the Glashütte work was held in such high regard that some English makers even had their escapements fitted complete. See Fig. 28 and Plate 67.

The Russian, Japanese and Chinese Industries

The challenge which made the Swiss accept free enterprise again came from two countries, Russia and Japan.

Russian Watchmaking

When Russia overran Germany in 1945 she acquired both the men and the machines to boost her industry in a way that few thought possible. She decided from the start not to make pin pallet watches and by as long ago as 1968 she was producing 35 million watches a year. These were produced in five major factories, the biggest employed 6,000 people! Each of these factories was virtually self-sufficient and competed rather than co-operated with one another, and concentrated on a few models to satisfy the home market whilst supplying a surplus destined for the markets of the world. A large development and research organisation was built up. Eventually Russia even produced a marine chronometer, to the surprise of many.

Up until the 1930s Russia had no watchmaking industry. Protracted negotiations with the Swiss in 1935 to obtain their help to set up a factory led to nothing. The Russians had, however, already turned to America. The Amtorg Trading Corp. purchased practically all of the equipment in the Duber-Hampden Watch Works, Canton, Ohio in 1930. Mr. A. Vladimirsky of Moscow, Director of the Russian Watch and Clock Industry, superintended the dismantling of the plant and its removal to, and setting up in, the Russian capital. No less than twenty-four departmental heads of the Canton Plant accepted contracts from the Russian government and worked in Moscow for about a year, after which they were replaced by the men they had trained. Apparently sixteen ligne chromium-plated pocket watches with fifteen jewels were sold in the shops for the equivalent of twelve dollars.

The Rise of the Japanese Industry

Japan had no record of serious watchmaking until the close of the 19th century, although the Paperweight Clock (Plate 56) is really a watch. In the 1960s, however, watches of such quality began to be turned out that the Swiss markets began to be affected. Probably the most famous firm is that of Seiko, where every single part is made by the company. This firm was also the first to produce a quartz wrist watch in production quantities.

Chinese Watches

As if to underline her place as a major power in the world, Chi-
also created a watch industry. Two wrist watches, both for r
have been created and represent a very creditable effort for a you
industry. What her intentions are in the future is not known.

4 Special Watches

Cheap Watches

Until about 1750 owning a watch was a sign of wealth. Obviously a great market remained untapped, as long as this situation continued. Some cheap watches were being made in Geneva in the mid-18th century, but it was not until 1810 that serious attempts were made by Frederic Japy in France to produce watches by factory methods. These still required a fair amount of hand finishing, however. It is to Georges Frederick Roskopf (1813–89), that the credit is due for the first 'poor mans watch'. Roskopf was German born and was quite determined to succeed in his dream of a watch that could be made to suit a slender pocket. The first Roskopf watch, the name stuck to the type of watch until quite recently, was assembled in Chaux de Fonds in 1868. It was keyless wound but had no provision for keyless setting of the hands. These watches are now a collector's item. The example shown in Plate 62 is typical of the true Roskopf. It has distinctive hands and an enamel dial. The chief characteristics of the movement is that there is no centre wheel and that the escapement is pin pallet.

It is not surprising that the Americans were soon in the thick of the battle to produce and sell cheap watches. Amongst these were the 'Waterbury', probably the most ingenious cheap watch ever produced, the 'Auburndale Rotary', the 'Ingersoll' and the New York Standard Watch Co.

'The Waterbury' was designed by D. A. Buck in 1879 and the first sold for three dollars and fifty cents (about seventeen shillings and sixpence at the time). The early watches were 'long wind' with mainsprings twelve feet long and the movement revolved within the case, thus giving a 'tourbillon' effect. There were only fifty-seven parts in the watch, probably a record that has never been beaten. The watch broke all the rules and was obviously the work of a genius. The escapement employed was the duplex, an escapement considered then (and now) as too delicate to perform properly for long, the slightest wear resulting in difficulties. A 'Waterbury' wound today will usually start and perform without difficulty. Epicyclic gearing was employed and the layout is in fact difficult for most people to understand. The 'Waterbury' cost five shillings in 1900, the same as the 'Ingersoll' watch.

The 'Auburndale Rotary', produced in 1877, was also designed to have a tourbillon action. This was sold at ten dollars to the trade. Once again the whole movement rotated in the case. Unfortunately, a basic design fault caused the majority of these to be withdrawn by the firm and this no doubt contributed to the demise of the factory in 1883.

The New York Standard Watch Co. also tried to produce a cheap watch. This was characterised by a movement with a worm-driven escape wheel and with a curious lever escapement, with the escape wheel mounted like a verge escape wheel. This design was abandoned within the year (see Plate 66).

Robert Ingersoll sold his first dollar watch by mail order in 1892. By the time the American company failed in 1922 over 70 million had been sold, still at the same price that they were in 1892. The early Ingersolls had a dummy winding button but improvements were soon made.

The fascination of the tourbillon led the Swiss to produce the Mobilus. The design was patented in 1905 by J. Burtin. The revolving escapement was usually displayed at the dial centre or through the glazed centre of the back. The balance was not at the centre of revolution of the carriage and was small for the size of the watch. These watches now sell for prices that would astound their original makers! (See Plate 74.)

France and Germany also produced cheap watches, as would be expected. Japy Frères exhibited one at the Paris Exhibition in 1889, but it would appear that none have survived. Many watches were made by Junghans, but are mostly just marked foreign. Thiels produced an imitation 'Waterbury' in the 1890s but it needed winding every twelve hours, a return to the characteristic of the earliest of watches.

England also made an attempt to combat the imports of cheap watches by producing the 'John Bull', made by the Lancashire Watch Co. in 1909. They retailed at five shillings each, the trade price being three shillings and ninepence. The movement was marked 'British made by British Labour'. The undertaking was not a success, however, and the factory as a whole failed in 1911 after 5,000 had been sold.

The Automatic Watch

The automatic watch has a longer history than one might think. It is possible that there were earlier self-winding watches than those produced by Abraham Louis Perrelet of Le Locle in 1770, but there is no doubt as to his contribution. Breguet and Recordon were the first to purchase his watches and it is to these three men that the development of the self-winding pocket watch must be attributed. The winding device consisted of a weight, pivoted in the centre of the movement. The weight rotated through a full circle, with winding in both directions through the fusee. Breguet produced a number of self-winding watches after 1777, calling them 'Montres Perpetuelles'.

In 1780, Louis Recordon, Breguet's business associate in England, took out patent No. 1249 in London. Subsequently, the winding device became known as the pedometer wind. A number of makers were to produce such watches in the years that followed but nothing much happened until the idea was taken up again for a short time when A. Von Loehr, a Viennese engineer, took out his patent in 1878.

The self-winding wrist watch was what the world was really waiting for, once the wrist watch came into being in about 1910. It was John Harwood, an Englishman, who began experimenting in 1917 and eventually arrived at a self-winding wrist watch, the design of which suited mass-production techniques. His Swiss patent covering this was applied for in October 1923. The idea was to house a 10½ ligne movement in a 13 ligne case. Hand setting was accomplished by turning the bezel, thus doing away with the necessity for a stem passing through the space around the movement needed for the housing of the rotating weight. The weight was pivoted in the centre of the movement and moved between stops. One could not wind the watch without shaking it since there was no manual wind provided (see Plate 79).

The 'Wig Wag' and the 'Rolls' watches

The patent for the 'Wig Wag' was taken out in 1931 and it was manufactured by Louis Muller and Cie SA Bienne. The movement was held by two arms which were pivoted in a framework fitted in the case. The movement had a possible lateral displacement of about 2 mm and as it moved, self-winding took place. The 'Wig Wag' watch was relatively short lived but another watch, the 'Rolls', built somewhat on the same lines was produced by Messrs. Leon Hatot SA, Paris. Here again, the movement slid freely in a carrier and was located by ball bearings. Self-winding was affected through levers and a ratchet. Hand setting was by a normal button, but could only be done once the outer case had been opened. The movement had a total displacement of 3 mm.

The Blancpain SA factory at Villeret in the Bernese Jura produced 6,000 of the 'Rolls' watches up until 1932 (besides 14,000 Harwoods).

The Rolex Perpetual Movement was the first really practical and long-lived automatic. Made in 1930 it had a semi-circular weight, pivoted at the centre of the movement. It moved through the full 360° but wound in one direction only. The reduction between the weight and the barrel was achieved by gearing and this eventually proved to be the favoured method.

The Bidynator was made in 1942 by Felsa of Grenchen, Switzerland. This watch represented the next phase of development, when the weight rotated the full 360° and also wound in both directions. This was achieved by the use of a rocking pinion, which is urged by the pinion mounted on the weight, into mesh with either of the two first gears in the self-winding train.

The Ultra movement represented the first of the last fundamental group of automatic watches. Instead of a gear there was a cam mounted at the weight centre. A long double spring, shaped like a W, reached across the block that carried the self-winding work. It was mounted on a steel plate and could slide backwards and forwards by a limited amount. The back and forward movement was caused by the cam moving two small jewelled rollers that were mounted on the same steel plate. The two extremities of the W spring were shaped into clicks and these alternately pushed and pulled a fine-toothed ratchet wheel. This had a pinion integral with it that drove the barrel ratchet wheel direct. Here the major reduction between the weight and the barrel was achieved through the geometry of the moving or sliding parts, as opposed to through the gearing.

Refining the Automatic Watch

Thereafter changes to self-winding work concentrated upon the following refinements.

1. Changing the geometry of the weight to achieve maximum winding torque with minimum mass.

2. The modifications of the slipping attachment in the barrel to give uniformity of torque output at the barrel. (Early attempts to put clutches on the barrel ratchet wheel were soon to become obsolete.)

3. Shock protection for the weight by design of the weight support, so as to make it flexible, by designing the weight so that it was flexible, or by mounting the weight on a ball race that could take the forces imposed without damage.

4. Easy disassembly from the main part of the movement.

5. Indication of the state of wind by inclusion of an up, or an up and down mechanism.

It is interesting that despite all the progress made and the near mechanical perfection of the automatic watch, the last problem comes back to lubrication. The more efficient the self-winding is, and it needs to be efficient for sedentary people, then the more the mainspring will slip when the watch is worn during active periods. This slipping of the mainspring can lead to serious wear in the barrel. There must be restraint or the mainspring will not be sufficiently wound and this restraint means friction and probable wear. As long as the lubricant is present, and is not contaminated with wear particles, all is well. Once it becomes contaminated a rapidly deteriorating set of conditions arise.

The last experiments along these lines include permanently sealed barrels. The spring is frequently dry lubricated and a heavy grease introduced between the spring and the barrel wall. In the event of failure the barrel is exchanged as a complete assembly.

The self-winding watch appeared to be in an extremely strong position at one time, so much so that it could have been assumed that eventually nearly all watches would have become automatic. However, the advent of the quartz watch has changed all this and appears likely to completely supersede this extremely interesting family of mechanical watches.

Complicated Watches

Watches not only tell the time of day. One of the first complications was not unnaturally striking work and watches that strike, both in passing (and later at will), have been made from the earliest days. The same comments apply to calendar work, where the phases of the moon were often displayed at the same time. In the past, of course, the question of whether or not any particular night would be moonlit was much more important than it is today. Watches also played tunes, gave sidereal time, the equation of time, the time in selected cities of the world, the night sky, the temperature, and had alarm work fitted. Others might have singing birds. Some special watches combined nearly all of these features, a fantastic tour de force by the most eminent of makers.

Thomas Mudge, already mentioned in connection with the lever watch, was a man who was very much at home with complicated work. Recently the British Museum obtained a perpetual calendar watch made by Mudge in 1764. It is probably safe to assume that this was the first successful perpetual calendar watch. A perpetual calendar watch corrects for the differing lengths of the months, including February 29 every four years, and was a feat only attempted in a few clocks prior to Mudge's triumph. Mudge was also the first to make successful minute repeaters. One was supplied to King Ferdinand V of Spain and was made to fit into the head of a walking cane. This watch was also a clock-watch. Another was sold at Christies in 1960 and was housed in a beautiful triple case, pierced and engraved to allow the sound of the striking to be clearly heard.

Mudge was to suffer a tragedy similar to that suffered by Beethoven, for at a relatively early age his vision began to fail. However, he was such a clever and determined craftsman that one can detect virtually no difference in his work as his sight progressively worsened.

Breguet was also a master of complicated work, as can be seen in the watch he produced that was intended for Marie Antoinette. This was ordered in 1783 by an Officer of the Queen's Guard and was to contain every complication known at that time. No limit on the time taken to manufacture it or on its cost was imposed and all parts normally of brass were to be of gold. It was not finished until 1820 and by that time had cost 16,864 francs. Some idea of what this means is given by the fact that the gifted pupil, Michael Weber, made most of the mechanism for which he was paid ten francs an hour for 725 hours work. Thus it could represent 1,686 hours work, which would these days represent about eight years work. Such a highly skilled craftsman would expect today to earn about £8,000–£10,000 a year, so that the total cost today would be £64,000–£80,000. When one considers that currently the Audemars Piguet triple complicated watch costs £22,500 this sum is not surprising. Breguet's watch contained the following complications:

   Perpetuelle winding
   Perpetual Calendar
   Equation of time
   Thermometer
   Centre seconds marking whole seconds

Indicator for state of wind
Minute repeater

The plates, bridges and all the train wheels were of polished pink gold. The dial, back and front covers were of rock crystal.

Breguet did not sell the watch. It remained in the family until, in 1887, it was sold by the widow of Louis Clement Breguet to Sir Spencer Bruton for £600. It is now on view to the public in the L.A. Mayer Memorial Foundation, Jerusalem, Israel.

A Patek Phillipe watch made in 1932 had a dial back and front and gave the following indications:

Mean time
Chronograph with split seconds
Up and down work for both barrels (going and striking)
Perpetual calendar
Phases of moon
Sidereal time
Equation of time
Sunrise and sunset
Night sky

In addition it was grand sonnerie, minute repeating, carillon on four gongs. The watch contained 110 wheels, 50 bars, 430 screws, 90 springs, 120 pieces of mechanism, 70 jewels, 19 hands and discs. It took five years to make, excluding the time taken to design it.

How such a watch was designed at all is something of a mystery. The parts for each complication cannot occupy their own separate space in the watch, but must be interconnected and although, in so far as possible, occupy separate layers, must encroach and interleave in very many instances. It is highly probably that many of the detail difficulties can only be worked out as the watch is being made.

A Dent watch, which may well be one of the most complicated English watches made, recently came up for sale in Switzerland. It is No. 32573 made in 1904. It has a gold case, a gold and silver dial one side and an enamel dial the other. It has the following complications:

Clock watch with grand and petit sonnerie
Minute repeater
Perpetual calendar on one dial

On the other dial

The signs of the Zodiac
Equation of time
The morning and evening stars
Moon dial
Sunrise and sunset
Moonrise and moonset

An ebauche in the British Museum suggests that these English watches went in the rough to have the complicated work done in the Vallé de Joux, in Switzerland, and on being returned were finished in the English workshops.

Even today a triple complicated watch is being made by a firm of Audemars Piguet. This is a minute repeater, has chronograph work and is a perpetual calendar. They are made at the rate of one or two a year and at the moment sell for £22,500. There is a waiting list of five years production.

Complicated Wrist Watches

In the late 1920s a small Swiss minute repeater, possibly the most complicated watch of its size ever made (the size is 11 ligne), was custom-built for an American, one James Schulz of New York in the late 1920s. It was made in a small Swiss home workshop in the French part of Switzerland just outside Geneva. Three Swiss watchmakers worked on it for three years. The watch is perpetual calendar, has phases of the moon, is a minute repeater and has chronograph work with a thirty minute register. The tonneau-shaped case is of platinum. When last recorded this watch belonged to a Robert B. McConnell who acquired it in 1964 and who prizes it above all others in his collection. He believes it to be the world's most complicated watch for its size and I am inclined to agree with him. Plate 78 shows a modern chronograph with phases of the moon and date work.

An outstanding achievement in the way of a modern complicated wrist watch is a self-winding date watch with chronograph work. This watch has been designed so cleverly that it is possible to lift off the chronograph work complete, this being carried by a sub-plate that can be removed by loosening just three screws. (See Plates 84a and 84b.)

Libertine Watches

For the first time a book is being produced on these watches, for sale on the open market. This underlines the change in attitudes today. In 1954 there was a sale of a number of these libertine watches. Nowadays catalogues show the scenes in question, but in 1954 the harmless aspects of the watch were shown and guarded statements made such as 'concealed automata', 'animated scenes', or best of all 'with interesting automata scenes'. And this was a mere twenty-four years ago! Only one of these watches, although there were about thirteen, bore an English maker's name – Johnson of London.

Such watches were mainly made by the Swiss and were of two types. In one, erotic scenes are disclosed when a cover is raised. The second type had automata, driven by repeating work. Amazingly enough there is now a modern development of the libertine watch. The crudest of statements appears on the dial of a wrist watch at intervals of fifteen seconds. The exhortation is inscribed on a nearly nude woman. One is assured that the watch is dustproof to ensure accuracy!

Small and Flat Watches

Very small watches are not a new thing. In the Chaux de Fonds Museum in Switzerland is a pre-balance spring, anonymous verge watch with gut fusee of 12 mm in diameter! Yet more astonishing is an even smaller watch, once in the celebrated collection of Sammlung Marfels. Again anonymous, its date is about 1650 and it is an astonishing 9 mm in diameter. Both dial and case were enamelled on gold. The whereabouts of this watch is not now known.

Much later, John Arnold produced a ring watch for George III, which was additionally a quarter repeater. It had a cylinder escapement and the cylinder was made of ruby. George III paid Arnold £500 for his trouble – which must have been considerable. Arnold was subsequently asked by Tzar Alexander to make another of these. Patriotically he refused, saying that he wished King George to be the only man to own such a watch.

Very flat watches are still being made by the firm of Golay in Switzerland. Some are worn as wrist watches, but others are set into gold coins. When finished, no sign is visible of the presence of the watch within the coin, except to those with a very keen eye, who know what they are looking for and can just distinguish the outline of the catch in the milled edge of the coin. When this is pressed one face of the coin flips up, as in a hunter watch, revealing the watch, complete within an inner case.

A revolutionary new movement has been produced by a Swiss firm, Bouchet-Lassale. The basic movement is only 1·20 mm thick and the self-winding version *with the rotor at the centre* is only 2·00 mm thick! The revolutionary feature is that all the moving parts are supported on one side only with the exception of the escapement. The barrel is edge supported by rollers and the other wheels by ball bearings. The claimed advantages of this design are as follows:

1. No alignment problems between bridge and plate
2. Fewer frictional losses
3. Simpler lubrication
4. Simpler assembly

The diameter is 20·40 mm (9 ligne). The movement has a fast beat rate – 28,000 per hour with a fifty-hour reserve.

Coin Watches with Skeleton Movements

Not only are ordinary movements, if one can call them so, fitted into coin watches, but so are skeletonised movements. It is as if to say, now that we have done the improbable let's do the impossible.

The plates, bridges etc. are frequently made of gold. This is also true of an automatic watch made by Patek Phillipe. The self-winding weight is 22 ct. gold, so as to give the maximum winding power with minimum size. Such watches are nothing less than miniature works of art.

The Electric Watch

The electric watch first appeared on the scene in a satisfactory form in 1957, made by Hamilton of America (see Plate 81). It is fitting that the firm who managed to produce 10,000 chronometers in three years without previous experience (and yet of the highest quality ever), should be the company to first succeed with the electric watch. Of course, the pundits prophesied that an electric watch was just a nine days wonder, but thinking people realised that it was but the start of the long road to the death of the mechanical watch as an everyday item. Admittedly, the Hamilton electric watch had a delicate contact system and no watchmaker could really undertake its repair without guidance, but nevertheless it was a tour de force. However far seeing anyone was at that stage it would have needed second sight to realise that within twenty years the quartz wrist watch would be commonplace, sold even in the supermarket. Such is the present speed of progress.

When the electric watch first arrived, it posed no real threat to the mechanical watch. Its timekeeping could be shown to be marginally better, but against this it was more difficult to get serviced and needed a new battery every year.

The arrival of the first truly electronic watch, the Bulova 'Accutron', changed this and the mechanical watch was in jeopardy. However, the advent of the quartz watch finally put an end to the hopes of those who made mechanical watches since a good quartz watch can be guaranteed to keep time to a minute a year, a feat no mechanical watch can rival.

The 'Accutron' was the first watch to move away from the balance and spring as the controlling device. Instead it employs a tuning fork. This is made of Ni Span C and vibrates at 360 cycles a second. It drives a ratchet wheel directly. This has 300 teeth which are so fine that a 30× magnification is required to see them with any degree of clarity. At this speed of indexing many feared that either the indexing jewel or the ratchet teeth would wear rapidly, but in fact nothing of the kind has happened. This is to say the least surprising, until one realises the tiny forces involved. Even so 30,000,000 indexes a year is a daunting figure. The author's 'Accutron' has now completed 240,000,000 indexes! (See Plate 82.)

After the 'Accutron', nothing was ever quite the same again and before long the Swiss produced the first production quartz pocket watch. Not long after this the Swiss were pipped at the post by the Japanese, who were the first to put a quartz wrist watch on to the market.

From then on, efforts were mostly in the direction of making quartz watches less expensive. In the course of a few years prices fell from £900 to £30. Currently quartz watches of the LED type (light emitting diode) are on sale in some shops at £14. The market is in a turmoil at the moment with unreliable and reliable models indistinguishable by the public. Wild claims are made for watches fitted with cheap crystals and inadequate circuitry incapable of the timekeeping ability credited to them. However, this stage will pass. There is little doubt that reliability is really the prime consideration, since few people actually need the sort of timekeeping that the best quartz watches can provide. Ebauches SA have produced a very thin quartz watch that they call the 'Flatline'. This watch is 3·70 mm thick, thus combating the arguments of those who say that for flat watches the mechanical watch will never be replaced. Omega have also produced a 6 ligne ladies quartz watch which was shown at the Basle Fair in 1977. The battery is only 6·00 mm in diameter. Thus, all requirements are now being covered and still we are only at the beginning of the quartz watch story.

The day is probably coming when most quartz watches will be purchased set to time, to be thrown away before the need is ever felt to correct them. The watch repairer as he is known today will disappear to be replaced by those capable of restoration work on antique watches, which description will cover the mechanical watch and the electric, as opposed to the electronic watch. Quartz watches are also being produced with many complications, perpetual calendar, chronograph and some are, in addition, miniature calculating machines. It is, of course, impossible to predict what the future will bring. Perhaps a watch that is set into a tooth that will give the time audibly when desired – who dares to laugh!

Glossary

Adjusted Refers to work done on the balance and spring towards eliminating timekeeping errors due to changes that occur in position, temperature or the state of wind. Unadjusted does not mean to say that nothing has been done about these problems at the design stage and in the choice of materials, or that careful poising has not been done. What it does mean is that no further work, other than bringing to time, has been done in view of the individual behaviour because of the changes mentioned.

Adjustable Potence see Potence.

Affix A small bimetallic strip fitted to the main balance which may or may not be bimetallic, so as to affect small changes in the moment of inertia of the balance. This may be to overcome middle temperature error or to make the small corrections required, due to the residual errors of a 'self-compensating' balance spring and balance combination.

Airy's bar A fine adjustment arrangement for bimetallic balances invented by Airy. Two weights lightly sprung against the inside of the balance rim can be slid around the rims, so that they add to the amount of compensation as they approach the free end of the cut rim. A very useful adjunct which found favour among chronometer makers.

All or nothing piece A piece in a repeating watch designed to prevent incorrect striking. If the slide is not pulled all the way round or the push piece fully depressed, so as to ensure that the full number of blows are struck, the watch will not strike at all.

Amplitude The arc of swing measured from zero position to extreme position. Thus, a pendulum which has a total movement of 3° has an amplitude of $1\frac{1}{2}°$.

Anti-friction wheels Wheels arranged so that their outside diameters are the bearing surfaces of the pivots of balances or of wheels in the gear train. Thus, the frictional restraint is reduced by a factor given by the ratio of the outside diameter of the anti-friction wheel to its pivot diameters.

Anti-magnetic Having the property of resisting the effects of an applied magnetic field both during and after the application of the field – the latter being the more important. Without definition the term is valueless.

Apparent solar time The time as given by the sun, i.e. as would be shown on a sun dial. To convert this to Mean Solar Time one needs to know the Equation of Time.

Appliqué Applied ornament to a case, or chapters, numerals etc. to a dial.

Arbor A shaft with bearings. If integral with a gear it is called a pinion.

Arc The arc of a balance is twice the amplitude often denoted as 'turns' by watchmakers. A balance 'doing one turn' has an arc of 360° and an amplitude of 180°.

Assortiment A complete set of escapement parts.

Atelier Workman, especially in horology or allied trades.

Attachment The position that the inner termination of the balance spring bears to the watch.

Automaton watch A watch with pieces that move, usually at will when causing the watch to repeat.

Auxiliary compensation The extra compensatory device fitted to a compensation balance to help to eliminate middle temperature error.

Backslope On an arbor, the part that slopes from the shoulder to the next larger diameter. On a staff, the tapered portion below the balance seating and also the slope behind the pivot blending radius.

Balance Used to control the rate of revolution of the gear train. This is a wheel with one, two, three or four spokes known as arms. Used without a spring in early timepieces, it was not until fitted with a spring that good timekeeping became possible.

There are three main types of balance:

1. Plain, where the rim may or may not be furnished with screws.
2. Cut, where the rim is bimetallic and is cut so that there are two, three or four circumferential strips.
3. Ovalising, where the material is chosen for its unequal expansion in two directions at right angles to one another or is made of two different metals when either the arm or the rim is usually made of Invar.

Moving screws and or weights enables the degree of compensation to be changed, i.e. by moving them nearer to or further away from the point at which the rim is anchored.

Balance cock The cock that supports the balance staff.

Balance screws The screws that are provided around the rim of the balance and that are used to poise the assembly, to bring it to time, to affect the amount of temperature compensation or to enhance the appearance; all or any combination of these.

Balance spring The spring that in conjunction with the balance provides an oscillating assembly. It may be flat spiral, helical, have an overcoil, be a tapered helical, spherical, or be a combination of certain of these, and made of various materials.

Balance-spring stud The stud is the fixing for the outer end of the spring, or the top end in the case of a helical or spherical spring (that is the end that is fixed to the balance cock or bridge). The fixing to the balance is known as the collet. This is normally mounted friction tight on the balance staff.

Balance staff The arbor on which the balance is mounted is called its staff.

Banking The part against which the lever in a lever escapement, or the detent in the detent escapement, rests once escapement action is over.

Banking pin A pin used to provide banking.

Barrel The barrel that contains the mainspring.

Barrel, hanging A barrel that is supported at one end only, namely the top.

Barrel, resting A barrel that is supported at one end only, namely the bottom.

Barrows regulator See Regulation.

Bascule escapement A loose term for the pivoted detent escapement.

Basse-taille enamel Translucent enamel on a surface that has been engraved.

Bassine A smooth rounded-edge case.

Beat The escapement sound or 'tick'.

Beetle hand The type of hour hand that vaguely resembles the shape of the stag beetle. Used with a 'poker' minute hand.

Bezel The rim holding the glass.

Bimetallic Formed of two metals, in horology usually brass and steel, but not invariably so.

Black polish A polish so perfect that at certain angles it looks jet black.

Bottom plate See Top plate.

Bouchon A brass or nickel bush used as a bearing for pivots.

Bow The loop at the top of the watch by means of which it can be lifted or attached to the albert, chain, chatelaine or what have you.

Breguet spring A flat spiral spring with the last turn raised from the body of the spring and formed into a terminal curve, capable of manipulation with the object of reducing positional and isochronal errors.

Breguet hands The moon hands much used by Breguet. These hands tended to be more delicate than those used before Breguet introduced a new look to the watches of the time.

Breguet key See Tipsy key.

Brevet The French equivalent of Patented.

Bulls-eye glass A domed glass with a flat ground in the middle.

Bush See Bouchon. Also the act of bushing a piece to correct a bad hole or to lengthen the bearing surface.

Button, winding The serated cylindrical or spherical piece that is rotated by the fingers to wind the watch or set hands.

Cadrature The work beneath the dial.

Calibre The type of watch often including the size. It is really the brief specification of the movement.

Cam A piece which when rotated is so shaped that it can move another piece in a controlled manner. The shape may be on the edge of the cam or on its face.

Cannister case A drum-shaped case, similar to the tambour case but not hinged.

Cannon pinion The part of the motion work mounted on the centre arbor and able to move relative to it during hand setting. It meshes with the minute wheel in normal layouts.

Cap jewel An endstone.

Capped movement A movement with a dust cap.

Carriage The piece in a tourbillon that rotates and contains the escapement.

Cartouche dial A dial that has cartouches. Cartouches are shield-shaped pieces usually of enamel, which are applied to the dial but may be produced on the dial by engraving and different finishing (as on a matt dial when the maker's name is on a polished oval).

Centre wheel and pinion The wheel and pinion at the centre of the watch; it usually rotates once an hour.

Centre seconds A watch with the seconds hand at its centre – also in modern watches called sweep seconds.

Chaff cutter See Ormskirk and Debaufre escapements.

Chaise watch A very large watch, also called a travelling watch.

Champlevé A hollowed-out area of metal that can be filled with enamel or niello.

Chapters The hour numerals or marks on a dial.

Chapter ring The ring on which the chapters are put, and also the minute and possibly an hour ring with quarter-hour divisions.

Chasing Engraving in relief.

Châtelaine A chain for suspending a watch or a piece of jewellery. As well as the watch, the winding key, seals and trinkets were also often attached. Very often the decoration on the châtelaine was made to match the watch.

Chinese duplex A form of duplex escapement invented by C. E. Jacot in 1830. Commonly used in Fleurier watches intended for China. The teeth on the locking wheel are doubled so as to resemble a fork. Each of the two prongs is held in turn by the locking roller, so that impulse is given on each alternate full swing of the balance. Thus, if the train is 14,400 beats per hour the seconds hand will move forward once a second. Thus, the watch appears to beat seconds, although there is a slight movement of the hand each half second as the locking changes from one fork of the tooth to the next. There was even one version of the escapement that had three prongs on each tooth!

Chronograph A watch with a centre seconds hand that can be started, stopped and returned to zero at will. Also usually provided with a minute counter and sometimes an hour counter to show how long the centre seconds hand has been in operation. All these hands are returned to zero together. See also Split seconds.

Chronometer In England a chronometer is understood to be a watch or marine timepiece that has a detent escapement (although the word was used before this escapement came into use). Unfortunately the word has been misused by the French and Swiss to mean any watch that has obtained an official rating certificate. This has resulted in great confusion in the public mind.

Collet A ring-shaped piece. In watches it may belong to a hand, a balance spring or to a wheel.

Compensated Taken to mean temperature compensated. The balance and balance spring are so constructed that over a certain range of temperature errors are reduced, these errors being due to dimensional changes and to stiffness changes in the spring.

Compensated balance Usually taken to be a balance that has to provide all the compensation required, but could be a balance that only has to provide the residual compensation for the so-called self-compensating balance spring.

Compensation curb A bimetallic strip that carries the curb pins, thus moving them in some manner that is meant to compensate when temperature changes occur.

Compensation screws Screws that can be moved along the balance so as to distribute them in the manner that, in conjunction with the movements of the balance rim, will provide proper compensation.

Compensation weights Weights that provide the same facility as the compensation screws.

Complicated work Usually taken to mean additions to a timepiece other than striking work, e.g. calendar work, phases of the moon, equation of time etc.

Cone pivot A pivot shaped like a cone. Nowadays used in cheaper watches. Although known as conical, the acting end of the pivot ideally has a carefully controlled radius.

Conical pivot The name given to the normal balance pivot, which is in fact not conical at all, but has a parallel portion with a radiussed end and is blended into the next diameter of the staff with a curve.

Constant force escapement A special escapement with subsidiary spring providing motive power. This is wound at frequent intervals, thus the force at the escapement is virtually independent of fluctuations due to the imperfections of the gear train and the variations in the main motive force.

Consular case Understood to be the double-bottom case fitted with a high rounded glass, although the term is used somewhat loosely.

Contrate wheel A wheel to transmit motion from one arbor to another that stands at right angles to it; the teeth instead of projecting from the periphery stand out from the face of the wheel.

Conversion An escapement substituted for the original. Generally a lever escapement supplants a verge, a chronometer or cylinder escapement. Nowadays important pieces are being re-converted by replacing converted escapements with one closely similar to the original.

Coqueret A steel end plate mainly found in French watches after 1735. Screwed to the balance cock, it provides the end bearing for the top pivot of the balance. By 1770 it was in general use but was then gradually supplanted by a jewel bearing as was the English practice.

Count wheel See Locking plate striking.

Coupe-perdu escapement One in which unlocking of the escape wheel does not always lead to impulse. The Chinese duplex is such an escapement. Usually this is so that the seconds hand can move forward in an interval longer than that given by a normal escapement, usually one second with a Chinese duplex.

Counterpoised pallets Those that have an appendage specifically to help to poise the pallets.

Crank lever escapement A form of lever escapement in which impulse is conveyed to the balance through what is really a single-gear tooth. The notch in the end of the lever is in the form of a gap between two gear teeth, and the projection on the roller is made as a single pinion leaf. Invented by Massey of Liverpool.

Crank roller See above.

Crescent or passing hollow. The clearance cut into the roller of a lever escapement for the passage of the dart or guard pin.

Crown wheel escapement Another name for the verge escapement.

Curb pins or index pins. The pins that embrace the balance spring and when moved along, affect regulation.

Cut balance See Compensation balance, although not all compensation balances are cut. Some modern balances merely have affixes or become oval to affect compensation.

Cuvette An inside cover to protect the movement, hinged and sprung, often of brass even in good quality gold cases. Used on continental watches and often engraved with maker's name, directions of winding, hand setting, number of jewels, escapement etc.

Cylinder escapement or horizontal escapement. Perfected by Graham in about 1725, the balance is mounted on a hollow cylinder large enough in the bore to admit a tooth of the escape wheel. Nearly half of the cylinder is cut away where the teeth enter, and impulse is given by the wedge shape of the teeth as they enter and leave. The escapement is dead beat, frictional rest. The pieces inserted in the hollow cylinder on which the pivots are formed are known as plugs.

Dart Another name for the guard pin, from its shape on high quality hand finished English and Swiss watches; they were often screwed in position. See Guard pin.

Daily Rate The amount a watch varies each day from correct time.

Damascene Ornamental finishing of watch parts, especially on keyless wheels and the barrel bridge. This was a speciality of the American watch industry.

Dead beat escapement First used successfully by George Graham in 1715 but possibly preceded by Tompion. Its feature is the elimination of recoil in the escapement by making the locking faces of the pallets circumferential with the pallet pivots. Although applied to the Graham clock escapement it is also a generic term for escapements without recoil.

Dead beat verge An escapement belonging to the Debaufre family, where two bevelled edge pallets receive impulse from a verge-type escape wheel.

Deaf piece A push piece in a repeater that when pressed prevents the watch from striking by taking the hammer blow. By this means the blows can be felt instead of heard. Not just for the deaf, since there are occasions when the noise could be a nuisance.

Debaufre escapement Invented by Peter Debaufre in 1704. Two ratchet tooth escape wheels are on the same axis, the teeth being staggered in relation to those on the other wheel. The balance staff passes between the two wheels and a pallet is fixed to the staff.

Deck watch A precision watch for use on a ship when establishing its position. It is normally large, say 18–24 lignes, and is used to transfer the time from the ship's chronometer or other time standard to the position where sightings are being made on deck. Also used instead of a chronometer where the vibration would otherwise be too much for the normal chronometer.

Depth The degree of intersection of two parts that work together, such as gear wheels or escapement parts.

Detached escapement An escapement which is not in contact with the balance except when unlocking, impulse or run to banking is occurring. Thus, the lever and chronometer escapement are detached whilst the duplex, cylinder and verge are not.

Detent A loose term for a stop generally confined nowadays to the detent of a chronometer escapement. Also, however, the fusee detent and the warning detent in striking.

Detent escapement Another name for the chronometer escapement, pivoted or spring detent.

Dial plate The plate to which the dial is fixed. May also be the bottom plate or pillar plate.

Differential dial   Here the centre of the dial is a disc marked 1 to 12 and makes $\frac{11}{12}$ of a revolution per hour. An ordinary minute hand revolves concentrically with this disc once an hour and is thus always passing over the current hour.

Differential up and down work   Differential gearing is required for one form of up and down work on going barrel watches.

Discharging pallet   The pallet that affects unlocking in the chronometer escapement.

Divided lift   In an English ratchet-tooth escapement, all the lift, or impulse, as on the pallet. In Sylvain Mairet's lever escapement all the lift was given by the teeth of the escape wheel. In the divided lift escapement, lift is shared so that some is given by the wheel teeth and some by the pallets. This is the family to which the club-tooth lever escapement belongs.

Dome   The inside cover of a watch case which is like a second back.

Double bottom case   The form of watch case most used to house full plate movements. The inner bottom or back is in one piece with the case band, and to inspect the movement this has to be swung out from the front of the case on its hinge, or as it should be called, 'joint'. Before this can be done the bezel must be opened and the bolt released.

Double roller   The type of roller used in the modern lever escapement; it has one table that carries the ruby pin and another that provides part of the safety action arrangement.

Draw   The characteristic of an escapement that keeps the lever or detent safely in the rest position once escapement action is over, despite all but the most severe jolts and jars. The part is impelled against the stop or banking by utilising the force that is needed to recoil the escapement. This is obtained by having suitable geometry at the pallet, so that in moving away from the stop or banking, as it is called, the escape wheel is forced to move slightly backwards. Although the knowledge of the feature draw was known, early makers, including Breguet, were reluctant to use it in the lever escapement since it seemed to go against what they believed in; that recoil escapements were bad and equally so was any recoil in any other escapement. John Leroux, in 1785, was the first to introduce draw in the lever escapement, but it was in fact present from the start in the chronometer, merely by the accident of the features of Arnold's particular design.

Drop The necessary small free movement of the escape wheel as it moves from one pallet to the other. Without this the escapement geometry would have to be perfect for the escapement to act without jamming, a manifestly impossible thing. However, the higher the quality – and by inference the more perfect the geometry – the less drop there can be and its amount is in fact a design decision. In a good-quality lever escapement drop is usually $\frac{1}{2}°$ which at a diameter, say of 5 mm, means a linear movement of about $\frac{2}{100}$ mm. Drop is also the amount the chronometer escape wheel moves before it catches up the impulse pallet on the roller.

In a cylinder escapement, drop is the amount the wheel tooth moves forward on to the outside or the inside the cylinder after impulse is completed.

Dumb repeater A repeater without bells or gongs where the hammers strike a block mounted in the case.

Duplex escapement Commonly an escapement whose wheel has two sets of teeth. One long and pointed set provides the locking function by working with a small roller with a passing notch that is mounted on the balance staff. The second set of teeth stands up from the rim of the wheel and gives impulse to a pallet (which is sometimes jewelled) that is mounted on the balance staff.

Less commonly, two separate wheels are used to perform the two functions. Like the chronometer, the impulse teeth do not need to be oiled but oil is, however, required at the locking jewel. Although a frictional-rest type this escapement can, if not worn, perform extremely well.

Dust cap A cap to help to exclude dust fitted mainly to the movements of watches that are hinged to the case. They came into use in about 1715. Usually made of brass, though sometimes of silver. As a rule found in English watches.

Ebauche The movement blank or rough movement. In the early 19th century they consisted of the plates, pillars, cocks and bars with barrel, fusee, ratchet, ratchet wheel and assembly screws.

End shake Axial play. The clearance between the pivot shoulders and their bearing surfaces.

Endstone A thrust bearing made of jewel, against which a pivot end bears.

Endless screw See Tangent screw.

Engine turning A regular pattern machined with a special-purpose lathe. Even when the pattern consists of straight lines it is still called engine turning. Often covered in clear or translucent enamel when it is called Guilloché.

English lever escapement The pointed-tooth lever escapement where all the lift is on the pallets.

Entry pallet The pallet in the lever escapement where the escape-wheel teeth enter. If one looks down on an escapement and the wheel is rotating clockwise, then the entry pallet is on the left.

Equation of time The difference between solar time and mean time. Only at four times of the year do mean time and solar time agree.

Escapement The element in a timepiece that transforms the rotary motion of the gear train into the oscillatory motion required by the timekeeping element.

Escape wheel and pinion The wheel that gives impulse to the oscillating member, the balance, foliot, or balance and spring, either directly or through an intermediate.

Figure plate Another name for the Index Dial used with a Tompion regulator.

Finishing The work required to bring a watch from the ebauche state to the finished condition.

Fire gilding An amalgam of gold and mercury is used to coat the article to be gilded and the mercury driven off by heat to leave a strongly adhering film of gold.

Five minute repeater A repeater that strikes the hours and then a number of double blows for the number of five minutes past the hour.

Flags The pallets of a verge. See Verge escapement.

Flirt A lever or some device that causes a sudden movement to occur. It is usually raised slowly by a cam to be suddenly released, or may be under manual control.

Floating hour dial See Wandering hour.

Fly A governing device that consists of a vane fixed to a pinion, which in sweeping through the air slows the rate of rotation of the train of which it is part. Used in striking, repeating work, and in remontoires and constant-force escapements.

Fly back hand   A hand that is caused to, or automatically flies back to, a zero position or to coincide with another hand.

Fob chain   A short chain with a swivel or bolt ring to fix it to the watch and usually with a bar at the other end to pass through the button-hole. It hangs outside the clothing.

Foliot   The earliest form of controller. It is bar shaped, and in watches usually has fixed weights at its ends. Its purpose is to increase the moment of inertia of the verge to slow its operation.

Forgeries   The whole question of forgeries and fakes is excessively difficult, and becoming more so. Even top experts have trouble in this field. Many old forgeries are collected in their own right. Some, both old and new, are virtually impossible to detect.

Fork   The fork-shaped end of the lever in the lever escapement in which is the notch.

Fourth wheel and pinion   The fourth wheel is the wheel that normally drives the escape pinion. It often carries a seconds hand. It is a loosely used term. In an eight-day watch it may in fact be the fifth wheel, but would never be so called.

Form watch   A watch whose case is made into a shape recognisable as representing something other than a watch case. See Index.

Four coloured gold   Gold can be produced in a great number of colours according to its alloying constituents. Dials were frequently decorated with different coloured golds, sometimes as many as four. Cases were also treated in this way but less frequently.

Frame   The main parts of a watch that support and locate all the other parts.

Free-sprung   Without an index. Free-sprung balances have to be brought to time in the final stages by altering the moment of inertia of the balance by removing, adding or altering screws and/or by means of the quarter screws.

Frictional rest escapement   An escapement that is always in contact with the balance.

Friction wheels   See Anti-friction wheels.

Full-plate watch   One in which all of the parts except the balance are located between two plates. An inconvenient arrangement that took a long time to disappear.

Fusee A grooved tapered pulley which when properly made evens out the torque output from the mainspring. When the mainspring is fully wound it pulls on a smaller diameter than when it is run down. The best watches had their fusees matched to their individual spring.

Fusee barrel The type of barrel that is used in conjunction with a fusee. It has no teeth, the great wheel being mounted on the fusee.

Fusee chain The chain that connects the barrel to the fusee. The making of fusee chains soon became a separate trade. It was invented in about 1635, and by 1680 was almost universally used in fusee watches.

Gadrooning Ornamentation found on the edges of late 18th- and early 19th-century watches. It is a sort of pie-crust ornamentation either made by hammering or casting.

Gate The name of the decorative piece covering the fusee stop-finger support.

Gathering pallet The pallet that gathers up the rack tooth by tooth whilst striking occurs.

Gimbals The freely swinging supports that are designed to keep a deck watch or chronometer horizontal regardless of the attitude of the outer case.

Going barrel A barrel that carries the great wheel on its periphery or on its arbor.

Going fusee A fusee with maintaining power.

Going train The train that has to do with the timekeeping side of the watch as opposed, for example, to the striking, repeating or musical train.

Gongs Strips of steel, usually circular, that go around the outside of the watch plates. Usually of round section but sometimes square. Invented by A. L. Breguet. They are struck by hammers.

Grande sonnerie Striking both the hours and the quarters at each quarter.

Great wheel The first wheel in the train and the slowest moving. Attached to the barrel or the fusee.

Greenwich Mean Time (G.M.T.) Mean Solar Time at The Old

Greenwich Observatory. Since Solar Time varies according to whether one is east or west of any reference point it is of little use in modern communities where travel and rapid communication are common. As a result, in 1880 G.M.T. was established by law as the official time for the whole of Great Britain. In 1884 Greenwich was taken as the prime or zero meridian from which all others are taken and time zones established around the world that relate to it. Only small countries can have just one time zone. The United States of America is so large that it must have five time zones each differing by an hour from that next to it.

Grey Parts in the 'grey' are not yet finally finished or polished.

Grisaille A technique in enamelling similar to 'scraper board' where a dark ground is laid down and covered with white enamel which is then scraped away to a greater or lesser extent to form a picture or pattern. This could be rendered more subtle by hatchings and by varying the tones of the white (either by using a spatula or a brush).

Guard pin The pin that is part of the safety action in the lever escapement. It is attached to the lever and is centrally disposed with respect to the notch.

Guilloché See Engine turning.

Hairspring The common name for the balance spring. A loose term that can refer to springs not associated with a balance, as in an electrical meter for instance.

Half plate A watch in which only the barrel, centre and third wheels are under the same top plate.

Half quarter repeater A repeating watch that sounds single blows for the hours, a double blow for each quarter hour past the hour and another single blow if another $7\frac{1}{2}$ minutes have passed since the last quarter.

Hallmark A mark applied by the Assay Office showing the place of assay, the metal purity, the year of assay and the sponsor's mark. Applicable in the U.K. to gold, silver and recently platinum.

Hand setting In early watches the hand was set by pushing it. Later the square on which the hand was mounted was extended so that the hand could be set by a key. Eventually the hand was set by means of the pendant button by pulling out the button or by moving out or pushing in a set piece.

Hanging barrel   One which is supported at one end only, the top end; the other end of the barrel being in a clearance hole in the bottom plate.

Heart piece   The heart-shaped cam which is operated by a lever to return a hand to zero.

Helical spring   A spring which is in the form of a helix. The ends are normally incurved so as to obtain more uniform dilation of the spring as it works.

Hog's bristle   A bristle used in the regulation of the balance or foliot before the introduction of the balance spring. The arm hit the bristle or bristles at some point before the end of its excursion, the exact position being adjustable.

Hole   The bearing in which a pivot runs. May be of jewel, brass, bronze, lignum vitae, plastics, sintered material etc.

Hooke's Law   The law that says that for a given material the relationship of stress to strain is a constant. Stress is force per unit area, and strain the extension per unit length. This is only true within the elastic limit of the material, that is within the limit where any deformation due to stress is not permanent after the load is removed.

Horizontal escapement   Another name for the cylinder escapement.

Horizontal positions   The positions in which a watch is horizontal, i.e. dial up and down.

Horns   The extensions to the notch ends that form part of the safety action in a lever escapement.

Hour rack   The rack that falls on to the hour snail and dictates the number of hours to be struck.

Hour wheel   The wheel on which the hour hand is mounted, usually on a pipe extension. Normally the hour wheel rotates every 12 hours but sometimes it rotates in 6 or 24 hours.

Hunter   A later case that has a solid cover to the dial. If the centre of the cover is pierced so as to show the middle half of the dial it is called a half-hunter.

Impulse   The force applied to the balance and spring which makes good the losses due to friction and the fanning of the air.

Impulse angle The angle through which the balance moves during impulse is known as the impulse angle.

Impulse face The face through which the impulse is transmitted.

Impulse pallet The pallet through which impulse is transmitted.

Impulse pin The pin through which impulse is transmitted.

Impulse roller The roller through which impulse is transmitted or which carries an impulse pin.

Independent seconds A watch with two trains, one of which carries a seconds hand which can be stopped and started at will and whose rate of revolution is controlled by the other train. The independent train usually has its own minute and hour hands.

Index The piece that carries the index pins.

Index pins The pins that embrace the balance spring and can be moved along it for regulation purposes.

Intermediate wheel and pinion A wheel and pinion that lies between the great wheel and the centre wheel.

Isochronous The property of oscillating at a constant rate, despite the amplitude of oscillation. An isochronous balance will perform long arcs in the same length of time as short arcs.

Jacquemarts Figures that are moved by the watch mechanism usually on repeating watches.

Jewels The art of piercing jewels for use as bearings and applying them to watch work was perfected by Facio in 1701. At first the art was confined to England; it was not until later that it spread to the Continent.

Jumper A spring, or spring controlled piece, used to locate another piece.

Jumping Hours An hour hand that jumps forward once every hour. Breguet was fond of this arrangement in his repeating watches.

Jumping seconds A hand that moves forward in second jumps, despite the fact that the escapement moves forward at more frequent intervals, is said to be jumping seconds. Also a hand that each second completes one revolution of a subsidiary dial.

Karrusel A watch with a slowly revolving escapement. If it revolves in six minutes or less it is usually called a tourbillon.

Keyless watch A watch that can be wound and set without the need for a separate key.

Keyless winding Winding that can be affected without the need for a separate key. Early keyless winding watches still needed a key for hand setting. See Rocking bar keyless work.

Lepine calibre A watch movement in which the top plate is replaced by bridges and cocks. Introduced by J. A. Lepine in about 1770. This layout made possible a thinner watch.

Lever escapement The most successful of all the watch escapements, so called because a lever is interposed between the escape wheel and the balance. The balance first moves the lever to affect unlocking then the lever is pushed across by the escape wheel, impulsing the balance in the process. When the pieces that the escape-wheel teeth act upon are jewelled the escapement is known as a 'jewelled lever'. If the pieces are pin-shaped, however, it is called a pin-pallet or pin-lever escapement regardless as to whether the pins are pieces of jewel or steel.

The escapement was invented by Thomas Mudge in about 1754 and subsequently improved over a long period until it became virtually standardised in its present form, the club-tooth lever.

Lever notch In a lever escapement the opening at the end of the lever which works with the impulse pin.

Lift The travel of the lever during impulse.

Ligne $\frac{1}{12}$ of the old French inch and equivalent to 2.25 mm.

Liverpool jewels Very large jewels fitted to Liverpool watches during the first half of the 19th century.

Locking The amount required for safety of action of an escapement. It represents the amount that the piece that is moved to unlock the escapement has to move before impulse begins.

Locking plate striking An earlier type of striking which has a locking plate or count wheel to determine the number of blows struck. Appropriately spaced notches around the rim of the wheel determine how long the striking train shall run before it is locked again. Unfortunately, once the hour has struck it cannot be struck again as with rack striking and as a result the striking can get out of phase with the hands. This will happen if for instance the striking train runs down before the going train and to rectify the situation may require specialised knowledge.

Lunette   A rounded, slightly domed watch glass.

Mainspring   The spring which provides the driving power for the various trains in watches, going, striking, repeating, musical etc.

Maintaining power   A device for keeping a watch going when it is being wound where otherwise it would stop – as when it has a fusee. Usually Harrison's maintaining power but Arnold did fit sun and planet maintaining power in some of his early watches and chronometers.

Maltese Cross   A wheel of that shape which forms part of stop work fitted to going barrels, this stop work being known as Geneva.

Massey lever escapement   See Crank lever escapement.

Mean Time   The average of all the solar days in the year is the mean solar day. This used as the basis of time is 'mean time'.

Middle temperature error   The elasticity of the balance spring does not vary in the same way as the moment of inertia of the balance when the temperature changes. The error can be matched either at one or two temperatures which can be chosen at will. The choice is usually two temperatures, the extremes, which then results in errors everywhere between these two temperatures. This is called middle temperature error and can be overcome partially or completely by means of adding auxilliary compensation. By using a Guillaume balance middle temperature error can be avoided.

Minute repeater   A repeater that repeats the hours, the quarters and then the minutes past the quarter.

Minute wheel and pinion   See Motion work.

Modele deposé   See Brevet.

Moon hand   See Breguet Hands.

Motion work   The gearing beneath the dial which causes the hour hand to revolve twelve times (or unusually twenty-four times) slower than the minute hand. It consists of the cannon pinion, the hour wheel, the minute wheel and pinion.

Movement   The 'works' of a watch, that is a watch less case, hands and dial. For rough movement see Ebauche.

Musical watch   A watch that has a separate mechanism that plays a tune on bells or a steel comb. The pinned barrel, as in a musical box, is sometimes used and sometimes a flat wheel with pins protruding from its face or faces.

Niello   A process similar to Champlevé enamel but the depressions are filled with a black compound consisting of silver, lead and sulphur instead of enamel. May be on gold but is more usual on silver.

Nuremburg egg   A misnomer due to bad translating of Uhrlein (little watch) as Euerlein (little egg). These watches were not egg-shaped but spherical or drum-shaped.

Offset seconds   Small seconds where the seconds hand is not concentric with the hour and minutes hands and in addition not at the dial centre.

Oil sink   A depression around a pivot hole to help retain oil and to make the amount that can safely be applied greater; surprisingly not introduced until about 1715 by Henry Sully. Early jewels had no sinks but these were soon included.

Oignon   A popular name mainly applied to the large and bulbous French watches of the late 17th and early 18th century.

Open face   An open-face watch that has no metallic cover to the dial. Although the time can be read without opening the front cover of a half-hunter it is still not termed open face.

Ormskirk   A town in Lancashire, U.K. In the early 19th century a number of watches were made with a sort of Debaufre escapement and these are known as 'Ormskirk' watches.

Oscillation   A constant and repetitious sequence of events. A pendulum and balance oscillate, as do a tuning fork and a quartz crystal, provided that some source of energy is available to maintain the oscillations, that is, to make good the various losses in the oscillating system.

Outer case   The outer case of a pair-cased watch. Sometimes embellished, sometimes plain.

Overcoil   The coil of the flat spiral balance spring that is raised above the body of the spring and is then shaped so as to follow certain rules. Invented by A. L. Breguet.

Pair case   The standard form of the case for English watches between the mid-17th century and the end of the 18th century and beyond. The inner case contained the movement and was protected in its turn by an outer case. The outer case was often decorated in the style of the period; inner cases more frequently being plain. At the end of the period the outer case tended to be more plain.

Pallet Specifically the part through which the escape wheel impulses the balance. When this part is made of jewel it is called the pallet stone.

Parachute A shock-protecting device for the balance staff invented by Breguet. The balance endstones are not rigidly mounted but are held by long springy arms which can give under shock. The earliest form of shock protection.

Passing crescent See Crescent.

Passing spring Also known as the 'gold spring', because it is usually made of gold. It is a passing spring which allows the discharging pallet to pass the detent in one direction without moving it aside.

Pedometer watch This has different meanings. Sometimes taken to mean an early self-wound pocket watch whose self-winding weight oscillates at every step. Also a watch and pedometer combined.

Pedometer wind See Perpetual watch.

Pendant The part on top of the watch to which the bow is fixed. This can, by its form, help to date a watch. Latterly, the pendant carries the winding button in keyless watches, the winding stem passing through it.

Perpetual calendar A calendar mechanism that corrects the date according to the length of the months including the extra day in Leap Year. Usually shows day, date, month, these latter being on a four-year dial with Leap Year indicated.

Perpetual watch The English translation of the 'montre perpétuelle', the French term for a self-winding watch.

Pillars These locate, support and separate the plates or a plate, bridge, cock or potence. The earliest pillars were of square section, later, after about 1600 styles became diverse, Egyptian, tulip, pierced foliate, lyre shaped, square section baluster and then cylindrical.

Pillar plate   The plate nearest the dial to which the pillars are fixed.

Pin barrel   The barrel that carried the pins that play the comb in a musical train.

Pin pallet escapement   See Lever escapement.

Pinion   Usually the driven gear in watch work with six or more leaves, as the teeth are called.

Pinchbeck   An alloy of zinc and copper, named after the inventor Christopher Pinchbeck in about 1730. It had a close resemblance to gold.

Pin work   See Piqué.

Piqué or Pin Work.   Pins of gold, silver or brass which are used practically to secure a covering to the outer case of a pair-cased watch. By arranging the heads in patterns they were also made to serve a decorative purpose. Leather, shagreen and tortoise-shell were some of the coverings in question.

Pirouette   A staff with an integral pinion by means of which the balance could be given an exceptionally large arc.

Pitch   The distance between teeth along the pitch line.

Pivot   The bearing area of a rotating piece, usually, but not necessarily, at the end of the piece. Usually made of as small a diameter as is reasonable to reduce frictional losses.

Pivoted detent   A chronometer detent which is supported by pivots, as against a spring detent.

Planting   The process of determining the position of mating parts and making the holes in which they run or that take the jewels that form the bearings.

Plates   The main members of the watch. The frame that locates and supports all the other parts. There may of course be only one plate.

Poise   If the poise of a balance is perfect it will display no heavy point when supported on knife edges.

Pointed tooth-lever escapement   See Lever escapement.

Poker hand   The minute hand that usually matches the beetle hand, somewhat in the shape of a poker.

Positional error   A difference in rate that results from a change in position is known as a positional error. It may be dial up to dial down or between dial up and the vertical position pendant up, and so on.

Potence (or Potance)   A cock that lies between the plates.

Potence plate   An old name for the top plate, because in verge watches it carried the potence that supported the lower pivot of the verge.

Pouzait lever escapement   One of the first lever escapements with divided lift, invented by J. M. Pouzait in 1786. The escape-wheel teeth stand out from the wheel edge and these engage with a claw-shaped lever. The notch in the lever imparts impulse in the usual way to a steel impulse pin. The safety action was novel and used a ring with a gap on the staff that interacted with a pin on one arm of the lever. Thus, this pin would alternately be inside and outside the ring.

Pull wind   See Pump wind.

Pump wind   An early type of keyless winding. The watch is wound either by pulling or pushing a lever that passes through the pendant and terminates in a button. Massey and Viner both used this method.

Pulse piece   A pin that projects through the case edge that is made to move against the bell hammer at will, so that repeating the watch can enable one to feel the hammer blows instead of hearing them on the bell.

Puritan watch   Made between about 1625 and 1650, these watches were usually oval in shape and made of silver. As their name suggests, they were devoid of decoration.

Quarter rack   See Hour rack.

Quarter repeater   A watch that strikes the hours and the quarters at will.

Quarter screws   The screws in a compensation balance that are adjustable so as to alter the moment of inertia and/or the poise. Because they are set 90° apart they are called quarter screws. The screws are either made a close fit in the threaded hole in the balance or else the balance is slit, so that the hole may be closed slightly so as to give a springy grip, as in the Glashütte balance.

Rack   Toothed segment. See Hour rack.

Rack hook   In striking or chiming work the lever that engages with the rack. It holds it and prevents it from slipping back, whilst not, however, preventing the gathering pallet from lifting the rack as striking occurs.

Rack lever escapement A form of lever escapement first invented by the Abbé de Hautefeuille in 1722. It was later patented in a more practical form by Peter Litherland in 1791 (patent 1830). The lever terminates in a toothed segment or rack which is permanently in mesh with a pinion on the balance staff. Made in large numbers in Liverpool in the early 19th century.

Rack striking See Hour rack.

Rack tail The tail of the rack which on contacting the snail stops the rack from falling further and thus dictates the number of blows to be struck.

Ratchet wheel A wheel which in conjunction with a click or ratchet has teeth so shaped that it can move in one direction only, or such that some change in the position of the click must occur for it to move in the other direction.

Rate The amount by which a timekeeper varies from the true time that it is intended to show. A timekeeper can have a large rate but providing it is uniform and predictable it can still be a perfect timekeeper – a fact not widely appreciated in the eighteenth century.

Recoil The backward movement of an escape wheel during the normal escapement operation. All truly successful watch escapements have recoil, however small, as this is utilised to provide 'draw'.

Recoil escapement An escapement in which there is recoil.

Regulation In pre-balance spring watches regulation was mainly done by altering the set-up of the mainspring. One way (to begin with) was by using a spring ratchet with a ratchet wheel on the arbor, but later also by utilising a worm and wheel drive. The worm wheel, which was mounted on the barrel arbor, usually had a graduated disc mounted on it so that one could see what adjustment had been made. If the helix angle of a worm is sufficiently small the arrangement is self-locking, so that it can be turned both ways with equal ease. A very early regulation arrangement was the use of the Hog's Bristle. Here the supplementary arc of the balance could be altered by varying the position of two upright hog's bristles against which the balance arms banked.

The ratchet set-up lasted until about 1640. The worm and wheel method (often called the tangent screw and wheel) only gave way when the balance spring was introduced. It gave way to Tompion's arrangement. The index plate now covered a gear that meshed with the segment of a larger gear that carried the curb pins. These pins can be made to traverse the spring by turning a square fixed to the index with the winding key. As the spring is effectively shortened or lengthened, so the rate changes. This was an elaborate arrangement and needed a special bridge to cover and locate the parts.

Regulator See Regulation.

Remontoire (or Remontoir) A constant-force device placed in the train near to the balance. It supplies the power to maintain the balance and is rewound at short intervals by the main source of power. Thus, the main variations due to the gear train and the running down of the mainspring are eliminated.

Remontoire escapement A remontoire device that is mounted on the escape wheel or next to the balance. Usually called a constant-force escapement.

Repeat A watch repeats if one can make it strike at will.

Repeater There are many types of repeater. Quarter, half quarter, minute, five minute and half ten minute. The watch is made to repeat by pressing on a plunger, pushing a push piece or pulling round a slide. The hammers may strike a bell, on gongs, or on a block, this latter being known as a dumb repeater. Repeating work was invented by Daniel Quare in the 1680s.

Repoussé A pattern raised by hammering from the back so that the scene is in relief.

Resilient escapement A form of lever escapement in which when banking occurs the blow on the impulse pin is taken by a non-rigid part of the lever, or in which the escapement is so arranged that recoiling the escape wheel serves the same purpose.

Robin escapement A lever chronometer escapement made by Robin in the 18th century. Locking takes place on the lever and the impulse is given direct by the escape wheel to the balance. It is single beat.

Rocking bar keyless work The action of the keyless winding mechanism usually found in later going barrel English watches. A bar is rocked by means of a push piece to move gears into mesh for handsetting and out of mesh for winding. On releasing the push piece the bar moves back under the action of a spring into the winding position.

Roller The part of the balance staff that receives impulse, or carries the pin, jewel etc. that receives impulse.

Roskopf G. T. Roskopf manufactured the first inexpensive watches in 1867. They had a pin-pallet escapement and were keyless pocket watches. The name Roskopf came to mean a certain type of watch and the name is often inaccurately applied.

Ruby-cylinder escapement Because the steel cylinder of a cylinder escapement was found to wear, some cylinders in high quality watches were made of ruby. Breguet especially used many ruby cylinders and devised a special sort that hung down below the bottom pivot of the balance.

Run-to banking In a lever escapement the extra movement of the lever needed above the bare movement required to allow the escapement action to occur. The extra movement is required for safe action.

'S' balance An early form of compensation balance used by John Arnold. 'S'-shaped bimetallic strips caused weights to move nearer to or further away from the centre of the balance as temperature changes occurred.

Safety action See Lever escapement.

Safety roller See Lever escapement.

Safety dart See Dart.

Savage two pin A form of lever escapement developed by George Savage. Introduced about 1814.

Savonnette A watch with a front cover to protect the glass.

Scape wheel The wheel that delivers impulse directly to the balance or through an intermediary. It is the last of the train wheels but does not mesh with another pinion. Properly escape wheel.

Secondary compensation Compensation that is additional to the main compensation and that corrects small residual errors.

Seconds train A train so designed that one of its wheels rotates once a minute, and can therefore have a seconds hand mounted on it.

Seconds wheel and pinion The wheel and pinion in the train that rotates once a minute.

Secret signature Used by Breguet to protect himself against forgeries. Has to be looked for carefully and is usually near the XII. Other makers subsequently adopted the idea.

Secret spring The fly and lock springs of a hunter case.

Segment weights The weights that are slid along the arms of a compensation balance to adjust the amount of compensation. Called segment weights because of their shape.

Self-compensating spring Somewhat of a misnomer but nevertheless a convenient term for a spring that has a small thermal coefficient of Youngs modulus that can be manipulated so as to compensate for its own dimensional changes and those of the balance. For complete compensation there must still be some adjustable device attached to the balance, or else the balance must be of the Guillaume, or of the ovalising type.

Self-winding A watch that is able to wind itself through the movements of the wearer. See Perpetual watch.

Set up Since the bottom diameter of a fusee cannot be infinitely large it cannot give the correct torque when the mainspring is completely run down. In practice, the bottom diameter is dictated by the size of the great wheel and the need for a maintaining ratchet (or winding ratchet in early watches). Therefore, the mainspring must be set up so as to give correct torque at this diameter and an equal torque when the mainspring is fully wound achieved by a reasonable size of the smallest diameter at the top of the fusee. Working out the shape of a fusee is a complex matter and is seldom done other than empirically or by virtue of experience.

S.G.D.G. See Brevet.

Sidereal Time Time as given by the stars. This is uniform in a way that solar time can never be. Lack of uniformity in Sidereal

Time is so slight that only when quartz clocks came into use was it established.

Single-beat escapement An escapement such as the chronometer, where impulse is given when the balance is travelling in one direction but not the other. Usually considered to be a drawback in an escapement as increasing its liability to set.

Single-plane escapement An escapement that works in one plane as with a lever escapement.

Single roller See Lever escapement.

Six-hour dial An attempt to read to the minute with a single hand was made at the end of the 17th century by having a six-hour dial. This can be divided at two-minute intervals. Of course, to tell the time one needed to know which six-hour period one was in.

Skeleton dial A dial that is cut away so that one can see the work beneath it.

Skeletonised movement A movement cut away so as to disclose as much of the work as possible. Taken to incredible extremes in some modern work.

Snail A cam-shaped piece usually dictating the number of blows to be struck.

Solid banking Banking that is provided by part of the bottom plate as opposed to a pin. See Banking.

Solar Time Time as indicated by the sun, e.g. as on a sun dial. Of little practical use in modern life, but early clocks were checked against sun dials by using the equation of time and local time which was used until the introduction of Greenwich Mean Time.

Souscription Breguet's inexpensive watch ordered in advance by the customer. Characterised by a barrel at the centre and a single hand through which the winding square passed.

Spotting A finishing method consisting of a series of overlapping spots arranged in concentric circles usually in watch work. Applied to a previously polished surface.

Split seconds A chronograph watch with two centre seconds hands that can be used to time two distinct events. One hand may be stopped, then if wished the other. When next the plunger is pressed the second hand returns to its position over the first, or both may be returned to zero, or both may continue together.

Spring barrel A barrel containing a mainspring. It is not clear when it was first invented but probably before 1450.

Spring detent The detent of a chronometer escapement that is supported and located by the spring that returns it to the locked position. Preferred by the English to the pivoted detent although possibly not with justification.

Stackfreed The device fitted to early watches to help to equalise the force of the mainspring regardless of its state of wind. A cam, mounted on the barrel stop work, is so shaped that a strong spring that follows it robs the mainspring of power when the watch is fully wound and assists the mainspring at a later stage. A crude device that was soon supplanted by the fusee.

Standing barrel A barrel, supported at its lower end only.

Star wheel A wheel with triangular-shaped teeth that can be indexed and is located by a jumper. Often carries a striking snail.

Stones Another term for jewels.

Stop work The arrangement fitted to a fusee or to a going barrel to limit the number of turns of winding. Always at the top end to prevent the spring being fully wound, and with going barrels usually limiting the number of turns by also stopping the barrel before it is unwound.

Straight-line lever A lever escapement in which the pivots of the balance, lever and escape wheel lie in a straight line. Almost invariably (there are exceptions) the layout of modern lever watches.

Stud The outer termination (or top termination with a helical spring) is either pinned into, clamped into or latterly sometimes cemented into a stud. This in turn is then screwed or clamped to the balance bridge or cock or the top plate.

Sugar tongs An early compensated curb-pin device shaped in fact like latter-day washing tongs. Both blades of the tongs are bimetallic and carry a curb pin at their termination.

Sun and moon dial A popular type of dial at the turn of the 18th century. A twenty-four-hour dial carries both a sun and moon. One indicates the hours of darkness from 6 p.m. to 6 a.m. and the other, the hours of light, 6 a.m. to 6 p.m. Doubtless more useful in the tropics than in temperate latitudes!

Sundial Time See Solar Time.

Supplementary arc The arc that a balance describes over and above that minimum required for escapement action. Probably the greatest supplementary arc is found in pirouettes, since the action need not be confined as with more conventional escapements, the action in fact being only limited by the power that can be put in, and by the necessity to prevent the hairspring coils from touching.

Surprise piece A device fitted to the snails of repeaters to prevent incorrect striking just after the hour or after each quarter.

Sweep seconds See Centre seconds.

Swing wheel An old term for the escape wheel.

Swiss lever escapement The term loosely used to indicate the club-tooth lever escapement, to distinguish it from the English or ratchet-tooth lever escapement.

Table roller The roller of the lever escapement on which is mounted the impulse pin.

Tact A montre à tact has a stout hand fitted over the back or the dial of the watch, which can be moved in a clockwise direction, until it is stopped by the mechanism inside. The time is then read off by feeling the position of the hand relative to touch pieces on the case edge. These pins are in the hour positions. Breguet made a number of these watches. They are a less expensive alternative to a repeater.

Taille douce Fine line engraving.

Tambour case An early type of drum-shaped case with a hinged lid.

Tangent screw A worm used in conjunction with a worm wheel for setting up the barrel (see Regulation). After 1675 this worm was moved inside the plates, before this it was mounted on the top plate.

Tavan lever An early type of lever escapement notable for being the first to have divided lift.

Temperature compensation Since metal (or most metals) change dimensions and stiffness with changes in temperature, some sort of compensation has to be affected if the balance and spring are not to change timekeeping characteristics. From the first attempts, two centuries were to pass before the problem was solved in a completely satisfactory manner.

Terminal curves Called incurves when discovered by Arnold, these were first applied to helical springs and helped to make the spring expand and contract uniformly. Subsequently applied by Breguet to flat spiral springs the mathematics of the theoretical curve was finally worked out by Phillips. The object, in theory, of the terminal curve is to keep the centre of gravity of the spring on the balance axis as the spring dilates and contracts. In fact, for close rating these curves are only the starting point and normally need to be modified to achieve close positional rates. Also the point of attachment of the inner end of the spring has to be controlled for best results.

Third wheel and pinion Normally the wheel and pinion next to the centre wheel and pinion which in turn drives the fourth wheel and pinion.

Three-quarter plate The top plate of a three-quarter plate watch covers the barrel, centre wheel, third and fourth wheels, but not the escapement.

Timepiece A timekeeper, pure and simple, that does not strike.

Timing in positions See Adjusted.

Timing screws See Quarter screws.

Timing nuts See Quarter screws.

Tinted gold Also called coloured gold. Gold can be produced in various colours according to the metals with which it is alloyed. This fact is used to provide golds that can be decorative because of colour and the way in which this is used. Often called four-colour gold and used for dials and sometimes cases, although only three or even two colours were used on many occasions.

Tipsy key A key designed by Breguet that can wind in one direction only; it free wheels in the other direction and then no damage can be done by winding in the wrong direction.

Tompion regulator See Regulation.

Top plate The plate that is on top if one considers the plate near the dial as the bottom plate.

Torque A turning moment. It is the product of force times distance, and its units in horology are usually grams/centimetres.

Touch pins Pins were usually inserted in the dials of 16th-century watches at the hour positions so that the time could be established in the dark. The single hands were very sturdy and not likely to be damaged by feeling for them.

Tourbillon A. L. Breguet patented his 'tourbillon regulator' in 1801. This was a carriage that revolved at one-, four- or six-minute intervals and that carried the escapement complete. This nullified the vertical positional errors.

Train The wheels and pinions that are used to connect the barrel to all the other moving parts in a watch. It may be the going train, the repeating train, or the musical train etc., according to its purpose.

Trial number A number arrived at by multiplying factors determined during trials in such a way that this number indicates the excellence of the timekeeping performance.

Triple case A watch, usually made for the Turkish market, that had three cases instead of what was at that time, in England at least, the more normal two – the pair case.

Tripping If the amplitude of the duplex or chronometer balance becomes too high the escapement can be unlocked a second time and a second tooth can escape during the one excursion of the balance. This is called tripping.

Turkish market watches Large quantities of watches were made for the Turkish market around the end of the 18th century and the beginning of the 19th.

Two-pin escapement See Savage two pin.

Two-plane escapement An escapement that is in two planes such as the verge.

Under dial work The work that lies between the dial plate and the dial. Also called 'cadrature'.

Up-and-down dial A dial showing the state of wind of the main-spring. Usually only found in higher class work.

Verge See Verge escapement.

Verge escapement Sometimes called the crown-wheel escape-ment because the escape wheel somewhat resembles a crown. The teeth are roughly triangular in shape and protrude from the face of the wheel. There are usually an odd number of teeth in the wheel (eleven or thirteen usually in watches) and one tooth is always pushing on one of the two 'flags' on the balance staff – called the verge.

Since the verge crosses the wheel, and one flag is on the opposite side of the crown wheel to the other as the second flag is picked up by the crown wheel, the other flag is moving in the opposite direction and the crown wheel is recoiled.

Vertical positions The positions when the balance is hanging vertically as opposed to being horizontal. Normally the four quarter positions are designated pendant up, pendant right, pendant down and pendant left. The horizontal positions are dial up and dial down.

Virgule escapement An escapement of the horizontal type that followed the cylinder escapement introduced in about 1750. The balance staff carries a pallet shaped like a comma. Upstanding pin-shaped teeth on the escape wheel slide up the part of the pallet that corresponds to the inside curve of the tail of the comma to give impulse. When drop occurs the next tooth falls on to the top of the comma, subsequently dropping into the notch formed where the dot meets the tail. When the balance reverses, the pin eventually unlocks and runs up the tail again giving impulse. The escapement is thus single beat.

Volute balance spring The flat spiral spring.

Wandering hour dial A dial without hands. The hour shows through a hole in a semi-circular slot and moves around this slot, its position indicating the minutes against a semi-circular minute dial that lies outside it.

Warning The operation of the striking train that takes place a few minutes before striking actually occurs. The rack is allowed to fall and settle, the train runs slightly until it is held on a pin on the warning wheel, so that all is in readiness for the exact moment of release of the warning wheel when the time has come to strike.

Watch papers These were originally used to protect the inner pair case from the inside of the back of the outer, which is where they were placed. Towards the end of the 18th century they also served as advertisements and often carried sentimental rhymes or sometimes the equation of time. Watch papers (a loose term; they were made of a variety of materials) are collected in their own right – a shame, since they constitute part of the history of the watch and would be better left where they were.

Waterbury long-wind watch This was a series of watches characterised by the elegance of the design and by the small number of parts – this latter for cheapness. They had a duplex escapement and also an exceptionally long mainspring and took a long time to wind.

Winding square The square on the barrel arbor or fusee by means of which the watch is wound. This square may be internal when the designer wishes to reduce the overall thickness of the watch.

Winding stem The shaft which carries the winding button. See Keyless winding.

Wolf-tooth gearing Gearing which drives in one direction only may have a special tooth form called wolf tooth because of a fancied resemblance in shape. Although commonly met with in keyless wheels, it has been used throughout the gear train in some rare watches.

Worm wheel See Tangent screw.

Z balance An early form of compensation balance designed by John Arnold.

Description of the Colour Plates

Plate 1 – This 16th century gilt metal alarum watch is probably German. It is pre-balance spring with balance and has a verge escapement. The lid which originally covered the watch has been cut away and undercut to take a glass – glasses were unknown at this period. The alarm setting disc can be seen at the dial centre. The hand is not original. The movement is steel with rectangular pillars and open mainsprings. The diameter is approximately 64 mm. The watch originally had a stackfreed, now removed.

Plate 2 – This Dutch watch is by Daniel Van Pilcom of Amsterdam. The case is silver and gilt made in the form of a fritillary flower. The fusee (with gut) movement is pre-hairspring and has a silver pinned cock. The pillars are Egyptian. There is ratchet set-up. The single hand registers on a gold chapter ring on an engraved dial. The case is a mere 30 mm long (without pendant). The view is of the case back. (c. 1620)

Plate 3 – Silver Skull Watch. Made by J. C. Vvolf, circa 1620. These rather macabre watches were made to remind people of the fleeting nature of life. The dial of the watch is revealed by opening the lower jaw. Verge escapement, pre-balance spring.

Plate 4 – This Swiss astronomical watch was made circa 1620 by Gaspard Girod à Geneve. It is verge, pre-balance spring with a balance. It is a fine example of its type. Note the screwed cock. The barrel set-up is with ratchet and ratchet wheel both of blued steel. The calendar indicates the following: Age and phase of moon, month and sign of Zodiac. The four quarters of the day are also indicated. The case back was originally crystal but this has been replaced with silver.

Plate 5 – This French verge watch is in an oval gold case pierced, enamelled and set with jewels, the back being emerald glass. The dial face is engraved on white ground, with decorations in translucent enamels. At the dial centre there is a landscape in coloured enamels. (c. 1620)

Plate 6 – This Swiss watch has a verge escapement. The case is crystal with a decorated enamel rim and bezel. The scene on the dial shows a bridge over a river with a fisherman in the foreground. The movement is inscribed J. Sermand à Geneve. (1595–1651)

Plate 7 – This crucifix watch is French. The case is embossed silver and gilt. The movement is verge pre-balance spring with balance and bears the inscription O. Tinelly. (1630–35)

Plate 8 – The case of this watch is circular and is of gold, painted with enamel flowers in relief roses, tulips and pansies etc. on a black ground. The lid has a border and a centre of diamond rosettes in gold settings. Inside the lid there is a figure in grisaille. The dial is enamel being a landscape in colour with two figures. On the top plate is D. Bouquet Londini but the case probably came from Geneva. (1630–40)

Plate 9 – This French verge watch is very small for a watch of this period. (However, there is a smaller round watch in the Museum at La Chaux de Fonds in Switzerland of only 12 mm in diameter.) It is pre-balance spring with ratchet and ratchet wheel set-up for regulation. The case is gold and also serves as the dial. The chapter ring is white enamel and the case blue. The movement is inscribed A Bretonneau à Paris. (1638–43)

Plate 10 – This German watch is a rare item and has a pendulum balance with a straight hairspring. Made by George Seydell in the mid-17th century. The straight hairspring is now unfortunately missing. The case has a silver gilt band, silver bezels and is glazed front and back. It is an astronomical watch showing day, date and month, and with a lunar dial. The dial has silver chapters on an engraved gilt ground. This watch illustrates the interest engendered by the introduction of the pendulum into clocks.

Plates 11a, 11b and 11c – This English watch is verge, the movement being inscribed Isaac Pluvier Londini (1614–65). The case is gold and is enamelled. The dial has Roman numerals and a floral centre. There is a pastoral scene inside the front cover. This watch enamelling is exceptional because of the delicacy of the work. (c. 1650)

Plate 12 – This watch is painted enamel and on the back shows Venus and Adonis and is circa 1648. The movement is signed Estienne Ester.

Plate 13 – A French verge watch, dated 1630–40, made by B. Foucher. Scenes of the Amazons are shown in the enamelling which is attributed to Jean or Henri Toutin.

Plate 14 – A beautiful example of miniatures in enamel taken from the edge of the case of a French verge watch. The case is signed by the enameller André Père et Fils. The scenes are of houses in lakeland settings. Other views of this case are shown in Figs. 6 and 12. Note the dial with cartouches. The movement is inscribed Pierre Martin c. 1695.

Plate 15 – This Swiss clock-watch with alarum was made by Jean Baptiste Duboule of Geneva (1615–94). He was a master engraver as well as being a watchmaker so that he would have been responsible for the lovely dial which has phase and age of moon, sign of the Zodiac, date, rising and setting of the sun etc.

Plate 16 – This German clock-watch with alarm was made for the Turkish market. It has a single case of gilt finish, single hand, silver and gilt dial with Arabic numerals. Note the worm set-up for regulation purposes. The watch is pre-hairspring. (c. 1680)

Plate 17 – This French watch was made by L. Vautyer in the 17th century. It is a verge watch. The body of the case is enamelled with raised and pierced gold and enamel decoration.

Plate 18 – This German watch has a rock crystal case in the form of a snail. It is a pre-balance spring verge watch with fusee and chain. Made by Wilhelm Peffenhauser of Augsburg. The dial is silver with Roman numerals and there is a single hand. The dial has an engraved brass surround. (c. 1650)

Plate 19 – A pair-cased gilt metal watch by Tompion London – the 'father' of English watchmaking. It is a verge watch with alarm, 'onion' style. The concentric alarm dial has enamel cartouches. It has a single hand with bold roman numerals on the outer enamel chapter ring and dates from the last third of the 17th century.

Plates 20 and 21 – A French verge watch with pendulum cock. It is a clock-watch. The count wheel can be seen top right in the movement shot. The index-wheel regulator is top left. The bell can be seen in the case bottom. The silver case is pierced and engraved. A silver chapter ring is mounted on a gilt and engraved dial. The movement is inscribed Fardoil à Paris. (c. 1680)

Plate 22 – This watch although inscribed Barraud London No. 1419 is of Swiss manufacture. It is a verge watch with centre seconds. The enamel dial has a rustic scene and the sails of the windmill revolve, being mounted on the escape pivot. The pair cases are metal, gilt with paste-set bezels and enamelled back. (1756–94)

Plate 23 – This English watch, made in the late 17th century, has a verge escapement and silver wandering hours dial with Windmills London engraved in a cartouche. The movement is inscribed Jos Windmills 0717. It is pair cased in silver, the outer being engraved with the arms of King William III.

Plate 24 – This verge watch is by Fr. Stammer London and is numbered 699. It has a double six-hour dial. This was developed to try to give a single hand the same accuracy of reading as two hands. The outer ring is divided into two-minute intervals so that the time can be read to a minute. One of course had to know the time within six hours, or confusion could arise, say, for instance, between 4 and 10 o'clock. Silver Champlevé dial pair cases the inner silver. The outer is silver metal covered in shell and inlaid silver. (c. 1700)

Plates 25a, 25b and 25c – This English watch is double dialled, one dial has I–XII twice and shows the months with coloured signs of the Zodiac. The other side shows hours, minutes and the date. The dial is inscribed David Pons. The gold case is glazed both sides. There are two worm and wheel drives in the movement which has a cylinder escapement. (c. 1770)

Plate 26 – This English watch is so large that one wonders if one can call it so. It is cased as a chronometer but in all its details it is nothing so much as an overgrown watch. Made by George Margetts (1748–1908) it gives the following information: Mean Time hands at centre. The state of tide at eight ports also on this centre dial and indicated by the surrounding twenty-four hour dial. This latter dial also carries the moon hand. The moon indicates its position in the Zodiac and its declination on the outer circles on the large dial. These show from the inner to the outermost, declination degrees, sign and degree of the Zodiac, and date and month of the solar year. The sun hand indicates the date and as with the moon, its own declination and position in the Zodiac. The circular frame separating the outer circles from the constellations has the moon's latitude above or below the indicated declination engraved upon it. The dragon's-head pointer also indicates the position of the moon's eclipse nodes in the Zodiac. The outer curved frame represents the observer's horizon, and the space between it and the inner curved frame, the twilight period. All parts rotate clockwise except for the horizon frame and the Mean Time dial, which are stationary. Also through the hole in the twenty-four-hour dial is indicated eclipses of the sun and moon. Between eclipses the age of the moon engraved on the sun hand disc (1–29½) can be observed each day through this same hole. All of this is accomplished with just sixteen gears in the motion work. True watches on exactly the same plan were also made by Margetts. (c. 1780)

Plate 27 – This is a view of the back of the case of a Dutch watch with verge escapement. It is a quarter repeater with gold champlevé dial of typical Dutch design. The inner case is plain gold, the outer repoussé. Both cases are pierced. The movement inscribed B Van Der Cloesen, Hague (1688–1719). (c. 1710)

Plate 28 – This is an English watch case of gold, enamelled blue and white, with a portrait of Arabella Hamlyn, 1774. It was enamelled by Henry Spicer (1743–1804) who was appointed enameller to George, Prince of Wales.

Plate 29 – This English watch by John Arnold is full plate with spring detent escapement and is half quarter dumb repeater. The movement is inscribed John Arnold London Invt et Fecit No. 21/68. The movement was originally pivoted detent but has been converted (by Arnold probably) to spring detent. It has a double S balance with helical spring. The movement is jewelled throughout including the fusee arbor. The case is gold hallmarked London 1780, the dial enamel, hands gold.

Plate 30 – This French watch is one of Breguet's 'souscription' watches which were Breguet's inexpensive line. Ordered before they were made on a subscription basis they were as simple as they could be. The barrel is at the centre of the watch, the winding square can be seen in the centre of the single hand. Note the quiet elegance of the Arabic numerals and the fine hand. The number of the watch is 2267. It was originally numbered 267 and this number appears against the secret signature just below the 12 o'clock. This is not visible in the photograph. This watch has a ruby cylinder escapement with a three-armed plain balance. The regulator has a compensation curb. The movement is three-quarter plate. The case is plain silver with gold bezels and band 62 mm diameter. 1798.

Plate 31 – This watch shows the early enamel dial made up from cartouches. The case is a piqué case.

Plate 32 – This watch is unusual, inasmuch as a portrait is painted inside the front cover.

Plate 33 – This watch shows really superb enamelling where the flowers almost seem to stand away from the surface.

Plate 34 – This Swiss anonymous musical watch is of the Fleurier type, and strikes on five bells. The case is gold and has what are apparently forged English assay marks. The dial is enamel. The cuvette is very beautiful being pierced and engraved with an urn of flowers. The bezel, pendant and bow are decorated with split pearls. The back is of translucent blue enamel on a guilloché ground and is also decorated with split pearls around the edge, with a reticulate motif of split pearls at the centre. (Early 19th century)

Plate 35 – This anonymous Swiss watch is a quarter repeater with automata. Two cupids ring bells at the upper part of the dial and two figures operate a grinding machine in the lower part. The escapement is cylinder. The case is gold. (Early 19th century)

Plates 36a and 36b – A Swiss watch with verge escapement. The gold case is decorated all over with grains, filigree and amethysts. The dial is gold with numerals on oval plaques. The movement is inscribed Fx Pernetti à Geneve No. 13601. (c. 1810)

Plate 37 – This watch, originally made by John Arnold in 1774 or 1775, was fitted with a tourbillon mechanism by A. L. Breguet, and presented to John Roger Arnold in 1809 as a token of esteem from one famous maker to another. This esteem was mutual since at one stage there was an exchange of sons so that each could serve some time in the other's establishment. The silver plate attached to the top plate can be translated as follows: The first tourbillon regulator by Breguet incorporated in one of the first works of Arnold. Breguet's homage to the revered memory of Arnold. The escapement is spring detent of the Peto cross detent type, with a steel escape wheel. Breguet's records show that over the course of a year fourteen different workmen attended to the modification of the movement, to the making of the tourbillon, and the casing and dialling of this watch. This watch has sun and planet maintaining power similar to that in Arnold's No. 1 marine chronometer and in other pieces of his manufacture. As far as is known Arnold was the only one to use this type of maintaining power in watches or chronometers, which he only did in early examples. The case is silver, engine turned and is in a presentation case not intended for wear.

Plate 38 – This Breguet watch, No. 971, shows one of his attempts at escapement improvement. The watch is a repeater and has a vertical wheel natural lift escapement. This is a variety of the resting wheel or dead beat verge. However, the function of locking is transferred to another wheel mounted co-axially with the impulse wheel which is locked by a lever with upright pallets that has the normal fork and double roller arrangement. This watch survives as a movement only. (c. 1810)

Plate 39 – This Swiss watch is a quarter repeater with skeletonised movement and has automata. The dial has coloured gold figures and foliage. Made by Meuron and Co. the movement has a cylinder escapement. The case is gold. (1800–25)

Plate 40 – This club-tooth lever watch carries a well-known English name, Robert Roskell, Liverpool, but actually was imported from Switzerland and is of the Fleurier type. The enamel dial is later and has both a thermometer and a compass put into it. (c. 1836)

Plate 41 – This is a French cylinder watch with repeating. Two gold figures strike bells which are mounted on the dial. This is unusual, as the figures are normally only pictorial and do not strike real bells. The offset dial shows the hours and minutes, the whole is mounted on a blue enamel ground. The movement is fusee, and is inscribed Selliard Aine à Paris No. 4050. (1812–25)

Plate 42 – These watches show different styles seen in cylinder watches. The lower one is elaborately enamelled and engraved and has a shaped case, while the top watch has been designed with simplicity in mind.

Plate 43 – This watch is a musical (two tunes) quarter striking clock-watch. It has an engine turned silver dial with the age and phase of the moon. The going train is powered by a going barrel and has a cylinder escapement. The name Courvoisier appears on the dial. The gold case is also engine turned. (c. 1815)

Plate 44 – This French watch is an independent seconds watch. The dial is silver, the case gold and both are engine turned. The escapement is ruby cylinder, with steel escape wheel. (c. 1815)

Plates 45a and 45b – This watch made by Ls George & Ce. Hr du Roy à Berlin, is a quarter repeater, and shows the day of the week and the date. It has a Pouzait-type lever escapement and is centre seconds. The large balance covers nearly all of the top plate! The case is silver, the dial enamel. (c. 1815)

Plate 46 – This Breguet watch has a cylinder escapement and is 'à tact'. It has a gold dial and gold case. The movement is inscribed Breguet Horloge de la Marine Royale No. 3877. (c. 1820)

Plate 47 – An English clock-watch bearing the name French, Royal Exchange No. 4458. It has a duplex escapement. It is also a quarter repeater. The striking train has a most unusual refinement. A cam on the striking stop work alters the fly-pinion depth as the mainspring runs down, in such a way as to regularise the speed of striking. The balance cock and barrel bridge are beautifully engraved. The dial is silver. (c. 1820)

Plate 48 – This watch is probably French. It has a cylinder escapement and is very flat whilst still being hunter cased. It has a gold niello case and gold niello dial. Note the matching chain and key. Moving discs show the hours and minutes. (First half of the 19th century)

Plate 49 – This English watch was made by John Moncas of Liverpool and displays magnificently the 'Liverpool jewelling', with large, relatively clear jewels. The balance is gold and the escapement is of the later Massey type. The engraving is bold and striking, and the gilding rich. (c. 1820)

Plate 50 – This Swiss watch has a Tavan lever escapement and compensation curb. It is also a repeater. The dial is enamel and also shows the date. The movement is inscribed Jn. Ge. Remond a Geneve. (c. 1830)

Plate 51 – This English watch has a ratchet-tooth lever escapement. The movement is inscribed Ulrich & Co. Cornhill London No. 62. It is a half plate with exceptionally high numbered pinions and wheels. They are as follows: Fusee 104, Centre Pinion 14; Centre Wheel 112, Third Pinion 14; Third Wheel 105, Fourth Pinion 14; Fourth Wheel 96, Escape Pinion 12; Scape Wheel 15. The escapement has diamond endstones. The balance is bimetallic with three arms. (1828–32)

Plate 52 – This watch is inscribed Hunt and Roskell 156 New Bond St. London No. 10514 and is absolutely ravishing. However, it was probably J. F. Houriet (1743–1830) who made it. The watch is a one-minute tourbillon with a 21,600 beat rate – unusual in a tourbillon, especially at that date. The polishing on the carriage is as superb as anything ever seen. The escape wheel is gold. The movement is keywound fusee with continental stop work. The fine mainspring is signed Bandelien Frere. A brake for the train operates on the third wheel. The balance is unusual. It is bimetallic with special screws in the segment weights for fine adjustments of the compensation. It is free sprung with a spherical spring. The escapement is Earnshaw-type spring detent. An additional complication is the inclusion of a thermometer. The case is gold, the dial enamel. (1836)

Plate 53 – This is a ball pendant watch with enamelled case. The watch is wound by revolving one half of the ball one way relative to the other. Reversing the direction sets the hands. These watches sometimes have cylinder and sometimes lever escapements.

Plate 54 – This Viennese watch is a copy of a 1650 style watch. The case is crystal front and back, set in enamel bands. The dial is also enamelled and there is a single hand. Whether these were intended to be fakes is by no means certain. (c. 1840)

Plate 55 – This English watch has a right-angled lever escapement (club tooth) with split seconds. Made by E. J. Dent, it is marked: compound movement chronometer makers to the Queen, London 15430 Patent. It is an early example of a split seconds watch and works on an unusual principle. It has a bimetallic balance with gold timing and quarter screws, with an overcoil spring pinned to a

Breguet-type stud clamped under a steel plate. The movement is of Lepine construction. (c. 1846)

Plate 56 – This has been described as a Japanese paper-weight clock. This little gem has also been described in Japanese papers as a 'doctor's clock', and although it might well have been it really comes under the heading of a watch. The confusion really arises because it is modelled on the well-known Japanese Pillar Clock. However, this watch is spring driven thus making it portable, and it also has a balance and spring. The outer case is of Shitan wood (lid has been removed for photography and the watch removed from its outer case). As the watch is wound, the hour indicator, which is fixed to the fusee line, moves to the top of the hour scale. As the watch runs, the pointer moves towards the bottom of the scale indicating the hours. The hour marks are adjustable. (Probably 19th century)

Plate 57 – This Japanese Inro Watch is mid-19th-century with verge escapement. The inro, or medicine box, is eminently suitable for housing a portable timepiece and this example shows one way in which this was done. The kimono provides no receptacle for carrying a pocket watch, but of course the inro was attached to the girdle by its netsuke and ojine. The watch is really a miniature clock with rectangular plates and striking mechanism. The bell is visible through the slot near the top of the box. The box is of Shitan wood adorned with maple leaves, chrysanthemum flowers and butterflies. The ojine is decorated with a spray of leaves and coral fruit and has a mother-of-pearl cartouche, with the signature Furuya. The striking is based on the European system. The dial is gilt with moveable silver and steel numerals.

Plate 58 – This Japanese watch has a verge escapement. There is a twenty-four-hour dial with adjustable numerals striking on Japanese notation. Dial engraved, gilded metal and steel chapters which are moveable. Fixed hand. Silver open-face case back containing bell pierced and engraved. Whole in rectangular wooden case with sliding back. Diameter 81 mm. (Probably 19th century)

Plate 59 – This Swiss cylinder watch has a movement made completely of steel! The style of the movement is Bovet. The watch is centre seconds, the dial enamel, the case silver. (c. 1860)

Plates 60 and 61 – In 1825 a new era began for the Swiss watch trade in China. This was started by Edouard Bovet who had gone to China to represent a London firm. However, he soon became independent, and organised a trade that became of such proportions that the Bovets of Fleurier Switzerland became known as the Bovets of China. The calibre was distinctive, as can be seen in the illustration, and became known as the 'bovet'. It was characterised by the layout of the bridges and the beautiful engraving. After 1842 a few Neuchâtel firms Vaucher, Dimier Vrard, and later Juvet and the firm of Voumard and Courvoisier (both the latter of La Chaux de Fonds) undertook production of similar watches. (c. 1860)

Plate 62 – A Swiss watch, Systeme Roskopf. This was the first attempt to make a watch for the working man, a task undertaken by Georges Frederick Roskopf (1813–89). The watch has a pin-lever escapement and is keyless (rocking bar system). The case is nickel, the dial enamel. (c. 1870)

Plate 63 – This Swiss watch has a pivoted detent chronometer escapement. The movement is inscribed Albert H. Potter & Co. Geneva. Pat Oct 11 '75. Potter was a superb craftsman who left America to settle in Geneva in 1876, and was actually credited by the Swiss with raising the standard in the area! (c. 1876)

Plate 64 – An early American Waltham full-plate lever watch. This watch is only jewelled at the balance and pallets. Note the works safety pinion. The centre pinion is screwed on to the centre arbor and would unscrew if the force became too great upon a mainspring breaking in the going barrel. (c. 1880)

Plate 65 – This Swiss one-minute tourbillon with lever escapement has the movement inscribed J. L. Calame Robert Chaux de Fonds. It has day of the month indication. The fusee is reversed and is fitted with five-turn Geneva stop work. A chain guard is fitted to protect the carriage if there is a breakage in the chain. The lever escapement is right-angle club tooth. The balance is bimetallic. (c. 1880)

Plate 66 – An American watch with lever escapement but with the scape wheel at right-angles to the plates worm driven. The idea behind this was a long running simpler watch with fewer parts! The worm can be seen through the star-shaped hole in the top plate.

The dial is enamel. Movement inscribed New York Standard Watch Co. No. 29490. However, such a high torque was required to run the watch because of the worm pinion that this watch was a failure, and only about 26,000 were ever made and few of them survive today. (1887)

Plate 67 – This watch although bearing the name Bennett London is in fact a Glashütte watch by Lange. It is absolutely typical, with lever escapement, slits in the balance rim for tensioning the quarter screws, and the small screw that turns into a slot in the barrel arbor square to retain the ratchet wheel. The movement is numbered 6386. The case is later. (c. 1880)

Plate 68 – A German watch made in Dresden by the famous firm of A. Lange & Sohne Glashütte. The watch is numbered 29574 and has a lever escapement. It is a half quarter repeater and a fly back chronograph. It has an enamel dial. (c. 1890)

Plate 69 – This American watch has a crystal top plate and balance cock. It has a lever escapement and was made by A. W. Waltham & Co. No. 27. A letter written to an American in 1938 says that these watches were made fifty years before, and that one could still be obtained from Walthams for ten dollars. These watches must have been very difficult to jewel. Watches with crystal plates are very rare. This movement is in a later case. (c. 1888)

Plate 70 – This English watch is by Frodsham. It is an eight-day movement and has two barrels. The escapement is English lever. The bimetallic balance has a helical spring with duo in uno. The dial is enamel. The movement is inscribed Chas. Frodsham 84 Strand London FD FMsz. No. 06398. Frodshams were at this address up to 1897. The letter code indicates that the watch is of the highest quality. Much of Frodsham's work was made by the firm of Nicole Nielsen – whom they eventually bought in the 1930s. Nicole Nielsen supplied the finest watches of the day – indeed perhaps of any day. (c. 1890)

Plate 71 – This French cylinder watch is anonymous. The bars of the movement are so arranged as to spell out the word Paris. The dial is enamel. (Possibly 1890)

Plate 72 – This Roskopf watch is later than the previous example and has largely acquired the form that it was to keep for decades.

Plate 73 – This very flat Swiss watch has a right-angle club-tooth lever escapement. The bottom plate, the bridges, the barrel and the cocks are engraved all over. (Late 19th century)

Plate 74 – This Swiss tourbillon made by Fureur, and numbered 34394, is an inexpensive tourbillon. The centre of the back of the silver case is glazed to show the carriage. The balance is not of course at the centre of the carriage but this is of no importance. They are not of high quality and history does not relate how well they went, but without adjustments for isochronism the errors between the horizontal and vertical positions and those due to the watch running down would still be present. (c. 1920)

Plate 75 – This English watch is a Karrusel and was made by Yeomans. It is No. 85222. Britten lists a Joseph Yeomans of Cockermouth who died in 1905 aged sixty-five. This Karrusel watch has a sweep centre seconds hand, and gold minute and hour hands. The dial is enamel. The rough movement was made by B. Bonniksen and bears his patent No. 21421, and is of three-quarter-plate construction. The fourth wheel is at the centre. The going barrel has Geneva stop work. The carriage is revolved by a large pinion on the third arbor which meshes with the teeth on the edge of the carriage. The escapement is the English ratchet-toothed lever. The balance is two-arm bimetallic with gold screws and quarter nuts. The balance spring has seventeen and a half turns, is closely pitched and is free sprung with overcoil. The balance makes 18,000 beats an hour. The watch is keyless. (Early 20th century)

Plate 76 – This American watch was made by the Elgin National Watch Co. in 1918. It is 18 size with a 24-size dial. This precision watch was made to the highest possible standard for the United States Government. They were installed as navigational timepieces on destroyers – conventional marine chronometers were apparently unable to stand the vibration. Three hundred were made and sold to the Government at $275 each. This would then have been about £15 – a very high price. It is free sprung, has up and down indicator showing a reserve of forty hours. The balance is a Guillaume, and the escapement has diamond endstones. The number of jewels is twenty-one. The plates and keyless wheels are most beautifully damascened. The watch is engraved Father Time Elgin Ill. USA No. Adjusted 5 positions Safety Barrel 21 Jewel No. 21869977. The wheels are of low carat gold. The dial is enamel. Hand set is accomplished by means of a lever that is disclosed on removing the bezel. The watch was housed in a chronometer box with gimbals.

Plate 77 – This small Swiss minute repeater could be cased as a wrist watch, although it would no doubt have been a fob watch when first made. It has a club-tooth lever escapement. (c. 1910)

Plate 78 – This modern Swiss wrist watch shows the day, date and month, and the phases of the moon. Made by Matthey Tissot. It is also a chronograph with minute and hour recorder. (c. 1950)

Plate 79 – This English watch was the first successful self-winding wrist watch. Designed by John Harwood it has a compensation balance and lever escapement. Automatic winding is by means of a weighted segment which pivots at the centre and oscillates between buffer stops. The hands are set by rotating the milled bezel. (c. 1930)

Plate 80 – This self-winding watch prototype was made jointly by the author and P. W. Amis for S. Smith and Sons Ltd. The reduction between the self-winding weight and the barrel ratchet is obtained partly by a lever system and partly by gears. (1957)

Plate 81 – This American watch is the Hamilton 500A, the world's first successful electric wrist watch. It has a monometallic balance with special alloy spring to self-compensate and to resist magnetic fields. Impulse is given when contacts are made by the balance, due to the interaction of the magnetic fields caused in the coil on the balance and due to the permanent magnets beneath the coil. The battery has been removed but normally lies beneath the brass strap. (1957)

Plate 82 – The American Bulova tuning-fork watch. This marks the transition between the electric balance controlled watches to the quartz watch. Other tuning fork watches have been made by the Swiss. (1963)

Plate 83 – The Dynatron. This Swiss watch was the last of the balance controlled electronic watches. It had no contacts. The coil that does the triggering and the impulsing can be seen beneath the balance. The battery has been removed but lies normally beneath the cover bearing the name Dynatron. (1967)

Plates 84a and 84b – The dial of this self-winding chronograph has date work. This watch is called the Chronomatic. In the back view we can see the chronograph work. This is mounted complete on a sub-plate and this can be removed merely by undoing the three blued screws. This is an astonishing achievement. Note the unusual position of the winding button, this being at 9 o'clock. This watch is the result of a design exercise undertaken jointly by Buren Watch Co, Hamilton Watch Co, Breitling, Dubons and Dupraz, and Hever Leonidas. The performance is such that it can be rated to what the Swiss call 'chronometer' standard. The balance is large for such a watch, being 10·60 mm diameter. (1970)

Plate 85 – A Swiss watch, earrings and ring all matching. Made by Patek Philippe in 18 carat yellow gold set with diamonds, onyx and malachite. (1977)

Plate 86 – As Plate 85, but set with lapis lazuli and diamonds.

Bibliography

Baillie, G. H., *Clocks and Watches: an historical bibliography* (to 1800) (1951)

Baillie, G. H., *Watches: their history, decoration and mechanism* (Reprinted 1978 NAG Press)

Bassermann, Jordan *The Book of Old Clocks and Watches* (1964)

Berner, G. A., *Dictionnaire professionel illustré de l'horlogerie* (La Chaux de Fonds, 1961)

Britten, F. J., *Old Clocks and Watches and their Makers* ed. G. H. Baillie, Courtenay Ilbert, and Cecil Clutton, 8th edn, rev. Cecil Clutton (1973), 3rd imp. (1977)

Bruton, Eric, *Clocks and Watches 1400–1900* (1967)

Chamberlain, Paul M., *It's about Time* (1964)

Chapuis, A. and E. Jacquet, *The History of the Self Winding Watch* (Neuchâtel, 1952; London, 1956)

Chapuis, A. and E. Jacquet, *Technique and History of the Swiss Watch* (Bale, 1945) rev. 1970

Chapuis, A. and E. Jacquet, *La montre automatique* (Neuchâtel, 1952)

Chapuis, A. and E. Jacquet, *La montre chinoise* (Neuchâtel, 1919)

Cipolla, Carlo M., *Clocks and Culture 1300–1700* (1967)

Clutton, C., and G. Daniels, *Watches* (1965) new edition in prep.

Cumhaill, P. W. (Philip Coole), *Investing in Clocks and Watches* (1967)

Cuss, T. P., *The Camerer Cuss Book of Antique Watches*, ed. Terence Cuss (Woodbridge, 1976)

Cuss, T. P., *The Story of Watches* (1952)

Daniels, George, *Art of Breguet* (1974)

Daniels, George, *English and American Watches* (1967)

De Carle, Donald, *Complicated Watches and their Repair*, reissue (1977)

De Carle, Donald, *Practical Watch Repairing* (1946)

De Carle, Donald, *The Watch and Clock Encyclopedia* (1950), repr. (1976)

Fell, R. A., *Some Notes on the Balance and Spring* (1965)

Fried, H. B. *The Electric Watch Repair Manual* (New York, 1965) new edition (1972)

Fried, H. B., *The Watch Escapement: the lever, the cylinder, how to analyse, how to repair, how to adjust* (New York, 1974)

Gazeley, W. J., *Clock and Watch Escapements* ((1956), 3rd imp. (1975)

Gazeley, W. J., *Watch and Clock Making and Repairing* (1953), repr. (1975)

Glasgow, David, *Watch and Clock Making* (1885)

Gould, R. T., *The Marine Chronometer: its history and development* (1923)

Haswell, J. Eric, *Horology: the science of time measurement and the construction of clocks, watches and chronometers* (1928)

Howse, D., and B. Hutchinson, *Clocks and Watches of Captain James Cook 1769–1969* (1970)

Huber, Martin, *Die Uhren Von A. Lange and Sohne Glashütte/Sachen* (Munchen, 1977)

Jagger, Cedric, *Paul Philip Barraud* (1968)

Jaquet, E., and A. Chapuis, *Technique and History of the Swiss Watch from its beginnings to the present day* (Switzerland, 1953), facs. reissue (1970)

Laycock, W. S., *The Lost Science of John 'Longitude' Harrison* (Ashford, Kent)

Lecoultre, F., *A Guide to Complicated Watches* (Bienne, 1952)

Mercer, Vaudrey, *John Arnold and Son, chronometer makers* (Ramsgate, 1972–5)

Pellaton, James C., *Watch Escapements* (Switzerland, 1927), English Repr. (1949)

Pioneers of Precision Timekeeping, a symposium, Monograph No. 3, Antiquarian Horological Society (1965)

Rawlings, A. L., *The Science of Clocks and Watches* (New York, 1948)

Ullyett, Kenneth, *Watch Collecting for Amateurs* (1970)

Acknowledgements

The illustrations in this book are reproduced by courtesy of the following:

British Museum, London: Figs. 5, 6, 9, 10, 11, 12, 19 and Plates 1, 2, 3, 4, 5, 6, 7, 8, 9, 10, 11, 12, 13, 14, 15, 16, 17, 18, 19, 20, 21, 22, 23, 24, 25, 27, 28, 29, 30, 34, 35, 36, 37, 38, 39, 40, 41, 43, 45, 46, 47, 48, 50, 51, 52, 54, 55, 56, 57, 58, 59, 60, 61, 62, 63, 65, 66, 67, 68, 69, 70, 71, 73, 74, 75, 77

Graus Antiques: Plates 31, 32, 33, 42, 44, 53

Harold Malies: Fig. 28

National Maritime Museum, London: Plate 26

Patek Philippe S.A.: Plates 85, 86

SOME MUSEUMS WITH WATCH COLLECTIONS

ENGLAND
Bury St Edmunds Gershom-Park
  ington Memorial Collection
Greenwich National Maritime
  Museum
Liverpool City Museum
London British Museum
  Science Museum
  Victoria and Albert Museum
  Wallace Collection
  Museum of London (London Wall
  EC2)
Oxford Ashmolean Museum
  Museum of History of Science

FRANCE
Besançon Musée d'Histoire des
  Beaux Arts
Paris Conservatoire des Arts et
  Métiers
  Musée des Arts Decoratifs
  Musée National du Louvre
  Musée du Petit Palais

GERMANY
Munich Deutsches Museum
Stuttgart Württembegisches Landes-
  museum
Dresden Staatliche Kimstsammlung
  'Grunes Gewölbe'

HOLLAND
Amsterdam Rijksmuseum

ITALY
Milan Museo Poldi Pezzoli

SWITZERLAND
Basel Historisches Museum, Kirch-
  garten
Geneva Musée d'Horlogerie
La Chaux de Fonds Musée Inter-
  national d'Horlogerie
Le Locle Musée d'Horlogerie
  Chateau des Monts
Neuchatel Musée d'Art et d'Histoire

U.S.A.
CONNECTICUT
Bristol American Watch and Clock
  Museum

ILLINOIS
Rockford Time Museum

NEW YORK
New York Metropolitan Museum of
  Art

WASHINGTON D.C.
Smithsonian Institute

WALES
Cardiff National Welsh Museum

Index

INDEX TO COLOUR ILLUSTRATIONS

Figures in bold refer to the colour plates